The News Man

Published by Brolga Publishing Pty Ltd
ABN 46 063 962 443
PO Box 12544
A'Beckett St
Melbourne,VIC, 8006
Australia

email: markzocchi@brolgapublishing.com.au

National Library of Australia
Cataloguing-in-Publication data
          Walden, Mal, author.
          The News Man : Sixty years of television / Mal Walden.
          ISBN: 9781925367492 (paperback)
          Subjects:Television journalists--Australia--Biography.
          Television news anchors-- Broadcast journalism.
          Dewey Number: 070.43092

Printed in China
Cover design by Chameleon Design
Typesetting by Tara Wyllie

BE PUBLISHED

Publish through a successful publisher. National distribution, Macmillan
& International distribution to the United Kingdom, North America.
Sales Representation to South East Asia
Email: markzocchi@brolgapublishing.com.au

THE
NEWS MAN

Sixty years of television

MAL WALDEN

I remember (Mal) joining Network Ten in 1987 and in football parlance it was like picking up Nathan Buckley in the draft.

– EDDIE McGUIRE, television presenter

Mal you have been the public face of Victoria for so many years … I have no doubt you will continue in some shape or form … to continue your interest and more importantly your service to Victoria.

– JEFF KENNETT, former Victorian Premier

I have been a firm friend for a long time… and even before then … I was a great fan. Television is going to look very different without you there.

– BERT NEWTON, television personality

Mal they tell me you're retiring – it took a lot of convincing that it was so. Have a great life. You deserve it.

– RON BARASSI, former AFL player and coach

I remember at HSV7 doing a kids show 'Anything Can Happen'… You were a gods' gentleman … that Australia will miss and Melbourne TV will miss more than anything else.

– MOLLY MELDRUM, music journalist

He doesn't have regard for many rules — or anything — he just plays it his way, which I think is a very Melbourne trait.

- ROSS STEVENSON, 3AW

I remember my first interview (as a teenager) and thinking how nervous I was that someone as important as Mal Walden would want to come and see me.

- MOIRA KELLY, humanitarian

I grew up watching him and I know both Brian Naylor and Peter Hitchener always regarded him as the friendliest of foes.

- TONY JONES & PETER HITCHENER, GTV9

Mal is a giant of the news business. A communicator who always did the job with warmth and authority, but most of all … a gentleman.

- JENNIFER KEYTE, PETER MITCHELL & SANDY ROBERTS, HSV7

People love him and that was one of the secrets of his success. Happy retirement. May you never have to say phenomenon again.

- DAVID JOHNSTON, mentor and friend

REVIEW

Melbourne news anchor Mal Walden is one of the longest continually serving faces on Australian Television. In 2012 Mal submitted several chapters from his collection of memoirs as part of a non-fiction writing course at UCLA in California. The reaction was overwhelming.

"Mal, I have felt honored to have been a part of your process. Your stories are rich with anecdote that makes it not only relevant to Australians, but anyone with an interest in the news industry or history. I have never seen a project quite like yours with such a unique body of reference and such a fascinating mingling of news and memoir. I trust it has a great future in print."

- GORDON GRICE
Senior lecturer, author of *The Red Hour Glass*
and contributor to *The New Yorker* and *Harpers*

INTRODUCING
THE AUTHOR

SATURDAY, 23 NOVEMBER 1963

It was 4.30 a.m. in the Victorian town of Warrnambool when the first strident ringing of an alarm clock jolted the young man from his deepest pre-dawn cycle of sleep. At precisely the moment he reached to silence the offending sound, a fatal shot in Dallas Texas claimed the life of US President John F Kennedy.

The JFK assassination would not only influence the young man's life, but also establish a benchmark in journalism, setting parameters for an emergency handbook to be adopted by networks around the world in their race to be "first with breaking news".

Within 30 minutes of his sudden awakening, the young sleeper found himself in the blocks for the start of that race and at the beginning of his extraordinary life as a newsman.

Mal Walden was 17 years of age when he successfully applied for his first job in media. At age 70, he gracefully crossed the finishing line to be recognised as the longest serving newsman on Australian television. Each year he maintained a journal in which he recorded the many serendipitous and life changing moments woven through some of the biggest headlines of our times. Today they form a record – not only of his life as a newsman but an evolution of television news now in its sixtieth year in Australia.

In 1987, following an unprecedented public backlash against his sacking during the Fairfax takeover of HSV7 Melbourne, he became known within the industry as "a protected species", never to be sacked again.

However, everything in life is cyclical and even the "news clock" is ticking. Technology and the social media phenomenon are driving news at an ever-increasing speed into a new era – an era that has cast a shadow of fear over the industry.

Finally in 2013, after a career spanning more than six decades, Mal stepped down on the day of his choosing, something very rare in television. He left behind a network that had spiralled into "unmitigated financial disaster", a media industry in steady decline, and many proclaiming the imminent "death" of news, in all its traditional forms.

DEDICATION

One of the greatest fears among those in television is that careers can end at a moment's notice. One of the joys I discovered is that they can be restored just as unexpectedly.

My survival was directly attributed to my family: Pauline and our twins Sarah and James. They inherited a public spotlight but forever kept me balanced in its luminous flux. It was a local spotlight from a network stage, and I was a single cog in a much larger wheel. But at the end of each day there was little to show for my efforts. The news stories were kept on file but a newsreader's role always went out into the ether and, apart from an occasional blooper, was lost forever.

I dedicate this memoir to those whose achievements far eclipsed mine – my mentors. I also dedicate this book to all my former colleagues, some no longer with us, and the far too many who were killed while just doing their job.

I have been constantly reminded ... "There but for the grace of God ..."

REFLECTION

Fear of public speaking has always ranked as the world's number one phobia – second only to the greatest fear – death itself! But add the phobia of "just one black sheep" to the equation and suddenly there is a risk of being sucked into an unprecedented, overwhelmingly chaotic "vortex of fear".

"Just one black sheep" is a crude term implying that one indiscretion is enough to wipe out a lifetime of achievements. I have worked with a number of high profile colleagues who, sadly, are remembered not so much for their contribution, but for their one unforgettable stuff-up on air. Given the fears and phobias I have often wondered why in God's name I chose such a risky high profile profession as broadcast media.

Long before I made my career choice – before I was even in my teens – I deliberately maintained a low profile, not so much because of a juvenile shyness, but an extremely embarrassing nervous physical affliction called blushing. I am not talking about a reddening of the cheeks but a total scarlet-creep bordering on a full-blown hemorrhage. However, I discovered on radio no one could see a blush. I could hide with a comforting anonymity behind a microphone. Speaking on radio became the perfect vehicle to overcome this affliction and as the years ticked by my confidence grew unhindered. I also discovered I was not alone when it came to fears of public speaking. During my formative years on country radio in the early '60s I watched incredulously as ministers from each of Warrnambool's mainstream religions: Baptist, Presbyterian, Roman Catholic, Salvation Army and Church of Christ, fronted a 15-minute devotional program broadcast live each afternoon on 3YB.

Each minister would arrive at the studio with a prepared scripture, parable or message and I would play a hymn of their choice. These experienced public speakers, who preached so confidently from their Sunday pulpits, were out of their comfort zone and often reduced to nervous wrecks on live radio.

One afternoon I welcomed a novice to the studio who asked for any advice I could offer. Remembering I was little more than a novice myself, but feeling a little perky, I suggested if he bound the microphone cord tightly around each of his wrists, his message would sound more sincere.

'The tighter you squeeze the clearer the message.' It wasn't until I noticed his wrists turning white threatening his entire circulation that I gently unwound the lead as he read the lesson.

God wrought his revenge on me 18 months later.

It was late 1965 and while working on 7EX Launceston I was asked to host the live culmination of a massive breakfast radio competition – Key Mania. Listeners had been given clues in their search for a dozen hidden car keys around the city.

On the night of the presentation, those who had found a key were invited to insert it into a brand new car door. Whoever opened the door won the car. This presentation was also broadcast live on Channel TNT9. It was my first experience of live television and needless to say with a live studio audience and simulcast over radio stations throughout northern Tasmania I too, was well out of my comfort zone.

Under immense nervous pressure I began by welcoming everyone to the 'biggest competition ever conducted in the history of Tasmanian broadcasting.'

And that's as far as I got.

Standing in the spotlight like a startled rabbit I forgot the name of the competition. I could have simply glanced down at my scripts for a prompt – had there been any scripts. But to my inexperienced horror the scripts were well out of reach lying on the bonnet of the new car in the far corner of the studio.

I stood speechless as the camera moved closer. I heard the silence break as the audience gasped in surprise. I felt the sickness rise from the pit of my stomach, up through my chest and into my head, which was now numbed senseless. My first instinct was to run for the studio door. I would have run but the studio lights were so bright I couldn't see the bloody door. It was probably all of 15 seconds but felt like 15 minutes. I kept mumbling an apology and then stepped away from the spotlight and walked back to the car where I had left my scripts.

I then walked back to the little white mark on the studio floor and started again – this time reading every word from a shaking sheet of paper. It was by far the most excruciatingly terrifying experience of my life. In hindsight it was a "little black lamb" that could so easily have become my one black sheep had viewers not been so forgiving. I believe viewers became a lot less forgiving as television matured.

However, that experience had a profound impact and would live with me for the rest of my life. The lesson I learnt was never to attempt a live broadcast without a script, notes or a prompt within easy reach. Years later I inherited the role of MC for the

Miss Victoria Quest televised live on HSV7 from Melbourne's St Kilda Town Hall.

In the days leading up to the telecast I began to suffer from a severe bout of nerves. Two days before the event and unable to sleep I rang the producer Geoffrey Owen Taylor at 4 a.m.

'I can't do it,' I sobbed. 'I can't do it.'

'Don't be so bloody stupid,' he snapped, 'of course you can. I have a plan and believe me it wont fail.' His plan was to transfer my scripts onto small manageable cards, which I would read as the camera panned across the contestants. My co-host Honor Walters shared the duties and together we breezed through the live telecast without a hitch.

Gradually all these experiences became "grist for the mill" in what would become a lifetime of live television. However despite hours of preparation and reams of carefully prepared standby scripts, there are always those unexpected moments you can never prepare for.

In October 1979 I was invited to open the annual Korumburra Potato Festival south east of Melbourne. A simple task on the surface: an introduction, a short speech about potatoes and the festival was underway. I researched the history of the simple spud from the Encyclopedia Britannica discovering 346 different varieties of potatoes and 340 different diseases that kill them. Each potato, I discovered, had a name. Named after royalty, well-known political leaders or even a humble farmer who had cultivated a specific variety.

The local mayor stood at the microphone before a crowd of several hundred townsfolk in their Mechanics Institute Hall. His introduction was pleasantly brief.

'Now from Channel Seven would you welcome Mal Walden.'

I left my chair to walk the short distance across the stage to the microphone. In those six short steps the mayor continued, 'I don't suppose you know this Mal but there are 346 different potatoes in this world and 340 different diseases that kill them. Each potato has a name, named after royalty or even a humble potato farmer.'

My entire speech had just been pre-empted! So I stumbled through my experience harvesting potatoes on a kibbutz in Israel and a history of television bloopers including my own. It was live but thankfully not on live television.

There were many dozens of bloopers that poured from my mouth over the years. In 1986 during a live news update from the HSV7 newsroom two reporters began arguing in the background. In an effort to override their voices I raised my voice level. This obviously interfered with their argument, as they immediately raised theirs. In pure frustration I exploded. 'For Christ sake shut up. Can't you see I'm on air… Sorry about that.' There was not one viewer complaint.

Meanwhile the more confident I became the more memorable became the bloopers until … PHENOMENON. I couldn't stop the syllables, Phenomenonemonenon. If I was ever going to be remembered for any indiscretion then I have quite happily accepted phenomenon.

There is always the risk of becoming over confident in public life but despite a few off-the-cuff comments and a bit of fun following some news stories, in most cases I was surprisingly restrained. I attribute that caution to a conservative nature, a natural maturity that developed with age and of course the deepest respect for that one black sheep – wherever it may have been lurking.

CONTENTS

PROLOGUE

SUNDAY, 13 JULY 1952

The day dawned cold and grey. Drizzle was blowing across Port Phillip Bay as I stood on the rear deck of the *SS Orontes* trying to catch the first glimpse of my new home – Melbourne.

The bleak weather blanketed the low city skyline as our immediate destination slowly came into view, first the tin roof, then the pylons of Station Pier. The twin tugs soon took control and gently nudged us into berth. I still have memories of my slightly bewildered parents, already a little homesick, overly anxious but above all, like most migrants, hopeful that the decision to migrate to Australia from England was the right one and would provide their children with better opportunities. I was oblivious to all this. To me, this was the start of some great adventure not dissimilar to those of Enid Blyton's *Famous Five* who had occupied my shipboard reading time.

I remember my parents struggling through the Port Melbourne custom's shed. Brightly coloured labels pasted onto the sides of several bulging suitcases indicated 'W' for Walden, 'S' for Steerage Class (a slight improvement on tourist class as we had paid our fare) and the name of the ship. We filed down the steps from custom's hall and along the wooden-planked station pier to the nearby trains. The red rattlers were waiting like dirty cattle trucks. The smell of stale leather seats blended with cigarettes and oil while steam engines shunted nearby emitted a deep-throated horn rather than the high twin-pitched whistles of British rail. Then with a sudden jerk, we began the final leg of our journey – a 20,000-mile one-way trip to Frankston – a small beachside township on the Mornington Peninsula.

We were 20 minutes into that journey when a fellow passenger with bleary eyes and loud voice struck up conversation. He began by calling me "Bluey".

'All redheads are called Bluey, mate. Where are you from?'

'England,' I replied with a very northern accent.

'Well, lesson number one, you don't wear those things here,' he laughed, referring to my knee length gabardine Macintosh. 'That's what we wear in Australia,' he said, pointing to a young kid wearing a black shiny plastic raincoat. 'Furthermore, they're waterproof.'

There was silence for a moment. He took another draw from his unfiltered cigarette and then exhaled a foul breath and flashed his discoloured teeth.

'See down there?' He gestured as the red rattler sped over the

Caulfield Bridge. 'That's where he shot the young copper, my cousin. They got the bastard though.'

He spoke as though I should have known to whom he was referring. I was shocked. It was the first time I was confronted with details of someone who had actually been murdered. I was also stunned by the vehemence of this stranger.

'They got him, and they're going to hang him. I hope he rots in hell.' His spittle sprayed my coat.

It was a most memorable introduction to Melbourne for a nine year old and each time I crossed that Caulfield Bridge I always thought of that stranger and his cousin, Constable George Howell, who had been shot dead. I would also think of the man who shot him, William John O'Meally.

With his protestations of innocence, O'Meally became a household name and a symbol of evil. He broke down and wept as the jury pronounced him guilty and the judge handed down the death sentence. No one felt pity, other than his wife Connie. While his death sentence was subsequently commuted, he went on to become Victoria's longest-serving prisoner and the last man sentenced to 12 strokes of the cat o'nine tails to be delivered in one session.

Twenty-seven years after I arrived in Melbourne and first heard the name William John O'Meally, I met this so-called "Melbourne Monster". As senior TV news presenter at HSV7, I was into the third story of the evening bulletin when the studio doors opened and in walked O'Meally accompanied by news director John Maher. He looked heavier than his photo taken years earlier. The once thick black hair had turned grey but he still reflected a youthful boyish appearance. I had been made aware of the possibility of an interview during the afternoon. It was dependent on the outcome of a deal with O'Meally who had been released a week earlier and immediately gone into hiding. Remembering that stranger on my first day in Australia and his comment, 'I hope he rots in hell' I asked the man himself about life in H Division.

'The H stands for hell,' he said. 'Life was hell alright.' O'Meally continued to proclaim his innocence and to this day there are certain doubts as to his guilt. He admitted having a chequered career as a petty criminal but insisted he was at home at the time of the murder. He spoke of the flogging. Tied to a wooden brace and lashed a dozen times. He spoke of his arrest while trying to elude police. His vehicle crashed after the bonnet flew open obstructing his view. He was bemused at future vehicles of that make having their bonnets hinged from the front to prevent similar incidents.

The interview lasted 4 minutes and 25 seconds – significantly longer than the lead story and setting new standards for a 30-minute news bulletin. However, the subject matter created a furore among viewers with many complaining about what we call today "cash for comment", paying a convicted criminal. Others took exception to a newsreader becoming involved in such a story.

The attitude of a newsreader's involvement became more generally accepted following a major campaign promoting me as the first "journalist" senior newsreader on Melbourne television. However, Seven management became far more selective after the O'Meally interview as to the nature of future stories I would be allowed to cover.

Several weeks later I received a letter from one of O'Meally's former cellmates at Pentridge Prison (some believe that letter is another reason I survived in television as long as I did...)

Dear Mal,

I watch your news on Channel Seven every night and you seem to be a decent sort of guy. I was wondering if you could help me. I am currently serving 12 years for holding up a county court judge with a shotgun. In several weeks' time my Dad is celebrating his 70th birthday and I want to send him a photo of me. My problem is I have cut off my ears and was hoping you would have some footage when I had my ears. If you can help please let me know.

Regards,

Mark Brandon Read

I sought permission and was told: 'As long as it doesn't cost much.' I found several film clips including one of the prisoner being escorted across the road from Russell Street police headquarters to the magistrate's court. Then with instructions to delete the two escorting police officers I sent the film off for processing. Several weeks later I received two 8" x 10" glossy photos of Mark complete with his ears which I immediately forwarded onto Pentridge. Two weeks later I received his reply.

Dear Mal,

Thank you for the photos. You are one of the few people in this world who has ever done me a favour. If you need any favours. No matter what! (You know what I mean Ha! Ha! Ha!) Just let me know and I'll get it fixed.

Yours sincerely,

Mark 'Chopper' Read

I never once called in that favour but as you will soon discover there were many times when I was sorely tempted.

Big news stories are like popular hit songs
— you always remember where you were when you first heard them.

CHAPTER 1

BIRTH OF NEWS –
DEATH OF A MENTOR

1956

Melbourne's waterside workers strike
John Landy stops to help a fallen Ron Clarke in the Australian mile
The Suez Crisis
The Hungarian Revolution
The Melbourne Olympics

HITS

Don't Be Cruel – Bobby Brown
The Great Pretender – The Platters
The Wayward Wind – Waterboys

SATURDAY AFTERNOON, 4 NOVEMER 1956
MELBOURNE

It was around 3.15 when the story headed "Suez Crisis" suddenly flashed across the wire service. The sound of bells from a humming teleprinter echoed around the newly renovated building in Dorcas Street, South Melbourne. The smell of fresh paint failed to stifle the lingering staleness of the building's former life as a newspaper warehouse and within its reincarnated interior an air of tension was becoming palpable. Sharing a large wooden desk in the centre of the room three newspaper journalists pounded the keys of a black Remington and two pre-owned Royals.

Trevor O'Brien and Allan Bain were both veteran journalists from the Melbourne *Herald*. John Maher was a D grade journalist who had just returned from London after a short stint working for the *Herald* office in Fleet Street during which time he had also gained a minimal understanding of television news at the BBC.

At the sound of teleprinter bells Maher stopped typing, ripped the newsflash from the machine and read out loud.

'Middle East in post-war crisis ... STOP ... Egypt's President Gamal Abdel Nasser nationalises Suez Canal ... STOP ... Britain and France announce joint strike to seize control of crucial waterway ... STOP ...'

The three journalists were already into the final countdown of what was probably the biggest deadline of their careers. Now they were entering totally unchartered waters. Then, just as they transformed the news rundown to include the Suez crisis, another bombshell struck.

With the Middle East at flashpoint, Soviet forces were reported massing on the border of Hungary preparing to put down the so-called "Hungarian Revolution". For a weekend of news, the international events could not have been more threatening to world peace. However, overseas news was never going to lead their bulletin. Not this night anyway.

Priority for the three journalists was a local story, which was overshadowing all else. A story that was about to change our lives forever. The 4th of November 1956, was the night television came to Melbourne.

Exactly 47 years later, in November 2003, I arranged to meet up with John Maher, one of the surviving members of that pioneering trio of journalists. He was my mentor who had driven me painfully through my cadet years and then provided a form of paternal support, as best as he was able, throughout the rest of my life as a newsman.

At the age of 77 he was living alone on the outskirts of Melbourne, high in the hills of Sherbrooke Forest in a small town called Kallista. Several years had passed since we had last seen each other. This time I came armed with a tape recorder and grave fears I may have left it too late.

'Come in my boy,' was his familiar greeting. I was always "my boy", rarely ever Mal. Two protruding hearing aids and slightly glazed eyes were other signs of failing health. I was under strict instructions to arrive at exactly ten minutes past 10 a.m. God knows why, he had always been slightly eccentric. So I sat in the car for eight minutes before walking up to his front door – precisely on time.

'You'll sit there facing the garden, put your recorder on the table here and go and make some coffee.' He had taken control, as always.

Several minutes later I was instructed to start my recorder, to capture a time before tape could record our history. A time before scripts were kept for posterity. A time when there was no vision for the future. This left us with only scant memories of our past, and sadly, even they were now fading. It was my wish to capture a moment of media history before we all faded to black.

He began with a voice softer than I remembered, slightly sibilant and with just a hint of theatrics.

'John Joseph Patrick Maher,' he stated in a rather perfunctory manner. 'Born in 1927 … into a strong Melbourne Catholic family.'

We skipped gently through his early childhood to the time when he studied for the priesthood under the Order of Jesuits. However, he admitted the calling of the Church was not as strong as the calling of journalism so he then followed in the footsteps of his father, John Joseph "Jack" Maher, who was regarded as one of the best sporting writers on the Melbourne *Sun*. He chuckled at those early memories before saying, 'Nepotism was alive and well at the Herald and Weekly Times (HWT) particularly for those of the Catholic faith.'

His first break came as a cadet journalist in June 1952, following the mystery disappearance of an eccentric former socialite near Bairnsdale in South Eastern Gippsland. Seventy-year-old Margaret Clement was reported missing from her derelict mansion where she had been living as a recluse surrounded by scrub, tall blackberries and open swamps. She became known as "The Lady of the Swamp" and the intrigue surrounding her disappearance triggered an unprecedented media frenzy led by a series of stories written by a staff reporter on the Melbourne *Herald*. Maher quietly conceded *he* was that staff reporter but didn't receive a bi-line because he was still a cadet at the time. Once he had qualified as a D grade journalist he was sent for a brief posting to the *Herald* office in Fleet Street, London.

'I was very fortunate that on my days off I sat in on the BBC News to see how it was done … My ambition was to come home and join the ABC but then out of the blue came an offer to join HSV7.' He drew a deep breath then began recalling that first day in 1956 when the world was teetering on the brink of two major conflicts; the day John Maher's legacy was about to begin. As he continued to talk, an image began to appear of three young men who had 'not the faintest clue what they were doing' and a crisis unfolding overseas which almost paled to the confusion and fears that reigned in their newsroom that day.

'Newsroom was a very loose term ... It was more a common room used by all and sundry ... We had clowns coming in, dogs coming in, children running about and there we were trying to write copy for a news service ... No one could complain because those who complained knew less than we did, and we knew nothing.'

There was no film coverage of those two breaking international stories on that first night of television. That footage would arrive several days later by air from London and Los Angeles. CBS America had sent other stories by air the previous week. Some had arrived edited and some contained sound but there was just enough film to demonstrate their ability to produce a news bulletin. Not just any bulletin – this was Melbourne's first television news service.

Adding to the mayhem on opening night were the constant interruptions by senior *Herald* executives from the parent newspaper company, all were eager to have a front row seat into this new medium called television. However, no one realised how many of those executives were quietly eager to see television news fail. As the countdown clock swept towards the opening hour, a rehearsed choreography of lights music and cameras was about to focus on an elaborate aquarium of live fish.

In the build-up to this historic event no one had noticed the intense heat from the lights had been slowly cooking the fish. Frantic last minute efforts were made to revive them by pouring in cold water but it was symptomatic of the drama unfolding all around.

Finally, as the second hand hit the hour, director Ralph Clarkson called for a shot of the fish tank. It held for several seconds before camera two cut to the host presenter Eric Pearce sitting comfortably smoking his pipe, which would soon become his trademark. The 41-year-old radio broadcaster had just launched a strategic mid-life career change to television – a natural progression given his British culture and Hollywood persona – all the perquisites of a television news anchor.

In his cultured radio voice, the immaculately groomed Pearce began by welcoming viewers to Melbourne television. He then proceeded to introduce a number of station personalities before calling on Victoria's Premier Henry Bolte to officially open the station.

'It is appropriate,' said the Premier, 'given the *Herald's* leadership role in the community that its television station is the first in Melbourne.'

Very few were aware of the "true" reason behind the *Herald's* bid for a television licence. The *Herald* board was in damage control driven by a genuine fear that if successful, television would erode their newspaper's advertising revenue. Their bid for the TV licence was purely intended to protect their newspapers. Maher described it as 'a dog in the manger attitude'.

'The last thing they really wanted was a successful news service which they saw as competing directly against their bloody newspaper revenue.'

SIR JOHN WILLIAMS

Sir John was the media tycoon who inherited his position as chairman of the board after the sudden death of Sir Keith Murdoch in 1952. To enforce his position, he called a staff meeting in the *Herald* canteen shortly before the launch. He assured his staff not to worry about television.

'There will be virtually no news coverage on our TV station,' he said. 'News is for newspapers, not television.' As if to enforce those views it became apparent to those at Seven that obstacles were being deliberately put in place to ensure TV news would fail. Maher was among the first to be convinced that 'TV news was never going to be a priority in our programming' and very soon his worst fears were realised.

SACKING ERIC PEARCE
OCTOBER 1957

Eric Pearce, who was being mentored by Maher and was taking his news duties far more seriously than his Game Show *I've Got a Secret*, took his concerns to management. Unsuccessful, he decided to directly approach the chairman of the *Herald* board, Sir John Williams.

According to Maher, Williams listened impassively to Pearce's complaint and then politely said he would look into it. The meeting was said to have lasted little more than two minutes. Whether it was a perceived threat from television news to his newspaper or the sheer temerity of a complaint by a staff member, Williams responded with an immediate telephone call to Seven's station manager Keith Cairns.

'Keith! Mr Pearce will NOT be reading the news tonight.' There was a long pause before he continued, 'In fact, Mr Pearce will not be appearing on our television station again.'

Cairns told colleagues he was stunned by the decision but not for one moment was he prepared to question the merits of such a powerful figure as Sir John Williams and so was forced to sack Pearce later that afternoon.

'Yes that's right,' confirmed Maher. 'They just didn't want our news to succeed. We were against it right from the start.'

Pearce was said to have been devastated but philosophically quoted the law of karma: *For every event that occurs, there will follow another event, pleasant or unpleasant ... related to the original cause.*

'But not even Eric Pearce could have imagined the power of karma,' chuckled Maher. 'Imagine the irony, sacked by a knight of the realm then picked up by the opposition Nine Network and eventually elevated to a knighthood himself ... if that's not karma, then nothing is.'

GEOFF RAYMOND

Maher then set out to mentor a successor to Eric Pearce – former 3DB broadcaster Geoff Raymond. Meanwhile, HSV7 was undergoing major budget cut backs.

'The Chairman had now become embroiled in a terrible struggle with his board,' recalled Maher. 'Some members were openly accusing him of being irresponsible for getting involved in television in the first place ... I stayed on for a while to help Raymond but the cost cutting blitz forced our news back to seven minutes a night at seven minutes to seven on Seven ... It was bloody sacrilege and that's when I decided to leave.'

Against this background of financial restraints, bitter resentment and internal hostility, John Maher left Australian television to join a documentary company in Hong Kong. It was a stepping-stone to Granada Television where he became the Asian producer based in Tokyo. During those few years he honed his skills by producing a series of award-winning documentaries while biding his time for a return to television news in Australia.

It was at this point of our interview Maher asked me to stop the tape and refill our coffees. While in the kitchen I could hear movement, crashing and swearing from the adjoining room.

Returning with the two mugs of coffee, I caught sight of Maher doing a clumsy pirouette near his sideboard. Clutching his walking frame in one hand and holding a black and white photo in the other, he dropped it on the table with some pride then slumped back into his chair. It was a photo of Labor Leader Arthur Calwell signed: *Thank you John for your Labor of love.*

And so our interview resumed.

MAHER – THE SECOND COMING

In June 1966 John Maher returned from Japan to become press secretary to the opposition Leader, Arthur Calwell. It was during the Vietnam crisis and Maher was sympathetic to Calwell's philosophy.

'He told me right from the start that it wasn't a long-term job. "I don't have a dog's chance of winning the next election," he said, "and I do not intend to recontest the leadership."'

Calwell had just survived an assassination attempt in Sydney and public opinion on Australia's involvement in Vietnam was running strongly against him.

'A lot of things he said about Vietnam were absolutely right so I was thrilled when he gave me the job of writing his final keynote speech. I put my heart and soul into it. If I do say so myself, it was one of the best speeches he ever made. It made me feel proud that I had contributed to it.'

It was based on the fact that Australia was "not asked" to go into Vietnam. We "offered".

'Of course, that was denied at the time,' said Maher. 'But when the papers were eventually released it showed in fact it was the truth.'

Either way, the Labor Party suffered a crushing defeat on 6 November 1966 and Calwell subsequently retired two months later. John Maher then fulfilled his earlier ambition. Taking the advice of his best friend Dick Voumard of Qantas he joined the ABC in Melbourne, but it too became a short time job.

THE TELEVISION OFFER

In April 1968, Maher received a call from Keith Cairns, his former station manager at HSV7. They arranged to meet behind the Shrine. Cairns simply said to Maher, 'Would you like your job back – this time as News Editor?' Maher was a key appointment in HSV7's plan to launch a "Revolution" to end GTV9's dominance in news, headed by their popular two-reader format of Eric Pearce and Kevin Sanders.

A short time after Maher re-joined HSV7, Program Manager Norm Spencer approached him suggesting they too should have a two-reader format. He says he remembers how he had watched and admired Brian Naylor for some years and had always appreciated his flair for communication.

'So when Norm suggested that Naylor should be considered alongside Raymond, I thought it fantastic.'

Naylor had been with Seven since 1958 when he also made the transition from radio 3DB. He transferred his popular children's show *Swallows Juniors* to television where it was renamed *Brian and the Juniors*. In 1961 Naylor began honing his news skills on a magazine style program *The SSB Adventure Club*. Having already nurtured and produced Eric Pearce through those first months of television, and then chosen his successor Geoff Raymond, Maher was now about to seal the future of his next protégé, Brian Naylor. Within three weeks of making that decision Seven launched its tandem team.

BRIAN NAYLOR

Maher reflected with deep pride on Naylor's performance in that first bulletin. 'This is not being disloyal to Geoff Raymond who I had been producing, but it was most obvious from day one who the star reader was. This was equally hard on Geoff, because he recognised it too.'

Raymond fortuitously had already been offered a talkback job on Sydney radio. Seven management was well aware of the offer and made it easy for Raymond to move on. They simply let him go. Maher then began by co-coordinating the first satellite link in time for the Moon Landing. He also began shaping his team of four key reporters, cameramen and a senior producer; establishing a successful format and blueprint for television news well into the future.

THE FINAL WINDUP

I sat watching, listening and piecing together this tapestry of television history from my mentor. Suddenly, his voice began to fade from sheer physical exhaustion. I wanted to remind him of his many achievements. But then, as if reading my thoughts, he suddenly asked, 'I did have an influence, didn't I?'

'More than you will ever know, John,' I replied. As I began cleaning up the coffee mugs and checking my tape recorder he called out, 'You know I am so proud of you.'

I knew it of course, it was just something I would have loved to have heard 40 years earlier. I packed up my recorder, tidied the table and promised I would not leave it so long before we would meet again. I left him sitting in his favourite armchair overlooking his garden.

'You can let yourself out can't you, my boy?'

I did and I promised I would be back. But that was the last time I saw John Maher, he died several months later on 8 July 2004.

TRIBUTE

No news editor discovered and mentored so much on–air talent in Australia. No one suffered the loss of so much talent under his watch. Three colleagues killed in Balibo East Timor. Another four killed when the HSV7 news chopper crashed in 1982.

No news editor suffered so much humiliation as he did during the Fairfax takeover of HSV7 in 1987. And no director of news argued and fought so hard with management and boards to maintain the standards of television news – regarded as the template of bulletins – that continues to this day.

Maher's death inspired me to follow up several aspects of the history of television news, particularly the hitherto unreported sacking of Eric Pearce that would prove to have been a far more duplicitous decision than initially thought. Nigel Dick, former sales manager at GTV9 who succeeded Colin Bednall as general manager of GTV9 in 1962, says he was present when Nine made an offer to Pearce. It was made several months after GTV9 went to air in January 1957. However, due to restraints imposed by HSV7, Eric Pearce did not join GTV9 until 28 March 1958 (GTV9's public records).

'We had waited until after Christmas and watched the Seven experiment very closely … I remember clearly "our" first night of news read by Tom Miller who had a good voice but dirty fingernails.' Dick laughed at the way Miller used to sit with his hands clasped and fingers intertwined towards the camera. 'Miller was principal newsreader until we grabbed Eric, then Miller went on to weekends.'

Nine hiring Pearce was an inspirational move by its manager Colin Bednall. While Pearce was undisputedly the best presenter in town, he would be used as the main weapon in a battle between Bednall and the *Herald* board: 'a vicious and very personal crusade'.

NEWS BATTLELINES

One has to understand the background to this to fully appreciate the deep-seated hatred between Bednall and the *Herald*.

In 1954, Prime Minister Robert Menzies called for a royal commission to investigate the introduction of television in Australia – the system, the number of commercial stations (including government channels), and their charters. Bednall had not only been on the board of the *Herald* under Sir Keith Murdoch, but privately Murdoch had anointed him as heir apparent. However, Sir Keith suddenly died before the transfer of power had been ratified and Bednall was overlooked by the *Herald* board.

'Hell hath no fury like a spurned newspaper executive,' said Dick.

Initially Bednall went over to the *Argus* newspaper, where according to Dick, 'He rather stupidly tried to use the *Argus* to beat the Melbourne *Herald*. He over-spent and over-used his welcome.'

However, Bednall was well connected and Menzies soon appointed him as one of the royal commissioners into television. With television on the horizon, Arthur Warner, the transport minister in the Liberal Bolte Government and also Managing Director of Electronics Industries, the company that manufactured Astor television sets, decided to bid for a licence. There was never any doubt that Warner would be successful.

THE NUMBERS DRAW

The successful bidders, including Keith Cairns representing the *Herald* and HSV, Arthur Warner and executives of GTV and Government representatives for ABV, gathered in Melbourne for the numbers draw. Each pulled a number from a hat and that number would represent their station call sign.

Some years later General Manager Keith Cairns, who pulled out number 7, looked back on that moment in history, describing it in somewhat less than historic terms. 'It was like a bloody chook raffle on World of Sport.'

When asked why he was happy with the number 7, Cairns replied, 'It's my lucky golf club. The number 7 iron always drives higher and longer than the others.'

A short time after GTV pulled number 9, Warner (who confessed to knowing little about media) asked Bednall to find him a suitable general manager. The search proved more difficult than first thought, so eventually Warner offered the job to Bednall himself.

The pieces were now in place and according to Nigel Dick, 'Bednall gladly took it, seeing it as another opportunity to destroy the HWT … It was now very much a personal crusade and Eric Pearce would become his main weapon aimed at sinking Seven and his former *Herald* cronies once and for all.'

The battle began on 19 January 1957 with a small announcement in the Melbourne *Herald*.

GTV9 On Air Tonight
Television station GTV9 will be opened tonight by the Governor Sir Dallas Brooks who will drive his car into the centre of the main studio. Melbourne now has three television stations, HSV7, the first on air and ABV2, which have been operating for some time.

The opening will take place at 8 p.m. but the arrival of the official guests will be televised at 7.30. They will be interviewed by John McMahon. The variety show will be hosted by Terry Dear and Geoff Cork. The program is expected to end at 10 p.m.

In cold hard type, that was all the *Herald* newspaper was prepared to publish regarding the opening of Melbourne's second commercial television station. To further downgrade GTV9's profile, the *Herald* placed the article under a promotion for HSV7's movie of that night. It highlighted Nine's worst fears. There was simply no way they could succeed in the Melbourne market. Believing the *Herald*'s publicity machine was just too formidable, Sir Arthur Warner decided that GTV had to operate as a profitable number two – lean and mean – with minimal staff. However, Bednall saw it differently. According to Nigel Dick, 'He was determined to tackle Seven, confident Nine would become the dominant station … For a start, Bednall knew the *Herald's* executives weaknesses. He was a former HWT executive himself … He was aware of the structure that existed between HSV7's GM Keith Cairns and the *Herald* board; a structure that prevented Cairns from making day to day decisions without the board's approval … Bednall was also aware of the "pompous arrogance" of many board members and was under no illusion about the *Herald's* policy towards television, particularly their fears of television news.'

So while HSV7 had the potential backing of Victoria's largest publicity machine and newsgathering organisation, GTV9, led by Bednall, went in for the attack. Unhindered by GTV's ties with other media interests, Bednall made rapid decisions, capitalised on local events, captured the imagination of Melburnians, developed personalities, and relied entirely on word of mouth.

Within 18 months, GTV9 was number one and by then both

stations had also realised the potential of news in their programming line up. HSV7 was now regretting the day they let Eric Pearce go. It was too late to go cap in hand to get him back. Besides, he was signed and secure at GTV9.

Following the gap left by Eric Pearce, Seven's management hired a young announcer from radio station 3XY. Bert Newton arrived primarily to host an evening variety show called *The Late Show*. Bert's other task, which was not widely known, was also to read the news. But according to Bert, 'My first bulletin was my last. Seems the powers that be at the top of the *Herald* just didn't appreciate my quips and one line humour in the news, particularly when I referred to Prime Minister Menzies as "Ming". They were all too conservative.'

By 1958, Seven and Nine had been tinkering with their news services. Both had tried to go head-to-head with ABV2 at 7 o'clock, but that only incurred the wrath of viewers.

'That in itself was pretty remarkable at the time,' said Maher, 'because very few people ever complained about what we were doing. They still knew less than we did and we still didn't know much.'

Post-Pearce, Seven rotated a number of news presenters from their stable of 3DB radio announcers including names such as Geoff McComas, Roland Strong, John Eden and even General Manager Courtis Crawford (DB). Eventually former 3DB broadcaster, Geoff Raymond, who had just returned from overseas, became the regular news presenter although he had been initially hired to host the game show *Noughts and Crosses*. Similar musical news chairs had been taking place at GTV9. Among their presenters were, Tom Miller, Brian Taylor and even American wrestling commentator Jack Little. Jack read with Pearce in a double header for a short time, but it was Pearce who reigned supreme. According to Nigel Dick, 'Pearce had that X factor. People loved him. In fact in one of our surveys of 16 to 24 year olds he rated even higher in the popularity stakes than Nine's star performer Graham Kennedy.

'We found some of those viewers related to Eric as the father they didn't have, while others related him to the father they wished they had.'

By that stage the Packers had taken control of GTV9.

'You also have to remember,' said Dick, 'Nine was initially part owned by Sir Arthur Warner's Electronic Industries, the *Argus*, *Australasian Newspapers* and the *Age*.'

In January 1957, as GTV first went to air, the *Herald* bought the *Argus* and *Australasian Newspapers*. Under TV ownership legislation the *Herald* couldn't hold an interest in two television stations, so it sold off its newly acquired GTV9 shares to Sir Arthur Warner giving him brief but absolute control. However, in 1960, Philips in the UK bought a large shareholding of Warner's Electronics Industries. This turned it into a foreign company forcing Warner to sell his shareholding in GTV to Sir Frank Packer. So began a new "dynasty" with as much drama and deal making as its US soapy namesake.

By 1963, ABV2 had secured its news position at 7 o'clock and as the nation was maturing so too was its appetite for news. Seven and Nine had expanded their services to 30 minutes and moved to 6.30 but GTV9 with Eric Pearce was the clear leader. According to Dick, this was the year 'that GTV 9 out-manoeuvred HSV7 and secured their dominance in news for years to come with exclusive control of a coaxial cable'. It had been made clear to the Post Office (the organisation responsible for postal and telegraphic services) that GTV9 in Melbourne and TCN9 in Sydney would only enter the deal if the Seven stations were excluded. The cost of the relay was 250,000 pounds for the use of 60 hours each way between Melbourne and Sydney. Packer grumbled at the cost but undoubtedly knew the advantages that would come from it. The advantages were instantaneous. The cable allowed simultaneous live broadcasts of the fifth test of the 1962–63 Ashes series to Sydney, Canberra and Melbourne and was also used in 1965 for a historic live split-screen link-up between Graham Kennedy's *In Melbourne Tonight* and Don Lane's *Sydney Tonight*.

While Seven Melbourne and Sydney were struggling to meet deadlines and forced to transport news stories each night by air or road, TCN9 and GTV9 exchanged stories right up to news times. It couldn't have come at a worse time for Seven and they would continue to struggle until the start of the '70s and the launch of the News Revolution led by John Maher.

And so amid this background of bitter resentment, corporate rejection and internal and external hostility, television was born and with it came the news. I watched its birth as a young teenager before being seduced in 1961 by its competitive sibling rival, radio. Then in the early hours of a Saturday morning in November 1963 another piece of a jigsaw came into play.

CHAPTER 2

ASSASSINATION –
THE STARTER'S GUN

1963

Profumo case rocks Britain
First flight of Boeing 727 Jumbo
Britain's Great Train Robbery
JFK assassination

HITS

Blowin In the Wind – Bob Dylan
Sugar Shack – Jimmy Gilmour
It's My Party – Lesley Gore

SATURDAY, 23 NOVEMBER 1963

Working the breakfast shift on country radio had turned me into a creature of habit. It was 4.30 a.m. when the twin-belled, chrome-plated alarm created that disturbing jolt to kick-start my new day. Only this would be like no other day. At precisely the moment I silenced my alarm, a fatal shot was fired at US President John F Kennedy from the School Book Depository in Dallas, Texas. It was 12.30 p.m. Friday, 22 November in Dallas.

As I crawled from my bed in search of clothes, Jackie Kennedy was cradling her dying husband and attempting to assist a bodyguard who was scrambling to board the moving presidential limo.

As I forced my feet into already laced up desert boots, threaded the wooden toggles on my duffle coat and hobbled for the door, Lee Harvey Oswald was walking calmly out of the Book Depository on his way home.

As the presidential limo was frantically driving through Dallas heading for the Parkland Memorial Hospital, I was starting up my 1952 Morris Minor convertible to drive the short distance from my bedsit to the local radio station 3YB in the Victorian coastal town of Warrnambool.

We both reached our destinations at the same time.

I headed up the cold grey winding stairs below the familiar tower of the T&G building and entered the first floor offices of 3YB. Switching on lights and grabbing a pile of records from the bin outside the studio door, which I had selected the previous day, I entered the studio and stood before a manual telephone dial attached to a wall mount. I began the morning ritual of ringing six predetermined digits. As each number spun freely around the dial, an audible clicking sound confirmed that the first stage of the field transmitter was coming on-line. Three minutes later I dialled another six digits to bring the transmitter up to full strength.

As the studio clock hit the top of the hour I sat behind the console, flicked the red mike toggle switch to ON, hit four notes on electronic gongs and welcomed listeners to 3YB's *Saturday Morning Country Music Show*. At the very moment I released my finger to spin in the "yodelling jackeroo", a priest in Dallas Texas was administering the last rites.

As Buddy Williams launched into *I'll Stroll Down Memory Lane with You*, doctors in Dallas were pronouncing the 35th American President dead.

During the next 30 minutes, Slim Dusty, The Singing Kettles and Tex Ritter yodelled and trilled throughout the milking sheds of Victoria's Western District while chaos and confusion reigned in Dallas. Within six and a half minutes of the fatal shot being fired, New York's ABC radio anchorman Don Gardner was first to break the news. Gardner dictated information from UPI correspondent Merriman Smith who had been following the Kennedy motorcade a few vehicles behind. It was UPI that filed the first report for their international clients including radio 2SM in Sydney, which claimed to be first to break the news in Australia. However, the wire flash only stated that 'shots have been fired at the Presidential motorcade in Texas and first reports indicate the President may have been wounded'.

It was early morning in Australia and news staff at all major radio networks were only just signing on for duty. It would take more than 60 minutes before Australians became fully aware of the tragedy.

At 12.40 p.m. in Dallas (4.40 a.m. in Australia), just four minutes after America's first radio newsflash, the CBS Television Network with Walter Cronkite went to air with the first TV newsflash. However, as no cameras were available, it became a voice-over report only.

At 1.33 p.m. in Dallas (5.33 a.m. in Australia), just one hour and three minutes after the shooting, acting White House press secretary Malcolm Kilduff entered a nurse's classroom at the Parkland Memorial Hospital. In the room sat dozens of media representatives – to whom Kilduff made an official announcement:

President John F Kennedy died approximately 1.00 p.m. CST today here in Dallas. He died of a gunshot wound to the brain. I have no other details regarding the assassination of the President.

Meanwhile at CBS in New York, the studio cameras had now become fully operational and Walter Cronkite was seen to put on his glasses, pause, and then read that confirmation: *President Kennedy died at 1 p.m. CST 2 p.m. EST some 38 minutes ago.*

After reading the flash, Cronkite took off his glasses so he could consult the studio clock, which established the lapse in time since Kennedy had died. He paused briefly and replaced his eyeglasses, visibly moved. There was also a considerable lapse in time before any of this confirmation was reaching Australia.

Oblivious to the events unfolding in Dallas, I continued the normal breakfast shift. At 6.15 a.m. the studio door quietly swung open and in stepped Mickey Donahue. Mickey was a 14-year-old paperboy who delivered the Warrnambool Standard each morning from which I would select, edit and read local stories for our local news service. His visit had become a morning ritual of my breakfast show chatting briefly about trivial issues including which footy team in the Hamden League was expected to win in the next round. He passed me the paper as the record came to an end. I flicked the microphone back on to announce Marty Robins *White Sports Coat* before turning back to Mickey.

'Kennedy is dead.'

My hand automatically flew to the OFF switch. It was an involuntary action based on nothing more than if indeed Graham Kennedy, Australia's number one night time TV host, had died then it would have to be confirmed by someone with far more influence than just a local paper boy.

'You can't say that on air. Don't say that until it's confirmed.' I then switched the microphone back on.

'It's true,' he continued, 'President Kennedy has been shot. It's on Melbourne radio.' It was the innocent but convincing way he said it. I immediately queued up Connie Francis *Where the Boys Are*. My on-air conversation with young Mickey was over.

At 6.18 a.m. I rang the home of our station manager Eric Collins. Eric Collins was a frustrated chain-smoking thespian. When his interests in the local repertory theatre company lapsed, as they did between productions, he then turned all his efforts into running his local radio station. The timing of my call couldn't have been better placed. He was not only awake but between productions. His first reaction was, 'I'll call you back.' His second reaction was to call his chief engineer. Harry Fuller was responsible for rebuilding the station after fire destroyed the building back in 1946. However, in later years, Harry had become colour blind, making it necessary for an assistant to be on hand at all times to identify which wires he had laid were red, yellow or black.

Long before joining 3YB in 1939, Harry Fuller had become an established radio ham and for many years VK2HF was recognised by American operators as one of the best amateur radio stations in Australia. Within minutes of receiving news of the assassination, Harry Fuller tuned his receiver into Voice of America then relayed the transmission through a landline directly into the studios of 3YB.

At 6.29 a.m. Eric Collins rang me back just to confirm I was receiving the signal and then gave me instructions to use my own discretion in recording sound grabs and turning them around or putting them directly to air.

At 6.32 a.m. I crossed to the US having had no idea of the source, whether it was fresh news or a recap, or even if we were in breach of the PMG's Broadcasting Code, which of course we were.

Here is a bulletin from CBS News. Further details on an assassination attempt against President Kennedy in Dallas, Texas. President Kennedy was shot as he drove from Dallas Airport to downtown Dallas; Governor Connolly of Texas, in the car with him, was also shot. It is reported that three bullets rang out. A Secret Service man …was heard to shout from the car, "He's dead."

In between trying to listen to these static fading voice reports, I also sat juggling a stack of recorded commercials on 45RPM discs, cuing up specific individual sponsored tracks while also selecting music and reading live commercials. On a number of occasions when I became overwhelmed with programming duties I simply crossed live and let the American service run.

Government sources now confirm…we have this from Washington. Government sources now confirm that President Kennedy is dead. So that, apparently, is the final word and an incredible event that I am sure no one except the assassin himself could have possibly imagined would occur on this day.

Throughout all this chaos, and being the only person on duty, I was also trying to field dozens of phone calls from anxious listeners who were under a misguided belief that perhaps I knew more than the American reporters, or were simply ringing to confirm what we were putting to air was true.

Back in Dallas, Oswald arrived home a short time after the shooting then left to catch a bus. As he stood at the bus shelter, a passing police officer appeared to recognise a similarity to the description of the man wanted over the shooting of Kennedy. Moments later, Police officer JD Tippet was shot dead. An eyewitness then followed the alleged killer to the Texas Movie House Theatre where two hours and 20 minutes after shooting the President, Lee Harvey Oswald was arrested.

The Dallas Police Department confirms the arrest of a 24-year-old man, Lee H Oswald, in connection with the slaying of a Dallas policeman shortly after President Kennedy was assassinated. His initial comment was said to be, "Well, it's all over now!"

It was not over. It was just the start. We were not aware of it at that time but the assassination had just transformed the media industry, particularly in the US. It was the first time a major event had been broadcast live from the scene with a news presenter anchoring the coverage and letting images do the talking. It was the first time US networks went live with wall-to-wall coverage, suspending all commercial commitment. The next time commercial free news would be seen would be 11 September 2001. The coverage of the assassination proved that television could compete with radio in breaking news – at least in the United States.

As I walked from the radio studios in 3YB Warrnambool shortly after 9 a.m. that morning, most Australians were just waking up to the news. Melbourne's GTV9 had already opened the day's transmission with a newsflash and radio pictures transmitted from the scene for international newspaper affiliates. Channel 2 began their morning program with a bulletin of library vision and similar radio stills. HSV7 went to air at midday with a 15-minute bulletin including a packaged obituary. TV critics were unanimous in their praise of the Melbourne television coverage describing it as, 'The magic of modern communications... television at its greatest... the first prints of the history books of tomorrow'. They were not far wrong. The "tomorrow" had a more literal interpretation. It would be at least 24 hours before the vision arrived for television viewers by way of intercontinental airlines. Unlike the live reports, American viewers were witnessing, we had to wait for our vision.

Australian radio listeners were being far better served. No questions were ever asked by authorities or the PMG as to breaching broadcasting rules, I just followed the procedure we had established a year earlier during the Cuban Missile Crisis when Harry Fuller first tapped into Voice of America through his amateur radio station VK2HF from his home in Warrnambool.

The Soviet convoy heading for Cuba with war materials is showing no signs of turning back as massed US warships prepare to stop it — and start shooting if necessary.
The showdown is now just hours away...
—Voice of America, Wednesday 5 October 1962

The tyranny of distance meant it was some time before we actually saw the confrontation on television news, by then of course US President John F Kennedy had emerged triumphantly just as radio had.

The shots fired from the Dallas Book Depository were akin to a starter's gun in an international race to be "first with the news". Driven by technology, it was a race that would develop into a marathon.

Over the next six decades this marathon would gather such speed that it would threaten to derail like a multiple train wreck.

I look back on my notes from that day in 1963 – not only for its tragic consequences – but also for the part it played in the history of a country radio station in the Victorian town of Warrnambool and the roles of a naive newspaper boy, a novice junior announcer and a technically blind technician. I particularly remember the amazing sense of pride having been handed the responsibility of broadcasting such an event at such an early stage of my career.

My interest in news can be traced back to my childhood. December 1951, I was eight years of age, we were living in the Cheshire town of Poynton and, unlike my father, I was not an avid reader and took very little interest in daily news events. However, there was one story that did attract my attention. It involved a World War II Liberty ship *The Flying Enterprise* that became the victim of a late seasonal hurricane in the mid–Atlantic.

For more than two weeks the hero of this unfolding drama refused to leave his stricken vessel. Newspapers carried the pictures but it was the news story on radio that captured my imagination. It kept the entire nation enthralled as the ship began tilting at an ominous 30 degrees after its cargo shifted in the rolling seas.

Each night Captain Curt Carlson reported the latest developments from his ship by radio. Then we all held our breaths as a crack suddenly developed amidships across the main deck and down each side of its hull. A second sailor, who also remained aboard the stricken vessel, helped during dramatic attempts to attach a rescue line in a bid to tow them to safety. It was a real-life soap opera as we gathered around our radio each night in a bid to catch snippets of conversations despite static interference playing havoc with reception during this rare live broadcast from the mid-Atlantic. It ended as both men literally leapt from the smokestack to safety when the towline snapped and *The Flying Enterprise* sank beneath their feet. I still remember the image of Captain Curt Carlson clinging to the rails of his sinking ship and often wonder whether that indelible memory on such an impressionable eight year old had some later influence on my choice of career in broadcast news.

The event also happened to coincide with a large family gathering at my grandparents' home in Cheshire England. We were celebrating their golden wedding anniversary and the impending departure of our family as my father had announced his intention to migrate to Australia. I seem to remember Grandad's reaction to us leaving for Australia drew less of a celebratory response than his golden wedding anniversary. My grandad, James Baxter Walden, had many notable friends. Among them was TE Lawrence, "Lawrence of Arabia". In fact, so close was he to Lawrence that he named his son (my father) after him – Hugh Lawrence Walden.

My grandfather read out two telegrams that night. The first was from his good friend, American poet Professor Walter Pitkin, author of the bestselling book *Life Begins at 40*. It read: *With your son Hugh on his way to Australia it will soon be true that the sun will never set on its possessions.* I had absolutely no idea what it meant but everyone else appeared to be very impressed.

The second telegram read: *Wishing James Baxter Walden a continued healthy life. Captain Curt Carlson, Flying Enterprise.*

I often wondered how Captain Carlson, struggling against a tilting vessel being battered by the wildest Atlantic storm in 20 years managed to reach his bridge and send that cable. Then again, perhaps it was my first awareness of the term "journalistic licence".

There is no question in my mind, Saturday morning November 23 in 1963 was a major turning point in my life. There must be a moment in every addict's life when they experience their first hit. If so, then the rush of adrenalin I received from breaking the news of the assassination of JFK created an addiction in me that would last a lifetime. Of course, I was totally unaware of the significance that news story would have on my life at the time, just as I was unaware of the implications of another race taking place high above us – the Space Race involving sputniks and satellites.

And so in 1969 when man landed on the moon and the world stopped and watched in awe as Neil Armstrong made his "giant leap for man-kind", I was more impressed when President Nixon picked up his telephone in the Oval office and spoke to the American astronaut in real time. That was when I realised satellites had allowed television to catch up to the immediacy of radio. If there was any future in news then it had to be in television – but until then, radio still held the advantage.

RADIO

My interest in radio can be traced back to the art of gently flicking a cat's whisker across the face of a crystal in a desperate search for its sweet spot. It took a steady hand and a stubborn determination before the fine hair-like whisker eventually found its point of contact and a crisp clear sound filled my Bakelite headphones. As a 12-year-old, the crystal became my seducer into the mystery of radio.

By the time I reached the age of 14, transistors had energised radio – and like adolescent teens, it too was enjoying a newfound mobility and independence. At 16 years I won a secret sound competition on a country radio station and used the cash prize to begin a course in broadcasting. In 1959 the legendary Melbourne broadcaster and mentor Lee Murray began producing my voice.

'Forward and to the tip of your tongue,' he would boom to his class of budding announcers. However, I was soon to discover a deep voice was not the only prerequisite to a future in radio. A year later I successfully applied for my first job. Call it fate or serendipity, but on June 6, 1961 I began my career on the same station I had won the prize that had paid for the course.

3YB WARRNAMBOOL

It was the final week in May 1964 when 3YB station manager Eric Collins delivered my farewell speech in which he revealed how close I had come to failure.

Never had I heard anyone in radio so naive, immature, totally lacking in traditional music appreciation and basic general knowledge … The turning point came with the way in which you handled a very difficult day broadcasting the JFK assassination … You showed a maturity and professionalism I had not seen before, and Malcolm, that day not only saved your job but taught me never to be so quick to be judgmental again.

In hindsight, who could have blamed him for nearly giving up on me? After all, I married George and Ira Gershwin, butchered Chopin (Chopping) and lost a major sponsor when I introduced Tchaikovsky's *Bum of the flightily Bee*. I anointed Miss Victoria with her 'sophie and trash' (trophy and sash) and put the fear of God into Collins whenever I introduced his station's major sponsor Philpot and Tucker, threatening the grandest spoonerism of them all. But he persevered and for that I would remain eternally grateful. I only hoped future mentors and managers would be as equally magnanimous and supportive.

MONDAY, 1 JUNE 1964
7EX LAUNCESTON

Diary entry:

We gathered in the boardroom of the Examiner Newspaper office. Sitting around the table were company sales representatives, radio 7EX executives and Chairman Edmund Rouse. After personally welcoming me to Launceston, Rouse quickly went on to claim that my name was 'totally inappropriate' for the station's 'big sound' of top 40 and US imports.

'Something short, sharp and snappy,' he demanded. Names like Mike, (Mike on Mike) and even Fred were suggested. Station Manager Alan McClelland cleared his throat and meekly suggested Mel as in Mel Torme, at which I gently said, 'Why not Mal, as in Malcolm?' There was a pause and everyone seemed to agree on Mal Walden. June 6 1964, exactly three years to the day that I began my career at 3YB Warrnambool, I commenced my first shift on 7EX Launceston.

By then radio technology had advanced to cartridge machines replacing commercials on 45RPM discs. As the breakfast announcer on 7EX, I inherited the formidable challenge set by my predecessor Rod Muir who left to relaunch the "Good Guy" era on Sydney radio before becoming the founding father of FM radio in Australia. I began by taking over his live hosting gig at Launceston's premier Hotel Cabaret before increasing my profile by reading my first television news on TNT9 Launceston.

Diary entry:

I was led into the stark small studio and seated before a single automatic camera, which was operated by remote from a control room director. The switchboard operator applied my makeup; there was no cameraman, no floor manager and no auto cue. I was quickly briefed on a technique that evolved reading slowly, memorising every second line and attempting to make eye-to-eye contact with the viewer at least 40 (if not 50) per cent of the time. I soon discovered that (unlike radio news) the slower I read the scripts the more time I had to make emphasis, inflections and eye-to-eye contact with the camera. Of course, that all changed with the introduction of autocue.

MONDAY, 6 JUNE 1966
3DB MELBOURNE

I finally fulfilled my ambition of reaching a capital city radio station. The HWT station 3DB had emerged triumphant from the "golden era" of wireless in the '30s and '40s where it became a broadcasting institution in Melbourne. However, in the '60s, the next generation of 3DB listeners was accepting the next generation of announcers and I was chosen to be one of them.

I only met General Manager Courtis Crawford three times in my three years there. The most memorable meeting took place in the studio as I was playing The Beatles hit *Yellow Submarine*. No sooner had it finished when he stormed in and whipped it from the turntable. With a pair of scissors he scoured it across both sides and then muttered in a deep malevolent voice, 'My daughter was right, it's just rubbish'. Three weeks later it became number one and we had to go out and buy another copy.

3DB seemed to lurch from crisis to crisis and format to format. It never quite stamped itself as a station with purpose or identity – except for its consistency in the quality of its *Herald Sun* news service.

CHAPTER 3

A MISSING PM –
A MISSED OPPORTUNITY

1967

Ronald Ryan, last person to be executed in Australia, hanged
Referendum to end constitutional discrimination against Aborigines
Raging bushfires devastate much of Hobart and surrounding areas

HITS

To Sir With Love – Lulu
I'm a Believer – The Monkees
All You Need is Love – The Beatles

SUNDAY, 17 DECEMBER 1967

California has the Santa Ana and Canada has the Chinook. The wind in Western Australia is known as the Fremantle Doctor and in Melbourne it is simply referred to as a blistering northerly.

On the seventeenth day of summer in 1967, one week before Christmas, the northerly winds that whipped across Melbourne and swept down along the Southern Coast of Victoria helped create conditions that arguably changed the course of Australia's history. Little more than a gentle breeze was blowing just before dawn as I entered the radio studio of 3DB, deep within the basement of the city's major *Herald* newspaper building. The red ON-AIR light cast a warm glow through the double glass sound-proofed window. It appeared to reflect the theme of my program, which was coincidently all about reflection. Outside, the wind was increasing. Half-way into my shift I cleared my smoker's throat again:

You're listening to Mal Walden's Hits and Memories as we return to the year 1959 when Melbourne pop fans mourned the death of Buddy Holly and hang your head if you have forgotten the Kingston Trio and Tom Dooley.

Without warning, the heavy studio door squeaked open to reveal the station's veteran news reporter Bruce "Nobby" Turner. He was a caricature of the traditional pressman, complete with a hat that tilted at the same angle as the cigarette that constantly hung from a corner of his mouth. I was a menthol smoker, he was vintage untipped Craven-A.

'I'm leaving and I'll file a report for your midday news.' He then turned and left the door to slowly squeak shut.

What was the point of having soundproof doors if they squeaked? Turner was referring to the arrival of lone British yachtsman Alec Rose who was due to complete his around the world solo voyage later in the day. But Rose was battling huge seas which had been whipped up by the strengthening northerlies and there appeared to be little chance his tiny yacht *Lively Lady* would arrive in time for my midday news. I didn't care too much. I knew I would be reading that story later tonight anyway– but not on this station and not even on radio.

Several weeks earlier I had been asked to read my first news bulletin on Melbourne television and this was to be the night. Although I wasn't looking for a career in television I was hoping it would at least lift my profile and boost my radio career. The previous year, while presenting the breakfast radio shift on 7EX Launceston I read the Sunday night news on TNT Channel Nine so I was confident of having had some experience in television.

The Kingston Trio finished and I continued my *Hits and Memories* segment through to midday. I have always believed hit songs are like big news stories; you always remember where you were when you first heard them. Very soon, we would all remember where we were on this day in 1967. At the end of my music shift I read the midday news bulletin and then packed up my belongings. I wandered out through the adjoining newsroom where the only person on duty was a young cadet journalist. Phone held to his ear, he placed his forefinger across his lips to indicate he couldn't speak. So without so much as a goodbye, I pushed open the rear doors into Flinders Lane where I had parked my car. I left the doors to swing shut and click into security mode. That phone call was the first dramatic alert from a source in Canberra indicating the Prime Minister of Australia may be missing! No further details were available. Given the nature of the report and being unsure how to handle such claims, the young cadet then called the news desk of the giant *Herald* newspaper complex four floors above him.

As I was driving home, his call had been verified and further details were immediately relayed to the *Herald's* chief of staff John Fitzgerald. Fitzgerald was attending a family Christmas gathering at his home nearby. Within minutes the veteran newspaper boss had placed the entire *Herald* organisation on full alert, calling in all staff and implementing the "who to tell" from a major newsbreak handbook he had refined after the assassination of US President Kennedy.

Across town at Sandown Park, ATV Channel 0 sporting commentator Phil Gibbs was wrapping up a sports segment from the location of the previous day's live racing. The live eye truck was still linked up to the control room at the studios in Nunawading. Responding to similar reports, senior cameraman Morrie Pilens immediately swung his team into action. He rang Gibbs and cleared the Outside Broadcast truck to be dispatched to Portsea. The station's chief of staff then called senior newsreader Barry McQueen who was confined to bed suffering a severe bout of flu.

McQueen conceded 'there was no alternative' and agreed to be picked up on route to Portsea. It was now a race to be first with the news but at that stage the PM was only being reported as 'missing, feared drowned'. At GTV9 in Richmond, the early morning chief of staff had already chalked up Alec Rose as the lead story. The network's chief news coordinator journalist Michael Schildberger was attending a pre-Christmas cocktail party and being quite close to Nine was able to take control almost immediately. Channel Nine host and public affairs commentator Tony Charlton had already been assigned to cover the arrival of yachtsman Alec Rose at Williamstown. He was standing beneath the fluttering flags and banners of welcome at the Williamstown Yacht Club when Schildberger radioed him with the chilling news.

'Get out of there and down to Portsea ... Harold Holt is missing at sea.'

Charlton was about to say what about the yachtsman when Schildberger cut in, 'Just get the hell down to Portsea.'

Over in South Melbourne, HSV7 had the advantage of its association with the *Herald Sun* organisation and was able to combine their resources. The network's senior presenter Geoff Raymond and support presenter Brian Naylor were called in while part-time reporter David Johnston was already in the area covering the arrival of Rose. In fact, of all journalists that day, David Johnston was the closest to Cheviot Beach. Had he not been so violently ill in the bottom of the fishing boat he had chartered to cover the arrival of Rose he could have watched the PM several hundred metres away as he waded out into the surf.

Back in Melbourne, I returned home blissfully unaware of the crisis until my flatmate broke the news. "Big" Sam Anglesea was a DJ with the top rating radio station 3UZ and with a voice that bellowed from his boots he was yelling, 'The fuckin' PM is dead, man! Holt is missing, man, they think he's drowned!' My initial reaction was shock and then some disappointment when I selfishly realised that they wouldn't want a part-time radio newsreader tonight – they would bring in their big guns. I rang the chief of staff at HSV7 who suggested I still come in as they could use an extra hand. As I arrived and parked my car, the wind suddenly dropped and all was still. It was the antithesis of the chaos that greeted me in the television newsroom. Journalists and producers were shouting, women were typing and two-way radio speakers were crackling, as garbled messages were lost in broken transmissions. It was a common communication problem facing most TV reporters in the field. Many were forced to leave the scene near Cheviot Beach in search of landline phones – as well as sufficient coins to make a connection. All news crews were reliant on two-way radio systems in their news cars. However, they frequently failed in black spot areas and with the overload on frequencies during a major crisis such as this, they became even less reliant.

Amid the chaos and confusion at HSV7, I was handed a bunch of scripts and led to a small audio booth the size of a phone box with a microphone strung between four wires from the ceiling. Cardboard egg cartons lined its walls as soundproofing and a flickering 8-inch black and white monitor was provided as a guide for my voice-over commentary. My instructions were just to read the scripts whenever the red light above the microphone came on. A director's voice barked orders through another crackling speaker system and between scheduled news casts from the studio downstairs I followed developments providing live voice-over descriptions to pictures that were being beamed back by microwave-link from the search centre at Cheviot Beach. The coaxial cable, when errant backhoes were not digging it up, was the only other form of transmitting news stories and the Nine network had exclusivity to this.

So as the military combed the beach and commentators struggled to fill blank moments when seagulls and atmospheric conditions caused drop outs in our micro-link coverage, I stayed in my tiny studio box watching and providing a minimal contribution to this tragic moment in history.

There were many conspiracy theories raised over the following years including one involving the PM as a spy who had been plucked from the water by a Chinese submarine. Another had the PM swimming around to the next bay where a secret woman admirer met him and they both drove off to spend their lives together elsewhere. There was even talk of suicide. However, the general consensus was that he swam out into the extremely rough waters at Cheviot Beach in an act of bravado, which ended when the roaring surf collaborated with the surging kelp. He was dragged under to become the sixty-seventh drowning victim of the year.

The media frenzy lasted weeks and each TV Network claimed credit for their efforts. The new kid on the block, ATV Channel 0, was regarded as the first to transmit details of a live news story from an outside broadcasting facility, setting parameters that continue to this day. GTV9 claimed the most viewers with their popular news reading combination of Eric Pearce and Kevin Sanders. They were unaware at the time but in less than two years they would break all records with the longest live television broadcast of the Apollo Moon Landing. However, the last word of the night and the one that has gone down in media folklore was attributed to HSV7's Geoff Raymond. With all the reverence he could muster he finally summed up the historic but tragic day, announcing the search for the missing PM had been called off for the night 'after coming to a dead halt'.

1969

After eight years I was beginning to lose my passion for radio yet held little interest in television. I was aware but not interested in media reports suggesting Channel Seven was about to launch a News Revolution involving its nightly news and that John Maher had been re-appointed as director. I was already aware of Maher's reputation. He was the man widely known as having discovered and produced Melbourne's first TV newsreader Eric Pearce, then selected and mentored his successor Geoff Raymond. Little did I know that several years later Maher would anoint me as the final link in his chain of news anchors.

In 1969, after a touch of tedium from the fickle formats of Top 40, news, weather and sport, I decided to adjust my sail. They say travel broadens the mind and there was no doubt mine was in need of broadening. After a severe bout of throat infection I had my tonsils removed – double claimed through the HWT and Hospital Benefits Association. I made a profit of $300 and booked a one-way trip overseas. With a letter of accreditation to file stories for 3DB talk host Gerald Lyons and a vague plan of becoming a radio correspondent, I anxiously boarded the *Fairstar* at Melbourne's station pier on a journey that would end in a country facing far greater internal anxieties than mine – Israel.

You can never change the course of the wind but you can always adjust your sail.

– James Rohn

CHAPTER 4

THE ISRAELI INFLUENCE

1970

HEADLINES

First jumbo jet launched
Poseidon shares grip market
Vietnam moratorium in Melbourne
The Westgate Bridge collapse

HITS

Yellow River – Christie
The Wonder Of You – Elvis Presley
Bridge Over Trouble Water – Simon & Garfunkel

CHRISTMAS EVE, 1969

In the French harbour city of Cherbourg, a small group of men attached to the Israeli secret service, Mossad, began moving towards their targets. Masquerading as Norwegian oil workers, they had infiltrated the town in the preceding weeks to orchestrate what they codenamed "Operation Noah's Ark". They cut through the perimeter fence of the town's ship building centre and silently split into groups, each heading towards five newly built Israeli gun boats being held under a French arms embargo. At the stroke of midnight, church bells began to ring out in celebration of Christmas – this drowned out the noise of five powerful missile boat engines as they roared out of Cherbourg harbour. The boats were on their way to help restore Israel's balance of power against a threatening Russian-built Egyptian navy.

The following morning in London, the newspaper banners were as grim as the weather with warnings of war and threats of retaliation. My mood was even gloomier as I strode through the rain to Victoria Station having pre-booked a trip bound for the same destination as the gunboats – Israel.

Why was I doing this? At 25 years of age I had already been accused of being a bloody fool by throwing in my job as a radio announcer in Australia. I grabbed a paper from a newsstand to give me some background to the incident, hitched my backpack a little higher and stepped up my pace for the midday train. The paper was reporting the incident as "the most intense political crisis between Israel and France since Israeli forces had violated the sovereignty of Argentina to kidnap Adolph Eichmann". It did little to settle my nerves. It went on to explain how Germany initially began building the boats as part of reparations for crimes against Jewry. But when word leaked out, fearing Arab trade reprisals, the Germans then handed the contract over to the French.

In December 1968, Israeli commandos launched a strike on Beirut airport. French President Charles De Gaulle was so outraged he issued a trade embargo against Israel including the gunboats. After 12 months of frustrating political negotiations Israel decided to act and take what they believed was rightly theirs.

My train left Victoria Station on time and I arrived in Marseille the following day. I then boarded a rust bucket called the *MV Adelphi,* which ploughed the Mediterranean carrying small groups of passengers and unknown cargo to the Israeli port of Haifa. My mood of uncertainty was not helped by dark puddles forming on the ship's deck as rain water leaked from the rotting hulls of the hanging lifeboats. Shortly before our midnight departure, I stood alone by the ship's rail. As I watched these puddles form then slowly leak over the side, a black limo pulled alongside the wooden gangplank. A passenger was quickly hustled aboard and not seen again until several days out to sea. Rumours tend to spread at sea when small groups are confined to close quarters and aboard the *Adelphi* the rumour mill was in overdrive concerning a mystery passenger believed to be a Mossad agent wanted by the French over the "gunboat hijackings". When he eventually emerged several days later, his mystique matched his appearance. He appeared as a typical blond haired Scandinavian with blue eyes that flashed with intensity yet spoke in fluent Hebrew. No one introduced him around yet several Israelis greeted him in almost star-struck awe. The rest of us amusingly named him "Garth" after the comic book character that boasted similar features of a well-chiselled face and muscular physique.

Together with a small group of Jewish migrants, teenage Israeli conscripts and half a dozen fellow backpackers, we steadily ploughed our way down through the Mediterranean. Days were spent playing cards, drinking cheap wine and singing. In every group of backpackers there is always one who plays a guitar. We gathered each night after dinner in the ship's small mess room, gradually breaking down the language barriers by inviting each person to sing their national song. On one of these nights Garth emerged to take centre stage and the Israelis joined him in a beautiful rendition of the Israeli folk song *Hava Nagila*. As tears flowed among his followers, he spotted me calling out, 'Gin-Giy, Gin-Giy. Boh!' *Gin-Giy* apparently referred to my red hair and *Boh* I soon learnt was Israeli for "come".

'Sing, Gin-Giy ... Sing your country's song.'

All I could remember was the first chorus of *Waltzing Matilda* but it was enough to form a very strange bond between the two of us, which lasted the entire journey.

On the final morning as we entered the port of Haifa, I stepped out onto the rear deck to watch the tugs bring us in. A short distance from our wharf lay the five gunboats. Sheltering from the rain beneath one of the few lifeboats that wasn't leaking was Garth, rocking back and forth on his knees and uttering the words, 'Eretz Israel, Eretz Israel.' The rusty metal door squeaked as I opened it and stepped through. Tears were streaming down his cheeks as he stood to embrace me saying, 'Mail (he could never get my name right), Mail, I would die for my country.' And I suspected one day he would. He then strode off.

In that first week of January 1970, with a scant knowledge of Israel and my vague plan of becoming an international radio news reporter, I disembarked and headed for life on a Kibbutz. I arrived in Tel Aviv with Anne and Mary, two Melbourne nurses I had met on route and 23-year-old Phil Stone, a Canadian scriptwriter from Medicine Hat, Alberta who, with his guitar, had joined the

Adelphi in the Italian port city of Naples. As we had similar plans we decided to stay together if possible, registering with authorities and successfully applying to work on Kibbutz Gevim, via Ashkelon, near the Gaza Strip. It was a small settlement with a population of around 300 that specialised in growing roses for export. Of all the Kibbutzim in Israel we were assured that Gevim was one of the safest.

We caught an old British Bedford built bus, which took just over two hours before we reached the administration office where we were met by the elected head of the Kibbutz, 86-year-old German-born Shoshanna. With her silver-hair pulled back into a tight bun and a loose-hanging army fatigue shirt, she approached with outstretched arms. Her appearance was of a warm maternal grandmother welcoming her four favourite grandchildren.

'Welcome, welcome to our home, Gevim,' she said with a slight guttural accent. We stood not quite knowing if we should hug her or just grab one her hands and shake it. Shoshanna quickly explained how she and her two brothers hadover-r arrived in Israel in 1947 aboard a refugee vessel which ran the gauntlet of a British blockade in much the same manner as her sister ship the *Exodus*. We discovered she had not only lost most of her family in Hitler's Holocaust but her eldest brother was killed in the Israeli War of Independence in 1948 and her husband and youngest brother were both killed in the Six-Day War in 1967. Despite her personal tragedy, Shoshanna's first instruction on our arrival was to insist we maintain contact with our parents and families back home.

'You must write, I will insist on this,' she said, as she then outlined the free medical and dental plan offered to volunteers on the Kibbutz. 'You will be required,' she said, 'to work six days a week. After four weeks you will be given a week off to tour my country.'

The terms of employment included accommodation and a salary, the equivalent of $5 per week, as well as one packet of cigarettes every two days or one bottle of Israeli wine. As guests of the Israel Government we were asked to respect their customs, uphold their laws and comply with any new restrictions that may be imposed at any time. There was one final warning **No Drugs**. Any sign of drug taking would lead to instant deportation. Apparently two British volunteers had recently been deported for baking "hash" cookies and distributing them among the community, leaving many in such a state of unexplained hilarity they were unable to work. I chortled at the thought but was quickly rebuked. Phil and I were then escorted down a neatly trimmed path, which led to a very basic pre-fabricated bedsit where we met Sam from New York. We would share our lives with him for the next six months. Anne and Mary moved in next door.

Around 5 p.m. a large bell rang out. It was our cue to assemble in the communal dining room where I was introduced to the other dozen volunteers and the several hundred members of the Kibbutz. I again heard the term *Gin-Giy,* a reference to my red hair. The term was always followed by bursts of laughter. When I asked why, I was proudly told, 'Don't be offended, King David was a *Gin-Giy.'*

The following morning I was driven out to a small, three-sided tin shed in a distant paddock where several volunteers were sorting potatoes on a conveyor belt. I had replaced an American Jew called Zachariah who had been told to leave. It seemed Zachariah was convinced the Kibbutz would become the target of a bomb attack. Each time an aircraft took off from a nearby military airfield he would run down into our communal air-raid shelter. Israeli bombers had been intensifying their attacks against Russian built SAM 3 missile sites along the Suez Canal and the heavily laden bombers were flying low across the Kibbutz at regular intervals. Much to the amusement of his colleagues, Zach was spending most of his time underground so it was decided that it would be best for all if he should leave.

As soon as I took my place at the conveyor belt system, the exploits of young Zach were regaled in detail to howls of laughter as we sorted through the passing line of potatoes. But as I was being instructed in the art of looking for certain inherent black spots which would doom the spuds to compost, I suddenly became aware of another spot. This one was in the sky behind my newfound colleagues who were facing me with their backs to the open shed. I estimated it was several miles due south and no more than 5000 feet high and descending. As the laughter continued at Zach's expense, the dot became a plane and the plane appeared to be heading directly towards our tin shed. I was simply not prepared to become another Zachariah so I continued sorting potatoes. By now the plane had dropped to less that several hundred feet, the pilot was clearly visible as were the twin bomb-like containers on each wingtip. There was no other target in that area. Just our tin shed. I was about to drop to the floor when it suddenly unleashed its superphosphate on the nearby orange grove and disappeared over our roof. It was at that moment I realised I would have preferred to die than make a fool of myself.

Each night we attended Hebrew lessons and very soon I could ask for the salt and pepper at meal times. We were also being briefed on the latest crisis facing Israel. Following the 1967 Six-Day War, Egypt had commenced a policy of shelling Israeli positions along the eastern side of the Suez Canal, which Israel had captured. Egyptian President Gamal Abdul Nasser believed that because most of Israel's army consisted of reserves they could not withstand a lengthy war. He believed Israel would be unable to endure the economic burden and that constant casualties would undermine Israeli morale. This was his "War of Attrition". But he underestimated Israel's resolve to survive. Young people from around the world, both Jewish and Gentile, were now defying the threats and volunteering to work on Kibbutz settlements. This allowed the nation's productivity to continue in the absence of young Israelis who were being conscripted into the military.

The War of Attrition had already claimed more than one thousand Israeli soldiers and civilians. Meanwhile, the Palestine Liberation Organisation (PLO) were regrouping under new leadership and stepping up terror attacks from nearby Gaza. It was something not mentioned at the Kibbutz office on our arrival and for the first time I had the distinct feeling volunteers could become legitimate targets of attack. Had I known that on our arrival, I would not have tempted fate.

Perhaps it was naivety, the invincibility of youth or plain sheer stupidity, but on our first weekend on Kibbutz Gevim, Annie, Mary, Phil and I were invited to join a small group of veteran volunteer workers who had planned to walk across the occupied strip to the former Egyptian town of Gaza. They assured us it was a safe three-hour walk, which they took regularly. As it was our first Saturday on Kibbutz Gevim and given it was the holy day of Shabbat, I was surprised we were even given approval to leave our duties to members of the Jewish community. But there were no objections so the twelve of us filled our water bottles, filed out of the Kibbutz and headed off towards the occupied city of Gaza.

It was a cool morning but the sun was out and promising a top temperature in the mid-20s. The road to Ashkelon was lined with Australian eucalypts and their familiar scent triggered my first pang of homesickness. Within 20 minutes we had branched off the main road reaching a cyclone gate with twin vehicle tracks, which led off across open fields towards Gaza. We simply lifted the latch and walked through onto the strip. The only anxious moments came with regular signs of landmine warnings in the fields but as we were sticking to the vehicle tracks I was assured we would not be at any risk. As our group began to spread out, I settled in half way between the leaders and the stragglers – with Dan from Amsterdam, my roommate Phil and the two Australian nurses Mary and Anne. We were about 20 minutes into this section of our walk when I first noticed a clump of trees ahead and a van parked nearby. It wasn't until we approached that we noticed the men. The Arabs were sitting crossed legged under the olive trees. While it was not particularly hot, the trees were offering the only shade in that part of the "strip" between Kibbutz Gevim and Gaza. The van parked nearby had its bonnet opened, indicating it might have broken down. Several rifles leant against the vehicle while others lay casually between the men who seemed totally disinterested in our presence. We offered them cigarettes but they refused. Having smoked the Israeli brand I could thoroughly understand the rejection. But then I realised they were smoking something far stronger than tobacco. As we attempted to move on, all hell broke loose and they reached for their weapons. This triggered an immediate response that could only be described as panic.

We all ran. Given there were a dozen of us, we each ran in 12 different directions; including the girls who ran into the minefield. But it was our screaming, I believe, that helped defuse the situation as they appeared unsure what to do next. I think I called for my mother. I definitely heard others call for Mary and even Jesus – which I felt was a little inappropriate considering the men who were threatening us. But it was Captain Uri Bass of the Israeli Command who actually responded. Having been under surveillance since we first entered the strip, Captain Bass led a dozen troops in two half-track carriers. The troops jumped from their vehicles and quietly disarmed the Arabs. After guiding the girls safely out of the minefield, he began berating us all for being there in the first place. Most of the invective was in Hebrew, but we all understood the words "fucking stupid". We were then ordered to climb on board their military vehicles and instructed on how to place our feet on footplates while hanging on to metal handrails. We were then warned that there would be no stopping if anyone fell off. Our journey through one of the world's most squalid refugee camps was not without incident, striking the occasional chicken as people and animals scattered in our dust. Our klaxon horn sounded a warning, it also signalled we were coming. Occasional stones and bricks struck the side of our vehicle as we clung on hoping we wouldn't be hit.

Our arrival in the centre of Gaza contrasted starkly with the reception we had received en route. Dozens of young children greeted us with outstretched arms, waiting to gratefully receive oranges being distributed by the Israeli troops. Several hours of sightseeing were spent with our strange entourage of children until we heard the heavy throb of helicopters and distant sounds of sirens. Quickly returning to the local police station, we were led through a series of narrow corridors and passed a central courtyard where we spotted three of the Arabs we had encountered earlier that morning, all chained to separate poles. They even called out and attempted to wave as we passed. It wasn't long before we were informed a terrorist attack had been launched on a local bus depot killing several people and leaving dozens injured. We were also told a second group had planned a simultaneous attack but had been caught. It was believed these were the Arabs we had encountered on the track to Gaza.

As we were being driven back towards Kibbutz Gevim, we tuned the radio to the local news service. We listened as our driver interpreted the broadcast.

'You are indeed very lucky,' he said, 'the group claiming responsibility is called Palestine Liberation Organisation (PLO). They are bad people and its newly-elected leader is now vowing more attacks.'

This was the first time I had ever heard the name Yasser Arafat. Just three weeks, later I met his nemesis ...

Four dark vehicles with a military escort pulled into the Gevim driveway creating a huge cloud of dust from the gravel surface. I was returning from the milking sheds as several senior members of the Kibbutz rushed past to welcome their visitors. As the dust quickly settled one man emerged with his familiar swagger and an unmistakable visual trademark. The black patch over his right eye confirmed it was General Moshe Dayan, the man who had led the Israeli forces to victory in the Six-Day War; a hero to all Israelis. Several other men, including another instantly recognisable face, accompanied him. The leader of his security detail was none other than Garth from the *MV Adelphi*. Despite what I regarded as a reasonably close association during our voyage to Haifa he made no attempt to acknowledge my presence; not even showing an element of surprise. I stepped aside as they passed and even called out to Garth but there was absolutely no sign of recognition. Despite this, I followed them to the Kibbutz office where I put in a request for an interview with Dayan and produced my business card stating I was a representative of radio 3DB in Melbourne part of the Major Broadcasting Network in Australia. His visit to our Kibbutz was described as "unofficial and personal". General Dayan had apparently come to visit an old friend and former retired Commander from the Six-Day War. A few moments later I was informed he had consented to the interview.

An hour later, enough time to scribble down a few questions, Dayan emerged from the office. I fumbled with my hand-held Hitachi cassette recorder having already erased the flip side of Simon and Garfunkel's *Bridge over Troubled Water* for what would become one of the most memorable interviews of my life. I stood in total awe looking into a solitary eye that sparkled with power, charisma and just a trace of humour. Where the other eye should have been, a black patch was held in place, more by an unseen force than the single strand of leather which disappeared behind an ear to remerge across his head and back down to the patch again.

Dayan immediately took control, speaking of the importance of young people arriving in Israel to experience life on a Kibbutz. They were, he said, 'supporting the Israeli war machine', allowing young Israelis to complete their military training and 'enabling Israeli productivity to continue uncompromised.'

This confirmed my fears of becoming legitimate targets in this so-called war of attrition, however by now I was more concerned with my interview. He continued with many quotes some of which I felt he had delivered many times before, but I was now hearing them first-hand from the man himself.

'Our American friends offer us money, arms and advice. We take the money, we take the arms, and we decline the advice.'

Dayan surprised me by revealing his love of Australians, perhaps the reason he was giving me so much of his time. I asked him about his famous eye-patch and was told that during an operation with the 7th Division of the AIF they came under fire from Vichy French. I later discovered the Mufti of Jerusalem, the royal houses of Iraq and Saudi Arabia, together with the Shah of Persia, were all slightly disposed towards Germany. The position in the Eastern Mediterranean was becoming desperate. The allies feared a pincer movement of German forces could pass through the Vichy French territory in Syria. This could have secured the Suez Canal and over-run small Jewish settlements in Palestine. To forestall any such movement a campaign was mounted against the Vichy French in Syria and Lebanon, a campaign made up primarily with Australian forces from the 7th Division AIF. It was during one of these skirmishes that a patrol of Australians, including Moshe Dayan, came under fire.

Dayan claimed, 'I was looking through my glass when it was suddenly hit,' taking out his eye. He spoke proudly of his time with the Australians and even of the incident that left him with a living legacy. In fact, on the recommendation of his Australian commander he was awarded the DSO. He also spoke of another impending war which he claimed was inevitable – and he was right. The Yom Kipper War was launched in October 1973, but unlike the Six-Day War of 1967, this one cost Israel and Dayan dearly. By then I had arrived safely home. Dayan received most of the blame for being unprepared and resigned from the Ministry of Defence, returning as Foreign Minister in the Begin Government until 1980, a year before his death.

At the conclusion of our interview, Garth arrived to escort Dayan away. With a wry smile the General stopped, looked at the small cassette recorder in my hand and said, '*Gin Giy*, next time you interview me make sure it's with a camera.' Then, without so much as a shalom, he and Garth turned and left.

A camera? Was this a defining moment or what!

In the meantime I continued with my plan to use the interview as the basis of my first radio documentary. Physically shaking with excitement, I ran back to our room. Phil had gained some experience as a scriptwriter in Canada so we began planning the broader program. I was about to mail it back to Melbourne when a new crisis erupted in Israel.

The morning of 21 February we awoke to hear that Swissair flight SR330 leaving Zürich bound for Tel Aviv and carrying 47 people including passengers and crew, had blown up mid-air.

Almost nine minutes after take-off a bomb exploded on board in the rear cargo hold. As the crew attempted to turn the plane back towards the airport for an emergency landing, smoke clouded the cockpit and electrical power was lost. The aircraft crashed with no survivors. The Popular Front for the Liberation of Palestine (PFLP) was claiming responsibility

On the same day, the PLO detonated a second bomb aboard an Austrian airliner travelling from Frankfurt to Vienna. The bomb located inside a mailbag was due to be carried to Israel on a later flight. Despite a huge hole torn in the fuselage, the aircraft landed safely at Frankfurt and none of the 38 people on board were injured. Israel responded with a ban on all international flights into and out of Tel Aviv pending a review of all international airport security. As a result all mail into and out of Israel was suspended, highlighting a growing sense of terrible isolation. It also seemed pointless to try to leave the country so we hunkered down on the Kibbutz.

By May tensions had eased a little so we decided to travel again. Phil headed back to Jerusalem to catch up with some relatives. I decided to head north to the Golan Heights and joined a small group of tourists who packed into another familiar mustard coloured British built Bedford bus and headed off towards Mt Hermon.

It was an uneventful but enjoyable round trip through the Golan Heights to the source of the Jordan River and back down to Tiberias. The only disturbing moment came as we passed through the deserted town of Kuneitra, occupied by Syria before the Six-Day War. Our tour guide explained how an estimated 20,000 occupants fled as the Israelis advanced, Possessions lay scattered around Kuneitra, including prams and children's toys left abandoned in the driveways of their homes. He spoke of the Israeli forces, pleading with them not to leave but somehow didn't sound too convincing. Several years later in the Yom Kippur War Israeli forces all but destroyed the town.

The following morning on 8 May I left Tiberias en route back to Kibbutz Gevim – unaware yet another tragedy was about to unfold. As our bus rattled out of Tiberias, another similar bus (following the same route we had taken the previous day) was winding its way just below the Lebanese border. Unbeknown to Israeli security forces, the route had been secretly scouted by Palestinian terrorists over the preceding weeks. Just ten minutes after leaving the settlement of Avivim, the bus (with mainly young students aboard) was attacked by heavy automatic gunfire. The driver was amongst those hit in the initial fire, as were two other adults on board. The bus then crashed into an embankment as the gunmen continued to fire. Twelve passengers were killed, mainly children. If the War of Attrition was not taking its toll on Israel, it was certainly affecting me. Any feeling of the invincibility of youth that I may have enjoyed when I first arrived had now evaporated. It was time to leave.

Back in Jerusalem, I sold a pint of blood at the Hadassah Hospital in order to buy an International Student Card on the black market and a one-way airline ticket out of Israel. After a tearful farewell to the many friends I had made on Gevim, I caught the bus to the airport and flew to Istanbul. From there I headed back to London with my prized interview with Moshe Dayan. I had been given the name of a contact within the BBC and made an appointment. An agreement was soon reached and I received the grand payment of twelve pounds, eleven shillings and sixpence. I was told the program would be filed under "K" for Kibbutz but later learnt it was really destined for the one marked "D" for Dayan. Meanwhile, I kept my copy marked "L" for Lyons, which I mailed back to 3DB in Melbourne where it became a feature story on Gerald Lyons talkback program. The program would become the final chapter in my nine-year radio career. In those prophetic words of Moshe Dayan: *Next time you interview me make sure it's with a camera,* it was time to seriously consider television.

A man travels the world over in search of what he needs and returns home to find it.
- George A Moore, Irish novelist

CHAPTER 5

CADETSHIP

1971

HEADLINES

Former Treasurer William McMahon elected PM
First heart-lung transplant
Violent protests over Springboks Rugby tour
Student protest leader Albert Langer jailed

HITS

My Sweet Lord – George Harrison
Maggie May – Rod Stewart
Chirpy Chirpy Cheep Cheep – Middle Of The Road

The fresh-faced cadet journalist reported back to his editor after attending his first solo assignment. His story, containing all the basic facts, two dead in horror road smash, was appropriately placed well down in the bulletin.

That night the opposition channel led their news with the same story but with a different spin: Twin brothers die on their 21st birthday.

The cadet was duly castigated by his editor for missing such an important angle to the story. Having put the fear of God into his young charge, the cadet was assigned another road accident the following day.

As the medics were loading the semi-conscious victim into the ambulance, the cadet burst through, microphone in hand.

'I don't suppose today is your birthday by any chance?'

Whether or not that is a media myth is irrelevant. The fact was I empathised with the young cadet and lived in similar fear of my news editor …

SEVEN IS REVOLTING!

September 16, 1969 the Seven Network launched arguably the most innovative exercise of promotion and marketing in television history – The Seven Revolution. Seven was indeed "revolting" either way you looked at it; the station was simply reflecting its poor performance.

Bruce Gyngell a powerhouse and pioneer of Australian television had left the Nine Network as its program manager to take over Seven as managing director. His first task was to abandon the concept of Melbourne's HSV7 and Sydney's ATN7 to establish the single entity – The Seven Network. Nine had been well ahead of Seven in 1969 but four months after the revolution was launched the media landscape changed perceptibly. Built largely around British comedies and overseas specials, Seven won its first survey in February 1970 and, for the next decade, never looked back.

During my absence overseas, Ron Casey, a former radio colleague at 3DB had been appointed Station Manager at HSV7 so on the basis of "it's not what you know but WHO you know", Casey was the first person I contacted on my return. I was thrilled to be offered a job as booth announcer but any suggestion of working in news was diplomatically cast aside.

'News,' Casey warned, 'is a hard nut to crack... but at least you will have a foot in the door should the door open a little.'

June 6 1970, my first night as station announcer (and coincidentally the date of my start in radio back in 1961) the door opened – a lot. The late night newsreader British born Graham Purchess was suddenly taken ill. I was asked to fill in and that is precisely what I initially became – a fill-in newsreader. When Purchess returned to the UK a short time later I became a little more permanent but never once did it occur to me that I would continue reading news on television for the next 43 years.

In a desperate bid to secure my position in television, I accepted every opportunity that came my way including Seven's first foray into breakfast television hosted by affable pop star Johnny Farnham. That almost ended in disaster when Farnham, who had just ended a cooking segment, broke an egg on my head while I was reading the news. This incurred the wrath of Bruce Gyngell himself who had plans to morph the Farnham experiment into the more serious *Today Show* with Bruce Webster and Pat Lovell in Sydney. I remained on air contributing briefly from Melbourne where I co-hosted the *Miss Teenage Quest* with George Chapman, *Morning Women's* with the legendary Stephanie Deste until finally being offered the network quiz show *Jeopardy*. But then 18 months later and just one week before Christmas 1972, it all threatened to come to an end. I was sacked.

SATURDAY, 4 DECDEMBER 1971

The Willard King Organisation, producers of Jeopardy, had decided to dump me as host in favour of Sydney personality Andrew Harwood. Seven's production manager Dick Jones called me into his office to break the news. 'I'm so sorry, Mal, but we will have to let you go.'

It had been a fairly haphazard arrangement right from the start – a simple Q&A audition in front of a studio full of contestants during the taping of Willard King's other quiz show, *It's Academic*. The program's flamboyant producer John Collins, resplendent in white pants, white shoes and white cable knit cricket style jumper, paraded me out on stage and asked me to read a couple of cue cards. He then called on the audience of students, 'Hands up those who like him?' More than half responded, so I had the job. With my commitments reading the late news and booth announcing five nights a week, I took my three-week annual leave and recorded all 52 episodes for the year ahead. I received $20 for each episode and as I was already on a basic salary of $80 a week – *Jeopardy* was a cash bonus and a priceless boost to my profile. But if you don't have a job, what's the point of a profile? That same day it had been decided the newly appointed news producer Greg Shackleton would read the late news and a newly appointed voice over talent, Don Rainsford, had been employed as the station booth announcer.

Yes, I was stunned. But just as all the doors appeared to be closing, another was about to open. At around 4 p.m., while preparing for my final booth shift, I was suddenly summoned into the office of news director John Maher. I was sitting in the canteen dipping ginger nuts into my cup and feeling as pale as the washed out tea when the newsroom secretary rushed in to announce, 'Mr Maher would like to see you in his office.'

Maher appeared flustered as the 6.30 news deadline was approaching. A cloud of cigarette smoke hovered around his slightly balding head and two tuffs of unruly hair each side above his ears created an image of an almost comedic caricature.

However, as I entered his office, his face was devoid of any semblance of humour. I had met Maher in passing and was fully aware of his volatile reputation just as I was aware of his uncanny news sense and the knack of creating iconic news anchors.

'It seems I have inherited you,' he said without any hint of subtlety.

For Christ sake, I thought, *I have only been in television 18 months and already I've been sacked. Now I'm being inherited.*

'Mr Casey,' he said, overly emphasising the Mister, 'Wants to see if you have what it takes to work in news so we are offering you a cadetship.' It was clear that Maher saw this as management interference but that was not my problem.

Just as I was about to throw my arms around my newfound

mentor he continued. 'I personally don't think you have it, but time will tell.' Then as he was about to dismiss me he added, 'We don't carry baggage so your best friend in this newsroom will be the telephone directory. I just hope you can read.'

Welcome to television news! Now all I had to do was survive. I was quietly confident. I knew I had a variety of skills from years in radio and at least 18 months experience in television. I had hoped that one day I would be able to channel this experience into something more challenging and above all, more secure. Television news, I believed, fell into that security category. Yes, I was still a little naïve…

So, on 4 December 1971, I walked out of Maher's office to find a position on the long central news desk. I felt everything had now fallen into place. I had already established a relationship with most of the small closely-knit news team; all I had to do was prove my worth to Maher – and I knew that wouldn't be easy.

Cadetship was a loosely based term for "sink or swim". Within a week I was reporting stories regardless of their priority in the nightly bulletin. One night I would have the lead story, the following night I would be relegated to last before sport. While Maher would occasionally snap at me with, 'You're not a journalist's bootlace,' I brushed off much of his criticism. I blamed his outbursts on the effects of a long lunch – of which there were many.

During my first 12 months, his outbursts became more frequent and more vitriolic. No matter how hard I tried to impress, the more personal and abusive his attacks would become, always ending in a trail of spittle as he repeated, 'You're not a journalist's bootlace.' But his news service was gaining in popularity, reaching record ratings of 30 per cent of the total share in the competitive 6.30 p.m. time slot. His style of news reporting in the early '70s was becoming unashamedly personality based.

'I fully believe our success,' he enthused in one of his more conciliatory moments, 'is due to programming, production and promotion, but above all it is the personality driven news team.' I dearly hoped he also meant me.

Maher's name and reputation was becoming legendary within the industry helped in no small part by an incident with his political reporter John Boland. Boland had been covering a story relocating Koalas from the French Island penal colony in Western Port Bay. His original script had referred to Koalas as "Koala Bears".

'They are not fucking bears, they are marsupials,' Maher screamed. The tirade against Boland continued for most of the day. Maher ranted and raved, and paced and chain-smoked his way around the newsroom. 'Koalas are marsupials, they have pouches. Bears don't have pouches. Bears are fucking er... well, bears. It's like calling them an elephant-platypus.'

From that moment on John Maher simply became "The Koala" – a pseudonym helped by his surname "Maher-supial", which would last his lifetime. A short time later Boland was sacked and the small team (consisting of four male reporters) was forced to expand. The Women's Electoral Lobby had been putting pressure on all networks during licence renewal applications to correct the imbalance between males and females in television news. They called it an imbalance but in fact there were no women at all. HSV7 had acted by promoting one of its producers but while she was one of the most accomplished producers in the newsroom she sadly failed in the transition as an on-camera reporter. Although the position had been created, it took several more months before someone recognised the ability of a young, attractive female reporter at the *Herald* newspaper which resulted in Pamela Graham becoming the first woman to join the on–camera news team. Maher's mission was now to humanise his news. It perhaps began with reporter Danny Webb's April Fool's Day "Spaghetti Blight" story, inspired says Webb, by a similar story he saw on the BBC.

'We threaded black cotton through cooked spaghetti and draped it across vineyards near Berwick …We then proceeded to tell our viewers that the vines were in fact "spaghetti growing vines" and the spaghetti being produced was under threat from a black weevil.'

The reaction was enormous and far beyond anything he expected.

Several years later Australia shed the imperial system of measure and adopted metric. Miles became kilometres, pints became litres and pounds became kilograms. It was decided that on 1 April we would feature a story proposing "Decimal Time". One hundred seconds to the minute? Ten hours in the day? Ten months in the year?

Reporter David Hill was assigned the story featuring the bespectacled Seven News Chief of Staff Tim Parsons playing "Harvey Spiegleman" – a Melbourne jeweller who had conversion kits ready to slip over the faces of clocks and watches. The story triggered unprecedented reaction. One company director rang up threatening to sue as he had been ridiculed by his fellow board members after proposing they should be first to adopt this system. However, reaction from our Hobart affiliate exceeded that. After each bulletin we air freighted our news to affiliate stations around the nation in order for them to select stories for their news the following night.

'Mate, congratulations,' said their enthusiastic news editor on the phone the following morning. 'That was a bloody great story on decimal time.' They thought the story was so good, it led their bulletin the following night on 2 April.

My personal experience of Maher's personality push was highlighted by a visit from British guitarist Eric Clapton. Melbourne fans were disappointed by his brief performance on stage, which he reduced to less than 40 minutes. The complaints gathered momentum after the daughter of a city councillor was dissatisfied with Clapton's concert. Upon hearing the complaints, her father promptly rang the media. We received a tip-off that Clapton was due to leave Melbourne from outside Flinders Street station just before midday. My instruction was to get down there and interview him before his tour bus left.

The band was already on board and waiting for their tour manager who was running late. When he arrived I pleaded for a quick interview with Clapton in a bid to clear up the growing criticism. Clapton emerged from the bus in no mood to talk to anyone, least of all a television news crew. I began by asking why he cut short his performance to less than 40 minutes. He replied, 'Scrotum.'

I followed up by asking whether he was aware he had let down his fans.

'Scrotum.'

I then asked whether he was aware that pressure would be applied for all tour bands to guarantee a set time for their performances.

'Scrotum.'

The interview continued along that line for another three to four questions all with the same reply, 'Scrotum'. Believing this would never get to air and at best would feature in the end of year Christmas reel, I finally asked him what he had for breakfast that morning.

'Scrotum,' he replied with a wry smile and then turned and boarded his bus. When I returned to the newsroom and the film had been processed Maher insisted on looking at the interview. To our amazement he insisted, 'Run the entire interview, top and tail it, no edits, let the viewers judge what an arsehole he is.'

And we did.

American television executives would also discover the power of this "personality trend" in news, but not until 16 August 1977, the day Elvis Presley died. On that night America's highly respected and top rating *CBS News* led their bulletin with an eight-minute piece on the Panama Canal treaty. It was a worthy news story but not on the day the King of Rock 'n' Roll had died. Presley's passing was relegated further down in their bulletin. Their opposition networks saw it differently and led with the death of Elvis. The ratings vindicated their decision and CBS was forced to accept the pulling power of personalities over politics. To the critics this represented the start of "dumbing down" the news, 'pandering to inanity in a bid to capitalise on this personality trend'. Maher, who argued that "dumb" did not necessarily mean "stupid", countered this with 'news that entertains can also be news that informs'.

In Australia, the decade of the '70s signalled one of the most defining periods in the history of television news. Not only were satellites delivering domestic and international stories, we had made the successful transition from black and white into colour – and even more importantly, the transition from film to tape.

Electronic newsgathering was initially fraught with problems and each reporter made every excuse to not use the ENG cameras but there was no going back. The greatest advantage with tape soon became apparent in the area of production and with it came an element that would silently evolve into all aspects of our lives for the next 40 years – the "Ten-Second Sound Bite".

A RETROSPECTIVE ON THE SOUND BITE

Ten seconds may not seem a long time. However, in that time you can save a life, take a life, dial a phone number, mix an instant coffee, or (if you're an Olympic athlete) run the 100-metre sprint. Arguably, the most ubiquitous ten seconds is the Ten-Second Sound Bite on television.

This was justified by scientists who reported that nicotine from cigarettes reached the brain in ten seconds, they also discovered that information reached the brain at the same time. However, while the damage from nicotine continued after its initial burst, information begin to lose its impact. The short-term memory cells apparently failed to absorb information after that initial burst.

Television researchers latched onto this discovery in the early '70s when video replaced film in the TV news industry. Until then, news stories contained lengthy interviews linked by stand-ups (a reporters piece to camera) in stories lasting two to three minutes. But by using video, a news story could be re-packaged with a voice over the vision and the lengthy interview replaced by a ten-second sound grab to reinforce the same facts. TV news stories were suddenly reduced to half the original duration but with more than double the information.

Today, computer analysts say ten seconds is around the time users examine a web page before deciding whether to stay or move on to the next page. The first ten seconds of meeting someone may well be the most important ten seconds of the entire relationship, determining whether there will be any relationship at all. Career advisors instruct their students on the importance of job interviews. First impressions are the most important. Security experts warn how the first ten seconds of a confrontation are critical to survival. In the event of a siege, kidnap or terror strike, victims have just ten seconds to respond or lose the initiative. In Japan, the Government's earthquake warning system "Duck and Cover" reminds residents that the first ten seconds from the initial warning could save their lives.

Our future was being shaped into a life of sound bites, bumper stickers and slogans and it all began with the Ten-Second Sound Bite from the '70s.

As the early '70s continued to break new ground in television news I continued to lurch from crisis to crisis with my news editor. Yet I continued to wake each day with anticipation and excitement for the stories I would be assigned and the changes that were being pioneered. To work in a job that was challenging, fun, creative and totally self-satisfying was beyond anything I could have hoped for, despite whatever Maher thought of me. The weekly ratings continued to be dissected and analysed by the sales and management teams but rarely were they of any interest to those of us involved in news. However, that all started to change as we began winning by even greater margins and the written press began reporting it.

In 1972 HSV7 was transitioning its image towards a younger demographic and as a twenty-something myself, they felt I could perhaps play a part. To further improve my on-air interaction and interviewing skills I was asked to audition a group of young women from which two would be selected for hosting roles. Several weeks later Lucy Kirali was announced as co-host with David Johnston for the first Tattslotto draw on live television and a young 18-year-old model Trudy Jaworski was chosen to host an afternoon children's program, *Jet Set*. Trudy was blonde, bubbly and far from bashful. She was the antitheses of Seven's former children's show host Happy Hammond, an icon since the start of television, who was asked to produce her.

Happy would crawl across the floor, handing up prizes for Trudy to show on camera while I sat in the far left hand corner of the studio providing live voice over's. Happy Hammond rose above any indignity he must have felt and accepted the job with the grace and humility of a TV legend being put out to pasture – a gentleman to the end. On her second night Trudy enthused, 'Look boys and girls, look at the prizes I have for you. A Kookaburra brand basketball for a girl and a Kookaburra football for a boy.

Incidentally boys and girls, do you know why Kookaburras laugh? Well, you'd laugh too if you had balls like these!'

Happy would have fallen to the floor had he not already been lying there. Yet there was not one official complaint. However, the following night Trudy appeared wearing a see-through blouse and the entire telephone system collapsed under the weight of complaints. Such was television in the early '70s.

Meanwhile in those formative years of my cadetship, I continued to struggle battling huge waves of confidence then sinking under the withering tirade of my news boss.

'Television is like walking a tightrope between ego and insecurity,' Maher would insist. 'One slip either way will prove fatal and you my boy, are treading a very narrow rope.' And yet, he persevered with me despite my obvious failings.

One such incident of my gross stupidity involved an interview with Liberal politician Don Chipp. This was an interview Maher had personally set up at Melbourne's the Southern Cross Hotel. I was told that Chipp would emerge from a conference to comment on a change of government policy on pornography. For months a political row had raged over the ease in which pornographic material was available to youngsters. Liberal Government spokesman Don Chipp had been a strong advocate of tightening the laws. Now I was told 'the government was relaxing them'. I wrote down my questions and waited while the cameras were set up in the hotel foyer. By the time Chipp emerged, a small crowd had gathered to watch.

'Well Mr Chipp,' I began, 'why after everything you have advocated about pornography have you suddenly back-flipped?'

There was a pause. His eyes shifted slightly and I thought, *You beauty I've got you, Maher will be impressed.*

The small crowd moved closer so for their benefit I repeated the question a little louder. 'Why Mr Chipp after everything you have said about pornography have you now changed your mind?'

There was another slight pause and then he took a deep breath. 'I understand your indignation young man but I think you may have forgotten there was an election last year and we are no longer in Government. You may prefer to put that question to Mr Al Grassby who is now the Minister for Customs.'

I may have died right there in the foyer of the Southern Cross Hotel but the burial would take place back in the newsroom. How could I have got it so wrong?

'Look,' he said, 'I'm in a bit of a hurry so why not ask me what I think of Grassby's decision and follow up by asking me what I intend doing about it?'

My attempts to improve my relations with Maher continued to fail; the harder I tried the bigger the gaffe. I was beginning to believe failure was my destiny but drew some comfort from Eric Collins my first manager at 3YB Warrnambool who persevered.

In the last few weeks of 1974 confidence was returning again when Maher assigned me to track down two Federal politicians he believed were involved in a shady financial scandal. I was aware that Minerals and Energy Minister Rex Connor had been seeking funds for a series of national development projects and had proposed the Whitlam Government should borrow US$4 billion (at that time a huge sum of money). However, it was a requirement of the Australian Constitution that non-temporary government borrowings must be through the Loan Council. We were not aware that a week earlier on 13 December, Whitlam, together with ministers Cairns, Murphy and Connor authorised Connor to seek the loan without involving the Loan Council, although whispers were beginning to circulate. Maher had received a tip off that Cairns and Conner would be meeting at Melbourne's Bryson

Hotel in Exhibition Street around midday. I arrived just in time to see them entering the foyer and immediately gave chase with microphone in hand and camera crew tagging behind.

In a final lunge, I entered the lift with Cairns and Conner. I was expecting the camera crew to follow but the door shut, the mike cord snapped and I completed the ride to the seventh floor in total silence. John Maher made up for that silence when I returned. His rant lasted more than five minutes ending with, 'You're not a journalist's bootlace and you never will be, so just fuck off out of my sight.'

And I did.

A week before Christmas I was sent out to interview Melbourne's biggest Tattslotto winner. A Yugoslavian bachelor had won first prize.

'Let's see if you can get this right,' was Maher's parting shot.

We arrived at the winner's Yarraville home and immediately set up the gear for an interview. I asked him every conceivable question from what he had for breakfast to what he intended spending his prize money on. By the end of the 20-minute interview there was nothing I didn't know about the winner. What I didn't ask on camera I took down in notes for my voiceover. It was one of the most thorough interviews I had ever done. He was intelligent, humorous and above all very personable. I arrived back in the newsroom satisfied with my efforts and eager to see it edited into a package. Maher was waiting but that didn't bother me.

'How did you go?' he asked.

'Tremendous, it's a great story.'

'Thank Christ,' he muttered. 'How old was he?'

Shit! I should have just made it up. He wouldn't have been any the wiser. I ducked the first blow but was struck by the second ream of paper he threw. It scattered like confetti across the newsroom floor. The tirade of abuse that followed lasted for 30 minutes. Most of the typists were in tears and my career seemed doomed. I tried to thread the paper in my typewriter but was all fingers and thumbs.

'He can't even thread the fucking typewriter!' he screamed.

The following morning while sitting at my desk I became aware of a presence behind me. The cigarette smoke drifted down from the cloud that always surrounded his face. He never inhaled.

'Look,' he said, 'I may have overstepped the mark. Let's see if we can start again.'

A week later we did and neither of us would ever look back again. But it took a cyclone named Tracy and the devastation of Darwin to do it.

CHAPTER 6

DIARY FROM DARWIN

1974

HEADLINES

Sir John Kerr becomes Governor General
Heiress Patty Hearst turns bank robber
Australian Unions ban Frank Sinatra tour
President Nixon resigns
Cyclone Tracy devastates Darwin

HITS

She – Charles Aznavour
Seasons In The Sun – Terry Jacks
Dancing Machine – The Jackson 5

BOXING DAY, 1974

Apocalypse, catastrophe, devastation!

If I was to be truly accurate my first words were 'Holy shit!' Darwin appeared through the window of our charted Lear jet as we descended through thick clouds on Boxing Day morning. It was a surreal black and white image, sepia at best in the early dawn light, and very like the photos I had seen of post-war Hiroshima and Nagasaki.

Suburb after suburb was flattened beyond recognition. Streets were vaguely outlined but homes and buildings had been laid waste and scattered for as far as the eye could see. The "eye" in this case, more than 20 kilometres wide, had passed directly over the city and nothing in its path had been spared. Even houses that miraculously were still standing had been left uninhabitable. However, the sight from above could not have prepared us for the tragedy unfolding below.

The runway had been cleared of wreckage and as we touched down, aircraft lay scattered each side of the strip like toys discarded in a toddler's tantrum. Planes of all shapes and sizes had been tossed at random; some lay crumpled beneath damaged hangers while others lay where they rested intact but contorted at odd angles. We stepped from the comfort zone of our pressurised cabin into a humid atmosphere of unbearable heartache amid an omnipresent sense of tragedy you could see, feel and smell. Two army privates who had survived in the nearby barracks stopped. They invited us to join them on their way to inspect their own home in one of the worst hit suburbs of Nightcliff. Most roads were blocked by indistinguishable wreckage and we passed many residents searching through remains of their homes. Some called for help and were advised to make their way to the airport while we continued on.

Several moments later a dog ran out in front of our vehicle trailing a partly severed leg. We braked and swerved. I looked back as a man emerged carrying a large piece of wood, which he raised above the dog's head. I looked away, already knowing its fate. No one spoke. Trees were totally dismembered, stripped of foliage and each wrapped tightly by roofing iron like tourniquets squeezing out what little life was left. And there was little life left. No insects. No birds just an eerie silence and a pungent odour of decay which was already beginning to pervade the area.

We eventually arrived at the army boys' apartment to find the doors missing and a fridge lying on its side having spewed its contents from the kitchen to the bedroom. Most furniture and appliances were scattered, broken or simply blown away. Curtains were shredded, windows smashed and everything soaked in water. The boys kicked a broken television then just stood and wept. A neighbour arrived to offer sympathy then proceeded to describe how he had survived with his wife and two children.

'A loud explosion signalled the whole side of our home had been torn away.' Then a rending sound above warned their roof was about to blow and with it went the washing machine and the kitchen stove with the same ease of force that had already sucked all the Christmas decorations from their home. The boys then stopped crying, realising after a night like that survival was all that really mattered. Our first hour in Darwin was a nano-second in time. Yesterday was so far removed from the reality of this disaster. Surreal was a word that came to mind.

CHRISTMAS MORNING 1974

Like most Australians I awoke on Christmas morning 1974 to sketchy reports that Cyclone Tracy had struck Darwin: *Damage unknown, Communications down.* Nothing was being confirmed.

At 7 a.m. I walked into Melbourne's Channel Seven newsroom, which resembled its own mini crisis of chaos and clutter. Tired old Christmas relics from previous years had been dragged out again. Sagging streamers hung in low droops, an artificial Christmas tree featured an angel with a beer bottle-top as a crown and six red fairy lights glowed softly but twenty-four were broken.

The chief of staff was standing on his desk trying to disconnect a flickering fluorescent light complaining. 'It's giving me a bloody headache!'

On a blackboard he had chalked the name 'Darwin' but no one had been assigned the story. We knew a cyclone called Tracy had been due but expected it to veer off course at the last minute as its sister Selma had done the week before. No word had been sent out so there was little cause for concern. My concern this Christmas day was to save my job. While Maher may have handed me a lifeline, I was fully aware it could be withdrawn at any time. I was skating and I knew the ice was thin.

It was around 8 a.m. when the camera crew arrived for my one assignment, the Salvation Army helping the homeless and disadvantaged celebrate Christmas, then I was free to celebrate my own. As we left the newsroom I noticed the chief of staff on the phone and heard the name Darwin mentioned but not with any urgency. Certainly nothing that would indicate the most devastating natural disaster in the history of Australia had struck the Northern Territory capital.

She blew in just after midnight and despite warnings on local radio it caught many sceptical Territorians by surprise. The wind continued to increase until at 3.05 a.m. when the anemometer at the airport recorded gusts of 217 kph before it broke. Estimates have since put those gusts at 250 kph. As it moved across the city and suburbs it gave its victims a brief respite. Twenty minutes of silence from the roar and screams. Tracy teased the Territorians with a false sense of survival. Just when they felt it was safe to emerge from their damaged homes, she struck again with even greater force. This time the winds came from the opposite direction. Tracy left no part of the city untouched. Ninety per cent of all buildings were completely destroyed or left uninhabitable. As families huddled together in cupboards, under beds, in bathrooms and particularly toilets (the smallest and safest room in the house), the rest of Australia slept in glorious oblivion.

As we arrived at the Salvation Army headquarters in Bourke Street the local radio was reporting that General Alan Stretton, head of the newly formed Natural Disasters Organisation (NDO), was being dispatched from Canberra. I had met the General only weeks earlier when he announced the formation of the NDO. But that was another Maher experience I wished to forget. He had insisted I ask Stretton whether or not the NDO was an excuse to form a clandestine right-wing army.

'Don't be brushed off with any excuses he may give,' he snapped.

I asked Stretton several times and on each occasion he simply replied no. Then, just to cover myself, I asked him to elaborate.

'Son, what is it about the word "no" you don't understand?'

I left hoping never to see him again.

General Stretton had been awake since a 6.20 a.m. phone call from the Cyclone Tropical Warning Centre in Perth. Darwin had been hit but no further details were available. That single phone call triggered the start of the most massive relief operation in Australia's history. Just by chance, Stretton found a phone number for the Darwin police station and rang direct. The officer on duty, Sergeant Taylor, reported the roof off the station, the hospital still functioning, about 50 houses damaged and an unidentified number of dead. It was only 5 a.m. in Darwin so no vehicle had been able to leave his station to investigate further. That was one of the last calls into Darwin before all communications went down. It was all Stretton needed to mobilise his organisation. He would later write:

> *It was unbelievable that the defence forces with all the millions of dollars spent on signals equipment could not communicate with their units in Darwin. What if there had been an enemy attack?*

It wasn't until 10 a.m. EST that the Marine Operations Centre received a sketchy communication in morse code from the *MV Nyanda*, which had just entered Darwin harbour after riding out the storm at sea. The only other message out of Darwin came through the offices of the Overseas Telecommunications Centre at the airport, which reported massive devastation and the terminal filling with refugees. Then they too went off air.

In Canberra, General Stretton began by organising medical supplies, stretchers, field cooking equipment, refrigerators and tarpaulins, 200,000 rations had been ordered, enough to feed the population for four to five days.

Back in Melbourne, it was close to midday when I returned with my story. The newsroom now was humming quietly with typewriters and general gossip. The film editor had arrived and was busily finishing the first story of the day and was ready to start on mine. The third reporter David Hill (later to become head of Fox Sport in New York) had arrived. Boisterous and hungover, he quickly received his assignment and left. His deep gravelly voice richer from the previous night's drinking faded down the corridor. It would have been around the time of Hill's departure that another garbled message was received through the PMG at Mt Isa. It came from the Dr Charles Gurd, the Director of Health in Darwin, who reported at least seven dead including the senior anaesthetist.

Around 12.45 p.m. my story had been edited and I was preparing to leave when in walked John Maher. He immediately strode up to the desk and demanded to know what was happening in Darwin.

'Brisbane is sending in a crew,' replied the producer, 'but as yet we don't know how serious it is.'

Maher then began pacing and chain-smoking his way around the narrow newsroom, ducking the drooping streamers. 'Why have you left it to Brisbane to cover?' he snapped at the chief of staff. 'They are just dingbats, don't you know that? For Christ sake what's wrong with you all, we are supposed to be a fucking news organisation!'

Suddenly bells rang out from the teleprinter on a wooden shelf just behind my desk and in a desperate need to restore some credibility in the eyes of my mentor I ripped off the message and read it out loud:

Darwin completely devastated. Deaths number up to 20. Ninety per cent of houses completely or seriously damaged. Suggest National Disaster team be sent immediately.

Maher turned his back, trailing his trademark halo of smoke and disappeared into his office. Several moments passed in total silence. He then reappeared with a new cigarette hanging from a corner of his mouth and calmly announced he had hired a Lear jet. This we knew would put him at odds with senior management. Our network belonged to the austere HWT, which required that even a simple tram ticket had to be signed in triplicate. Now he had hired a Lear jet.

'We are going to Darwin,' he snapped. 'Who have we got to send?'

The chief of staff rattled off the names of three rostered reporters who for various reasons, were unavailable before adding, 'We have Walden!'

'God almighty,' was Maher's response. He then turned and in five slow motion strides walked straight to my desk. 'Mal, I am sending you to Darwin. Go home pack a bag and be at Essendon Airport by 2 p.m.' He then issued his final words – words that drove me to make decisions I would never have normally made and do things I would never have normally done. 'This story will either make you or break you son ... this is your last chance, don't let me down.' With that he turned and disappeared back into the sanctity of his office.

I silently pledged I wouldn't let him down but like tens of thousands of others touched by Tracy – our lives would never be the same.

CHRISTMAS DAY 1974 – 3.18 P.M.

Two aircraft took off bound for Darwin. As our chartered Lear jet roared into the Melbourne sky, a RAAF VIP BAC111 was taking off from Canberra. Aboard that flight was General Alan Stretton, a team of medical staff with supplies and one ABC junior cameraman who had hitched a lift at the last moment. Aboard our flight were two pilots, one of our most experienced senior cameramen, Mike Meahan, his assistant Loz Bowie, two journalists from the *Herald Sun* to help share costs and me; a cadet TV reporter desperate to save his job.

As we broke through clouds and turned into the mid-afternoon sun on a heading for Alice Springs, the RAAF BAC111 was en-route to Mackay to pick up the Minister for the Northern Territory, Dr Rex Patterson. They would later transfer to a Hercules at Mt Isa, which they believed would be better suited for an emergency landing in Darwin if it was found to be necessary. It was during the final leg of their flight that acting PM Jim Cairns contacted Stretton by radio giving him "supreme authority". Stretton would later concede, 'I knew the power was essentially of a de facto nature and could have no legal basis.' He therefore decided to rely on bluff.

Shortly before 6 p.m. we touched down in Alice Springs and began the agonising wait for air traffic control to give us clearance to continue. At around 9 p.m. the first flight of evacuees from Darwin arrived. They made a pathetic sight walking across the tarmac to an isolated hanger where emergency medical teams were waiting. Looking haggard and pale with children clutching bedraggled Christmas presents, some were still in a state of shock. We filmed from a distance. Some shouted obscenities at us, others pleaded to be left alone. But behind each shot I remembered that voice: 'This will make or break you, son. Don't let me down.' I tried to reason with them that news of the disaster must get through in order to get support and relief supplies moving. It was the only way I could justify encroaching on their tragedy.

Finally, we reached an agreement. A couple of volunteers would speak on behalf of them all and an impromptu press conference was arranged. As the plane would continue on to Adelaide and Melbourne we asked the pilot to carry our film and notify HSV7 shortly before he landed. This he agreed to and so a precedent was set for similar film transfer agreements throughout the next ten days in Darwin. By midnight the evacuees had left and the airport was virtually deserted. Between attempts to grab some sleep on the leather airport benches, I kept asking the chief pilot to check with air traffic control for possible clearance. Previous requests for takeoff had been refused.

At 3 a.m. the pilot returned with news that we could leave – but there was a catch. We only had enough fuel to make one pass over Darwin. If that failed we would have to return and make another attempt later. I knew other media would be on their way, so if a plane carrying evacuees could take off from Darwin certainly one could land. The pilot wanted to wait another hour for the cyclone to clear but there was still that voice: 'This will make you or break you, son.'

'Let's give it a try,' I pleaded.

Less than ten minutes out of Darwin, the turbulence struck. Not as severe as we were expecting. Suddenly the dark grey skies became lighter as we dropped beneath the heavier clouds giving us our first sight of the carnage below. It was raining as dawn broke on this new day.

The cabin silence was broken by a static voice calling from below. The only communication from the airport was a two-way radio in a military jeep. We were being directed from that jeep with instructions to land. The Lear jet bounced once or twice and came to rest at the end of the strip. It took little skill to gather our first story. Within less than an hour we had shot several rolls of film. The problem we would face was over-shooting. After our first interviews we made our way to the airport where I renewed my acquaintance with General Alan Stretton. Thankfully he didn't acknowledge our previous encounter as he gave an immediate assessment of damage and shocked us when he announced, 'I'm going to evacuate this city beginning immediately.' He then likened the scene of devastation to Hiroshima and several times during our interview became visibly close to tears. At the end he asked me what I was going to do with the interview and I told him it would be flown back to Melbourne on our plane.

'No, young man, I am the supreme commander here and I am commandeering every aircraft able to fly. The only time yours will take off is when it's full of evacuees.'

Tell that to John Maher, I thought as I ran through the crowd at the airport terminal calling out, 'Anyone wanting to go to Melbourne raise your hands.'

Within two minutes I had picked out ten evacuees fit enough to travel and located Stretton again for his official clearance.

BOXING DAY 1974 – 7.58 A.M.

Two hours and twenty-three minutes after landing in Darwin, I stood with the camera crew and watched as our Lear jet screamed down the rain-soaked runway and roared into the misty sky carrying the first two canisters of film the world would see of Cyclone Tracy's destruction of Darwin. It then began to rain again.

While Stretton was setting out his priorities, we set about organising ours. We began at the Avis car centre opposite the airport, selecting the least damaged vehicle. We requested one with air conditioning and got it. It was the only car with a windscreen intact. No other windows, just a windscreen. We then headed in the direction of the Travelodge Motel, which stood as a symbol of survival above a skyline that lay devastated beneath it. The foyer was scattered with hastily packed suitcases. Small groups gathered for evacuation after spending the night huddled in basements and in the dining room. It already smelt of stale tropical mildew. The pool contained at least one car and debris was scattered around the grounds but apart from that the hotel remained fairly intact. Many of its windows had blown out but one room on the fifth floor was habitable. The one requirement was to bucket our own water up the stairs to flush the toilet. Dry camp stretchers were brought in and the one broken window was sealed.

After a brief tour of the area we headed back out to the airport where the Salvation Army had set up food stalls. To my amazement I was greeted by the same Melbourne group I had spent Christmas morning with. Shortly after our interview they had apparently been alerted of the disaster and implemented a well-organised disaster plan arriving in Darwin six hours after us.

The relief operation was now in full swing. While supplies were being unloaded from the Hercules that had touched down moments before we arrived, General Stretton was convincing local authorities that he had the authorisation to take charge and no one questioned him. Priorities were food, water, local transport, searching for bodies and of course the massive task of evacuation. Of the 47,000 inhabitants, he decided to immediately reduce the number by 10,000.

That afternoon acting PM Jim Cairns and his wife Gwen arrived and we joined the cavalcade of local dignitaries and a growing band of media as they toured the worst parts. Not that there were any better parts. They both became visibly upset and Mrs Cairns broke down in tears on a number of occasions. At the end of the day, Stretton called a media conference on the steps of the police station. It was followed by a broadcast on ABC radio, which by then was back on air. As dusk quickly descended we drove back out to the airport to find a pilot on one of the many relief planes that would fly our film back to Melbourne.

FRIDAY, 27 DECEMBER 1974

The day began with another press conference during which Stretton pledged at all times to be honest with the media. There was already much speculation on the death toll and rumours that the true figure was being down played. This he assured us was nonsense. Dignitaries from all round Australia were now on their way. Politicians, union leaders, state leaders all eager to be seen and shown to be offering support. I wondered at times how Stretton found time to run the relief operation between pandering to the egos of his visitors.

Senator George Georges from Queensland was one who began to irritate the General with his constant presence and persistent advice. It didn't take long before a showdown loomed and he was told in no uncertain terms to keep out of Stretton's way or face deportation. These little asides were later revealed by Stretton himself who struck up a very close association with the media during his many "off the record" moments. He also praised our efforts, which he said were generating nationwide sympathy and support. We were totally unaware of any feedback as communication to our respective newsrooms was unavailable and any phone calls in those first few days were restricted to emergency calls only.

The body count had now reached 47 and the temperature was over 40 degrees. Stray dogs were being rounded up and shot and the decaying stench was getting worse by the day raising further health fears. We were now concentrating on human-interest stories with survivors who were telling amazing stories of clinging to what was left of their homes to stay alive.

Keith Jessop was one such man who had survived the cyclone of 1937, the Japanese attack in 1942 and now Tracy. He described his terrifying survival. 'There was just me and my wife … huddling under our bed until the room filled with water.' Then as the water rose we struggled to reach a wardrobe for support, '… moments later the whole ceiling crashed in on us.'

Others described moving from room to room as each one disintegrated around them. One story revealed how a mother grabbed her daughter's legs to prevent her from being blown away. There was also a wife who found her decapitated husband during those silent moments in the eye of the storm, but couldn't remember how she survived when the eye passed and the storm returned. Some were, in fact, asphyxiated by the pressure from Cyclone Tracy, leaving bodies totally intact.

The horrors were told in graphic detail, as survivors seemed keen to talk about their ordeals before they invariably broke down on camera. As we moved from one scene to the next, each story continued to erode the immunity of our own emotions.

SATURDAY, 28 DECEMBER 1974

This was our third day and I was becoming seriously concerned at our ability to operate as a news crew. The sniping and bickering intensified following false takes in stand-ups and equipment failures due to humidity. We were even arguing over whose turn it was to carry the water up the five flights of the Travelodge to flush the toilet. Water was a valuable resource and according to a notice pinned to the board in the Press Centre at the police station "ice and water would be made available for those wishing to queue". One light moment came as we queued. A newly arrived radio colleague strode up to the sergeant in charge of distribution and introduced himself as Ron Connolly from the Major Broadcasting Network in Melbourne. The sergeant apparently only recognised the word "major".

'Yes Major, what can I get you sir?'

Without blinking an eye Connolly asked for ice, water and beer and walked away with all three. The sergeant even saluted Connolly!

PM Gough Whitlam had flown in from Greece that day and after his press conference we then drove back out to the airport to find another pilot to send our story back to Melbourne. In ten days we never lost one report thanks to the pilots we had entrusted to carry our film.

SUNDAY, 29 DECEMBER 1974

A new cameraman had flown up to Darwin to replace my crew but no reporter had been sent to replace me. His arrival brought news that our first report had been syndicated around the world becoming the first story filed from Darwin. Maher apparently went out and celebrated. His decision to hire the Lear jet had been justified.

Stretton was now negotiating with the unions to get them onside for wharf duties in time for the arrival of the fleet. The evacuation had reached its peak of 8,000 in one day with the population now down to 16,000. The strain was now showing on Stretton. During one of his regular trips through the suburbs with the media in tow, a woman emerged to offer him a ripe mango.

'It is a gift for you,' she said. A gift she had saved to give him personally. He broke down and wept.

As we followed through the streets of Parap he stopped again when he caught sight of movement in a wrecked house. Emerging from the ruins stepped a man, his wife and two young children. They had been huddling there together, a family in shock since Christmas Eve when Tracy struck. Four days in the ruins with two children aged four and 18 months. With cameras rolling the media throng pushed closer as Stretton introduced himself to the father who then broke down.

'I have lost everything,' he cried, 'I have now no reason to live.'

We all cried at that moment. There was not a dry eye among the entire media contingent. The distraught husband's name was Sam who became a symbol of Darwin's survivors and the lead story around Australia once it was filed. Sam was originally from Syria so General Stretton arranged for his children to be flown back to Damascus until his house had been rebuilt. Six months later, Stretton took his wife back to Darwin where they paid a visit to Sam and his family who had moved back to their new home.

By now some journalists had dubbed Stretton the "Weeping Dictator" and the "Johnny Ray of Generals". His nightly press conferences invariably started "off the record" and in tears. Then as we quietly sat back and waited, he would compose himself and go back "on record".

MONDAY, 30 DECEMBER 1974

The day started quietly enough, although by now it was becoming more difficult to find new angles and new stories. We were only waiting in Darwin for the fleet to arrive in several days and for General Stretton to hand over his powers and leave.

Cameraman Chris Brown and I decided to see if there were any stories from the courthouse opposite the police station. There had been talk of looting and charges pending. The court we chose happened to be hearing a case against an Aboriginal man charged with obtaining whisky by impersonating a police officer. Those charges alone appeared disturbing, as the man who stood in the dock resembled anything but a police officer. He was grubby, bearded, longhaired, wearing tattered shorts and a dirty T-shirt. If there was one thing he could never have been accused of, it was impersonating a police officer. In fact, there were no Aboriginal persons in the NT Police Force at the time. Magistrate David McCann sentenced him to nine months hard labour, at which point we left the court. I then spotted Stretton at the police station and immediately rushed up to ask him whether the sentence could be interpreted as racial discrimination.

'Okay boys,' he said, 'roll that camera.' And on cue he ran across the street and up the steps of the courthouse until stopped by an officer of the court.

'Don't you know who I am?' he barked.

'I know who you are sir,' the young officer replied, 'but you have no authority over this court.'

Stretton backed off momentarily then continued. 'I demand to see the Magistrate.'

A moment later McCann emerged to investigate the shouting. Suddenly he saw our camera and became very angry. Stretton called on us to stop filming explaining he would meet us on the steps shortly.

An hour later he appeared with his arm around McCann and apologised for any discourtesy he may have shown. However we no longer had an exclusive story. The word had spread and a large media contingent gathered then quickly adjourned to the pressroom to file their stories. Suddenly the door burst open and Stretton's loyal advisor and assistant Colonel Frank Thorogood called us to order.

'Please,' he said, 'I beg you, do not send the story. They will crucify him in Canberra; you do not understand what this will do to him. He has brought Darwin single-handedly back from the brink. If you send this story it will destroy him. I will do anything … I implore you.' He was close to tears. No one spoke. There was an embarrassing silence until a single voice from the rear carried across the room.

'I have already filed.'

It triggered a mad rush for the phones. Thorogood's shoulders slumped as he left the room.

That evening, Stretton held his usual press conference. He informed us that he planned to hand over full administrative control to local authorities the next day, with the recommendation that normal civilian administration should resume. Stretton also paid a visit to Government House to discuss the impending visit of the Governor General, Sir John Kerr, for the official handover. The evacuation had been successful, essential services had been restored to an acceptable level and he felt his mission was almost complete.

TUESDAY, 31 DECEMBER 1974

I was quietly advised Stretton could attempt a low-key exit ahead of the hand-over. In fact I was about to discover he had no power to hand over anyway. He had no legal authority – it had all been bluff. We drove out to the airport and there he was. As he was climbing the steps to his aircraft I rushed forward. I wanted to apologise for my part in the courtroom incident. I wanted to tell him of the enormous regard I held for him and to thank him for the friendship and the experience we had both shared. I will always remember his final words.

'Well son, when you study the facts you will find you had as much power here as I did.' He then turned boarded the C130 aircraft and left. Two days later, after the official handover to the authority our mission too was over. Besides, Cyclone Tracy was no longer lead story.

SUNDAY, 5 JANUARY 1975

A bulk ore carrier ploughed into the Tasman Bridge in Hobart causing a large section to collapse onto the ship and into the Derwent River below. Twelve people were killed, including seven crewmembers on board the ship the *Lake Illawarra*. We were already on our way back from Darwin when the story broke.

As I walked into the newsroom the following morning, John Maher was standing by the door to his office, a cigarette in one hand and the familiar plume of smoke drifting above his face. 'The wanderers have returned,' he called, 'now all we have to do is justify the expense.' He then looked me in the eye and said the words I had waited three years to hear, 'Well done my boy.' As he prepared to turn back into his office he handed me an envelope. Then with a wry smile as the door closed behind him he muttered something about Cyclone Tracy having saved both our jobs. By the time I reached my desk I had opened the envelope and sat reading its contents with such a feeling of satisfaction I almost wept. It was confirmation of my first grading as a journalist. I was on my way.

Of course we were all unaware that within 12 months another story would develop just north of Darwin. An unimaginable tragedy which would all but destroy John Maher; it would break our hearts, test our resolve and question the very fabric of what journalism should stand for. It was the tragedy of Timor.

CHAPTER 7

TIMOR ON THE TOSS OF A COIN

1975

HEADLINES

Ship brings down the Hobart Bridge
Jim Cairns embroiled in the Juni Morosi affair
Vietnam War ends as Saigon falls to the Communists
Whitlam sacked
Civil War in Timor

HITS

Bohemian Rhapsody - Queen
Bye Bye Baby - Bay City Rollers
Sailing - Rod Stewart

WEDNESDAY, 1 OCTOBER 1975

A 20-cent coin spinning in a Sydney newsroom was about to determine the fate of three Australian newsmen...

John Maher and his Sydney based counterpart Bob Johnston were operating news departments under a very complicated and at times highly volatile de facto Network relationship. ATN7 was owned by Sydney Fairfax and HSV7 by Melbourne's HWT. The more eloquent and at times acerbic tongue of Melbourne's John Maher frequently won arguments on budgets and strategy between the pair.

The developing Timor crisis was a story that justified sending a crew but neither could agree on whom to send. Melbourne reporter Greg Shackleton had convinced Maher he had the research and qualifications necessary to succeed while Sydney reporter Brian Anderson – who at least had some Vietnam experience – had similarly convinced his boss he was the most qualified.

In a bid to avoid another heated clash Bob Johnston offered a compromise with a simple toss of a coin. Johnston elected to toss the coin in Sydney while Maher would soon deeply regret calling "heads" in Melbourne. There was a pause as the coin made its final spin. Then the voice of Johnston simply said, 'It's heads for Shackleton,' and hung up.

WEDNESDAY, 15 OCTOBER 1975

The strident ringing of a single phone pierced the silence of the almost abandoned newsroom. It was 7.25 p.m. and the rest of the staff had already left for the evening's post-news ritual at a nearby hotel where the topic would undoubtedly be centred on the latest outburst by John Maher. He had been incensed at seeing his reporter Greg Shackleton filing a story from East Timor while wearing an army fatigue shirt. It was similar in design to the independence movement known as Fretlin who were fighting pro-Indonesian forces in a civil conflict.

'What the hell does he think he's doing?' he said in a voice just short of a shout. 'He'll get himself killed. Send a cable immediately to Dili and get him out of that bloody shirt, he looks like a fucking Fretlin.' With that he disappeared into his office leaving a familiar pattern of smoke swirling in his wake.

The incessant ringing continued until I reached for the phone and took one of the most haunting calls of my life. Between inconsolable sobs, I listened to a grief-stricken woman reacting to an intuitive notion that her son was dead.

'I know what has happened … It's a mother's intuition,' she kept repeating '… I know it … I feel it … I just know he's dead.'

I was about to ask who was speaking when she identified herself as Greg Shackleton's mother.

'My son is dead, he's been killed … Oh my God! Please help!'

I began tying to console her and finally, I promised to convey her concerns to management who would contact her as soon as possible. I then hung up and left. She was wrong. Greg was very much alive when I took that call. I relayed that conversation almost word for word when I reached my colleagues a short time later at the hotel. Several laughed in a cynical dismissive way. Then we all had another drink.

There was no laughter the following morning, just an indescribable sense of dread. The first thing I noticed when I walked into the newsroom was the silence. There was no hum of teleprinters, typewriters or normal newsroom chatter. Small groups were talking in whispers and all bore a look of disbelief, bordering on despair.

'We've lost the Timor crew!'

My immediate interpretation of the term "lost" was simply out of radio contact.

'They didn't turn up for a planned rendezvous with Chris Santos (former Portuguese Consul) and apparently Santos is concerned. He and Jose Ramos-Horta (Fretlin leader) are trying to locate them but there has been no word and there are some rumours that westerners may have been killed or captured.'

I remembered the previous night's call from Greg's mother and rushed to my desk to find her phone number. I was intending to give it to Maher but saw through the glass partition into his office that he was already on the phone. At that very moment someone turned up an ABC radio broadcast half-way through a newsflash:

Radio reports from Kupang West Timor are claiming a number of Europeans have been killed near the Indonesian border.

It was immediately followed by a primal heartbreaking cry as someone ran from the newsroom. I saw Maher drop the phone and suddenly slump into his chair, burying his head in both hands. I realised "lost" meant something far worse than just missing. I was still sitting at my desk in a state of stunned disbelief when minutes later he emerged distressed and dishevelled.

'When you have a good reporter bursting to go and cover something, what do you do?' He was talking to anyone but no one in particular.

I couldn't think of anything to say. I just sat watching one of Australia's hardest nosed news bosses reduced to tears as he desperately tried to justify a decision he had made.

'I pleaded with them to be careful and not to be foolish.' His voice was now beginning to choke. 'But this was such a very big story and … it was … Christ Almighty, it was on our own doorstep for God's sake.'

'We don't know for sure,' someone said, 'they may have been captured, nothing is confirmed.'

He appeared to take some comfort from that and returned to his office. Moments later, Station Manager Ron Casey entered the newsroom and walked solemnly into Maher's office. I watched for some sign, some signal, some hope. They both stood facing each other. Maher was chain-smoking, Casey was doing the talking. They then both wandered to the window and stood gazing outside towards Melbourne's Shrine of Remembrance. Had they turned to their left and looked up towards the adjoining building, they would have been looking directly into the window of the Defence Signals Directorate (DSD). Unbeknown to both men that office of Army Intelligence had just received a cable that confirmed our worst fears on the fate of five Australian newsmen.

Across the Timor Sea, less than one hour's flying time from Dili, the Royal Australian Navy Station at Shoal Bay had listened in fascination and then horror to an Indonesian radio message, transmitted on a secret wavelength between two small towns in East Timor, Batugade and Balibo. The essence of that signal indicated that the incursion had succeeded and that 'all traces of the white men had been obliterated'. Shoal Bay was one of Australia's most highly sensitive listening posts operated by DSD that was the most important of Australia's Intelligence Agencies. As such, the Australian Government had no intention of letting the Indonesians know of our eavesdropping capabilities. The cover-up was just beginning.

As Ron Casey and John Maher gazed out of Seven's newsroom window and past Army Headquarters, the transcript of that signal was already being sent to Canberra where it would be buried. A short time later Casey and Maher, both red-eyed and grim-faced, left the newsroom. I was told later that Maher had gone to St Patrick's in the city where he lit three candles and prayed to Saint Jude, Patron Saint of lost causes. As he left he was heard muttering something about having tossed a coin and lost. In what order they died was not immediately clear but very soon the irrefutable evidence was they had been shot, bayoneted and burnt beyond recognition. They would become known as the Balibo Five.

Seven weeks earlier, I had arrived mid-afternoon to prepare reading the Sunday evening bulletin. The lead story centred on the growing crisis in East Timor. *Seven News* had backgrounded the crisis to our north since the government in Portugal had been overthrown one year earlier heralding a change of policy towards its colonies, including relinquishing power in East Timor. Three political movements were seen as possible alternatives: the Fretlin movement, a revolutionary front for an Independent Timor, which was advocating self-rule; UDT, the Timorese Democratic Union, which favoured independence but with links to Portugal; while Apodeti wanted full integration with Indonesia.

For 12 months Indonesia was becoming increasingly concerned at the political instability on its doorstep and the possible spread of communism, which they believed was linked to the Fretlin Party. They also suspected anyone who supported them were of leftist leanings, including western journalists. The events in East Timor were unravelling about as fast as the Australian Labor Government under Gough Whitlam. Deputy PM Jim Cairns had been sacked and replaced by Frank Crean throwing the Labor Government into further crisis. ACTU President Bob Hawke was openly critical of Whitlam accusing him of treating the ALP as "his own party". Hawke was also canvassing entering Parliament himself, pledging to 'go on the wagon' if he became PM.

As I had only recently travelled across from West to East Timor on my return from Israel, I had a first hand account of the tension along those borders so I took more than just a passing interest in the events that were unfolding. At the end of reading the Sunday night bulletin, I wandered back into the newsroom. As I gathered up a Sunday Press before heading for the door the chief of staff Cyril Jones called out, 'Before you go Mal, I think we are sending a crew to Timor. I suggest you pack a bag tonight and I'll give you a call.'

It had been four years since I was last in Timor backpacking my way home, lazing around the cliff top swimming pool at Bacau waiting for the once weekly Ansett flight to Darwin.

I arrived at work the following morning with my bag packed and a thrill of anticipation that immediately evaporated as soon as I saw the assignment board. My closest colleague and senior reporter David Johnston had already left for Timor. He had arrived for the start of his shift one hour earlier and was already at the airport preparing for his flight to Darwin. He would later describe it as one of the most frustrating assignments of his career.

Johnston never left Darwin. As civil war had broken out between opposing factions around Dili, Australia's Defence Minister Bill Morrison was reported to have secretly ordered the Australian Navy and Air Force to blockade Timor preventing anyone from entering or leaving its territorial waters. For ten days Johnston argued, bribed, pleaded and begged nearly every qualified pilot and shipping agent in the top-end of the NT, but no one would risk the repercussions of entering the restricted area.

To add to his frustration, the head of Network Nine's news Gerald Stone and his boss Kerry Packer, had chartered a restored Japanese trawler and sailed across the Timor Sea avoiding detection from Australian and Indonesian Naval patrols and landed in East Timor near the capital of Dili. Stone and his cameraman Brian Peters (who would become a Balibo Five victim) captured on film scenes of fighting between Fretlin and Apodeti supporters and then just as quickly withdrew. They not only arrived back in Darwin with their scoop but, according to Johnston, did so under the scrutiny of official military personnel. Packer and Stone were even escorted on board a plane in Darwin by security forces with guard dogs to keep opposition reporters at bay. Johnston was further frustrated when 'they flagrantly boasted of their success' which some believe was only made possible by sailing under the false auspices of the Red Cross. The final insult to his ten-day mission of misery culminated in the wrath of news boss, John Maher.

Back in Melbourne, Maher was grooming his latest acquisition to the *Seven News* team. Greg Shackleton was the epitome of fresh-faced youth, with dark chiselled features capped off by a deep-seated ambition. Greg Sugar had changed his name to Shackleton, married his live-in girlfriend Shirley and established a career in media by working as a radio reporter and newsreader at Melbourne's 3AW.

I took an immediate shine to this clean-cut, image-conscious 23-year-old father of one when he joined the *Seven News* team as late night news producer in '73. But within a short time the shine began to dim as he began to encroach on my territory, finally replacing me as late night newsreader. There was never any question he was a good acquisition to the newsroom. He could produce, write, report, present and above all was ambitious. It was perhaps that competitiveness that became his fatal flaw.

The knowledge that Johnston had failed to make it to Timor simmered in Shackleton. This now was his opportunity; a way of proving his ability to those in the newsroom who snickered at the mirror he kept in his top drawer to maintain his appearance. He also worked quietly and methodically to establish a high level list of contacts including one he often spoke of, Shadow Foreign Affairs Minister Andrew Peacock. Greg sat directly opposite me on the long narrow news desk separated only by a 12-inch high chipboard partition in which we pasted our personal photos, press clippings and little reminders. It provided us with some privacy but certainly not enough to prevent us hearing each other's conversations or phone calls.

It was early October 1975 when Greg made a point of allowing anyone within earshot to know he was meeting Andrew Peacock. It was his hope, he said openly, that Peacock might have the connections, which could help him in his quest to get to Timor. Peacock has since strongly denied any such connection to Shackleton to the point of threatening legal action at one stage. Greg theorised that Peacock needed information from Timor to help embarrass the Whitlam Government proving beyond doubt that Indonesia was officially backing a pro-Indonesian party push for control of East Timor. Maybe it was coincidence, but within less than a week of claiming he had met with Peacock, Shackleton made it to East Timor.

The coin was tossed, the announcement was made: Greg Shackleton, Gary Cunningham and Tony Stewart were going to East Timor. Wednesday night, 8 October 1975, I invited the three of them for farewell drinks at the Melbourne Musicians Club in St Kilda where I was a member. The following morning on Thursday 9 October they flew out of Melbourne on a 7 a.m. flight to Darwin. Precisely one week later, to the hour, all would be dead.

The night they left we ran a story in our 6.30 news showing Greg and the boys at Tullamarine ready to board their flight. The reason we shot that story was two-fold. We were promoting the fact that we were sending our team to Timor. We were also notifying government authorities of their presence knowing our news would be seen through our affiliate station CTC in Canberra. They arrived in Darwin that afternoon to be told their charter flight to Dili in the morning had been cancelled. No reason was given. However the following morning, less than 12 hours after our news item had gone to air in Canberra, the ban was suddenly lifted.

FRIDAY, 10 OCTOBER 1975

At 8.30 a.m. Greg and the boys took off for Dili, but not before Greg filed a short piece for our evening news:

With us we are taking the passport of Fretlin member Chris Santos from the Portuguese Consul in Darwin with instructions to pass it on to him personally by hand. The passport is Santos's go ahead to attend negotiations in Lisbon next week on the colonies future, talks the Indonesians strongly oppose. We are also carrying a sealed envelope from the Portuguese Consul to Fretlin leader Jose Ramos-Horta.

They arrived in Dili shortly before midday and immediately sought out the leader of the Fretlin movement, Jose Ramos-Horta, who spoke of a large scale Indonesian attack on the township of Batugade four days earlier. At 4 p.m. that afternoon, after initial difficulty in locating a driver they eventually departed with Fretlin support for the border region.

SATURDAY, 11 OCTOBER 1975

Fretlin forces lost the border town village of Batugade just ten kilometres from Balibo. The UDT attack was believed to have been led by Indonesian troops – just the sort of story Shackleton and the boys had come for. However, en route to that area they encountered a retreating Portuguese and ABC news crew who had been pinned down during that attack. Accompanying them was Chris Santos, for whom Shackleton had brought a passport from Australia. Santos later told reporters:

> *I asked Greg where they were heading. He replied, "To the border to film some action." "No you're not" I said, "it's very dangerous. That's why we are retreating back to Dili." Shackleton replied, "Do you think we have come all this way from Melbourne to film you and your colleagues in peaceful Dili?" I insisted, "No it's too dangerous. I'm telling you." I had the power to stop them. But I feared the nationalist forces of Fretlin would get bad press perhaps that we were trying to hide something. Instead I said, "Well if you want to go it's your responsibility but you must sign a document to this affect absolving us of any responsibility." Every year October the 16th is my day of guilt. If I had been firmer they would not have been killed.*

Greg confirmed that conversation in his next news report, which he recorded when he arrived at Balibo late that afternoon. This was Fretlin's forward position overlooking a bay and an Indonesian warship, which lay at anchor below.

Greg to camera: *Several kilometres back we had signed a letter absolving Fretlin of responsibility for our safety and well-being. This was the same kind of letter we had signed with the Portuguese Government to get us into Timor.*

SUNDAY, 12 OCTOBER 1975

Fretlin decided to withdraw from Balibo because they regarded it as unsafe.

> **Greg to camera:** *It was at this time yesterday the town was reportedly hit by mortar and artillery fire. We look like being the last people in the town and will make a decision shortly on whether we should pull back too. In the meantime, we have daubed our house with the words Australia. We are hoping it will afford us some protection.*

Later that day they pulled out and headed for the town of Maliana but that night Maliana also became unsafe so they moved on.

MONDAY, 13 OCTOBER 1975

Greg filed one of the most emotional stories of his series after interceding to save the life of a prisoner believed to be a spy. Fretlin was proposing to execute the young man before Shackleton spoke on his behalf. The prisoner was saved and sent to Dili for further questioning. Greg and the boys returned to Balibo to find the crew from Channel Nine, Brian Peters and Malcolm Rennie had arrived

Back in Melbourne, the reports were becoming less frequent and Maher was clearly becoming more uncomfortable and irritable by the day as concern was growing. Each film report was couriered by Fretlin supporters back to Dili where it was flown to Darwin and on to Melbourne, a process that took several days. It was one of these final stories that caused such consternation in the Seven newsroom, the one in which Greg was seen wearing army fatigues and when John Maher literally screamed, 'What the hell does he think he's doing? He'll get himself killed. Send a cable immediately to Dili and get him out of that bloody shirt, he looks like a fucking Fretlin.'

Several people began to chuckle. Maher turned on them and with typical vitriol yelled, 'If he gets shot because they think he's the enemy then be it on your bloody heads.'

WEDNESDAY, 15 OCTOBER 1975

A Portuguese film crew passed through Balibo and urged the Australians to leave saying an attack by Indonesia and UDT forces appeared imminent. They replied that they would stay on in the hope of getting some footage of fighting. It is believed both teams were considering a pull back, but each thought the other would then have the competitive edge.

THURSDAY, 16 OCTOBER 1975

Just before dawn on that fateful morning they were awoken by the sounds of artillery, mortars and tank fire coming from the direction of the town of Batugade. The attack consisted of three Special Forces teams supplemented by regular Indonesian Para Commandos. Supported by heavy bombardment from seven warships, which were now stationed off Batugade, the two teams wearing regular army uniforms but no insignias attacked Maliana and the coastal town of Palaka. Team Susi under Captain Yunus Yosfiah, also known as Captain Andreas, led the attack on Balibo. All members were dressed in civilian clothes but according to some eyewitnesses some were wearing distinguishing scarves. The partisan forces were ordered not to wear watches or anything identifiable.

At first it was believed that both cameramen, Gary Cunningham from Seven and Brian Peters from Nine, had moved out and began filming. While filming, eyewitnesses saw other crewmembers Shackleton, Rennie and Stewart emerge from the building shouting and gesturing to the advancing troops. They were calling out that they were Australians and pointing to the Australian flag that Greg had painted on the side of the house where they had been staying. All five journalists were outside when the first soldiers from Team Susi entered the outskirts of Balibo. The soldiers then began firing as four of the journalists turned and ran towards the Chinese house with their arms in the air still yelling 'Australian... Australian!' A cameraman who was seen filming, then nervously looked back. He suddenly fell. He was described as 'with balding head', which fitted the description of Brian Peters.

When the troops entered the square the four journalists who had made it safely to the house slowly emerged with their hands in the air repeating the words "journalists" and "Australian". The journalist at the front was then seen to have been either stabbed, shot or both, depending on eyewitness accounts. The others were herded back into the house and machine-gunned. However, it's believed one of them survived by hiding in a bathroom at the rear of the house. One eyewitness said he saw one man running from the back door trailing blood from a wound. He ran up the hill towards a nearby house where he tried frantically to open a door. He suddenly dropped, either shot again or died from his wounds.

Another version of events has only one Australian newsman emerging from the house. He was immediately struck down and killed by a knife blow from an Indonesian soldier. All eyewitnesses seem to agree on one point, that Indonesian soldiers poured machine gun fire through a window of the house. Another source claims one of the two newsmen who actually survived the machine gun fire was seen being forced to talk into a tape recorder by Indonesian troops. It is believed he was the last to die.

Eyewitnesses say the attack lasted just over 45 minutes. By 7 a.m. local time, it was all over. The bodies, including the newsman who fled up the hill, were then gathered up. There are slightly differing versions of events that followed. One has the Indonesians pouring liquid over the bodies and setting them on fire. Another has them being left in the house until later that afternoon when troops dressed at least one body in a Fretlin uniform and propped it up between Portuguese army machine guns where a series of photographs were taken.

Whatever the truth, by early evening the five journalists were lying burnt beyond recognition in a Chinese house across the street from the house where they pitifully daubed the flag and the word "Australia" in the hope it would afford them some protection.

At around 1.15 that afternoon I was sitting at my desk in the newsroom. I was close to tears as information slowly began filtering out of Timor. We still had a news bulletin to put to air and were clinging to some hope that the reports we were hearing were wrong or at best some had survived.

Meanwhile, the phones were ringing incessantly from viewers, friends and of course families who were hearing the same reports on radio news services. They were all seeking further information, which we just didn't have. Some families who had been notified were coming into the building to meet with management and those of us they knew. There was still no confirmation just unconfirmed reports from unconfirmed sources in East Timor. Maher returned to the newsroom and a short time later I saw Greg's wife Shirley enter his office. For several moments they stood speaking then she suddenly slumped into a chair and I realised now that hope was indeed fading. What we didn't realise was a cover-up had just begun.

That afternoon the report from DSO went to the Defence Department's joint intelligence organisation in Canberra. A senior Defence Department official later took it personally to Defence Minister Bill Morrison at Parliament House. This was 12 hours after the attack.

According to a *National Times* investigation, Morrison circulated the report to PM Gough Whitlam and Foreign Minister Don Willesee. None of the Labor ministers were in any mood to look at the contents closely. Opposition leader Malcolm Fraser had announced that because of the "loans affair" they would block the passing of "supply" in the Senate. Perhaps because of this political crisis the permanent head of defence Sir Arthur Tange argued successfully to Morrison against revealing what had been learnt about Balibo. To do so would reveal the level of signals that could be intercepted and invite Indonesia to take counter measures. So for whatever reasons, the cable simply disappeared.

FRIDAY, 17 OCTOBER 1975

Both Casey and Maher had made arrangements to fly to Canberra to meet with officials from Foreign Affairs. At precisely 1.23 p.m. a small communication teleprinter which sat next to the Reuters printer just behind my back, rang with three short bells. I snapped it up and read:

EDITOR

CHANNEL SEVEN NEWS

MELBOURNE, VIC

MOST CONCERN FATE THREE CHANNEL SEVEN

NEWSMEN – STP – REPORTS REACHING DILI INDICATE THEY WERE KILLED BY INVADING FORCES – STP – RADIO KUPANG REPORTED YESTERDAY THAT UDT FORCES CAPTURED QUOTE FIVE COMMUNIST JOURNALISTS WHO SUPPORTED FRETLIN AND THEY GOT A LESSON UNQUOTE – STP – PLEASE CONVEY TO FAMILIES CONCERNED OUR PROFOUNDEST CONCERN FOR THEIR FATE – STP – FRETLIN SOLDIERS ON THE BORDER WILL OBSERVE ONE MINUTES SILENCE TOMORROW MIDDAY RPT 12 NOON – STP – MY PERSONAL WARMEST REGARDS FRANCISCO XAVIER DO AMARAL PRESIDENT FRETLIN.

The words CAPTURED, KILLED and THEY GOT A LESSON indicated our worst fears. The killings had been confirmed and it appeared their deaths were deliberate. I walked quietly out of the newsroom and into a nearby toilet. There were sobs already coming from one of the cubicles so I left to find one downstairs where no one would hear mine. We were all in a state of shock and disbelief.

My first thoughts were for our young sound recordist and assistant Tony Stewart who had just celebrated his twenty-first birthday. Tony and I had only recently returned from an assignment on Lord Howe Island covering the last flying boat service before the airstrip was opened. Throughout our time together he kept us fully entertained, quoting passages from his favourite show *Monty Python's Flying Circus*. Gary Cunningham was our most experienced cameraman having spent time covering the Vietnam

War. He was a very close friend of Tony Stewart and would have been most protective in the last moments together. Then my thoughts turned to Greg: his love of his son Evan and his overall professionalism, which matched his compassion. This compassion was clearly seen in Greg's last report where he selflessly saved the life of the young Fretlin prisoner about to be executed.

That afternoon representatives from both networks, Seven and Nine, met with Foreign Affairs in Canberra, but received little or no information on the fate of their staff. Against the wishes of Foreign Affairs, Casey and Maher then decided to visit the Indonesian Embassy in person. According to Maher, 'We met a very young official, who was very sympathetic and indicated to us in a very round about way, that our boys had been killed.' He convinced them of their worst fears. Both Maher and Casey later claimed that unidentified member from the Indonesian embassy gave them more information than any member of the Australian Government.

MONDAY, 20 OCTOBER 1975

The Indonesian press carried a report of the bodies of four Europeans found in a house at Balibo but said, '… it could not determine their nationality although there was a sign nearby of Australia.'

TUESDAY, 21 OCTOBER 1975

Foreign Minister Don Willesee told the Senate that the Australian Government was gravely concerned about the fate of the missing journalists.

THURSDAY, 30 OCTOBER 1975

A fortnight after the killings, the Australian Government still maintained its position of ignorance.

FRIDAY, 7 NOVEMBER 1975

PM Whitlam wrote to President Suharto appealing for confirmation of the fate of the newsmen. Suharto received the letter six days later but no reply was ever sent. Even had a reply been sent I doubt it would have seen the light of day.

TUESDAY, 11 NOVEMBER 1975

Tuesday afternoon 2 p.m. all thoughts of Balibo were swept away in seconds. The Seven newsroom suddenly erupted with the simultaneous sounds of urgent bells on teleprinters, phones ringing and Maher bursting from his office yelling, 'The Government has gone ... Whitlam has been sacked ... Move ... get off your arses and move NOW, all of you!'

As instructions and scant details of the dismissal were being shouted to reporters, we all scattered to our designated assignments. I immediately grabbed a news crew and headed into the CBD to record vox pops of people's reactions. Regardless of their political leanings the news was met by a unanimous reaction of shock and disbelief. Within hours there was talk of widespread civil disobedience, CIA involvement and some extremists were even talking of civil war.

Six months later, all hell did break loose and we witnessed some of the ugliest street scenes since the violent anti-South African rugby union Springbok tour in 1971. The protests were provoked by the Governor General Sir John Kerr's first visit to Melbourne since dismissing the prime minister. Gough Whitlam had called on the people to "maintain the rage" and the people of Melbourne responded.

I jostled through the large crowd as several hundred demonstrators pelted Sir John's Vice Regal Rolls-Royce with eggs and paint bombs on his arrival at the Royal Commonwealth Society in Queens Road. Then before he left, Sir John challenged them to join him two weeks later at a law institute dinner at the Leonda restaurant in Hawthorn. They took up the challenge but this time more than a thousand protestors were waiting and so was I.

Learning from previous experience, police blocked roads for two kilometres around the venue, a move that angered the protestors more. Armed with eggs, rocks, paint bombs and flares they gathered at either end of the approaches to Leonda and waited. At 6.48 p.m. as Sir John's car arrived, the demonstrators surged forward towards a solid line of police. Smoke bombs were thrown in quick succession and marbles tossed into the path of advancing police horses. I was standing at one end of the bridge, less than 50 metres from the howling crowd of demonstrators when a bottle suddenly exploded on the bitumen less than a metre away. Then a rock the size of half a brick struck a young police constable in the back and he went down with a grunt. I had been talking with him just moments earlier.

The smoke bombs cast an eerie orange glow in the late afternoon sky. Police sirens wailed and the crowd responded with a deafening roar. It was great television but it was not live television and it would be too late for our 6.30 news, which was about to end. Police horses were stumbling on scattered marbles and a young girl was injured as one horse went down. Helmets and shields were out as police advanced. Having long since lost contact with my cameraman I ducked under the bridge railing and dropped onto a grassy knoll leading down to the Leonda car park where I joined other reporters sheltering behind parked cars. None of us had ever seen the likes of this.

More protests would follow but gradually, very gradually, life would return to some form of normality – although not so for the families of the Balibo Five. Any hopes they harboured of PM Malcolm Fraser taking a tougher stance on Indonesia would soon be dashed as the Coalition Government adopted the same position on Balibo as the ALP.

WEDNESDAY, 12 NOVEMBER 1975

One month after the Balibo killings, and a day after Gough Whitlam had been sacked as Prime Minister, the Australian Ambassador to Indonesia, Richard Woolcott, received a box containing bone fragments, some camera gear, notebooks and papers belonging to Shackleton, Rennie, Peters and Stewart.

FRIDAY, 5 DECEMBER 1975

A funeral service was held in Jakarta. The wreath from the Australian Embassy read:

> *They stayed because they saw the search for truth and the need to report at first hand as a necessary task.*

Back home, our grieving continued unaware that an infamous cover-up would continue for the next four decades. For Maher the events of Timor stayed with him until his death. The grief he felt was second only to that which must have been felt by the families as Maher, who never married, regarded the closely-knit newsroom team as his own extended family. Then to compound his loss and guilt, he was also accused of being a killer. The owners of a suburban tabloid the *Toorak Times*, Jack Pacholli and John Somerville-Smith, launched a personal attack in their paper accusing John Maher of being a "murderer". For weeks its banners ran such scathing headlines as *The Killer News Boss Who Sent His Reporters To Their Deaths*. Only Maher would know the pain this caused which he revealed to me just before his own death.

'I went to see Casey,' Maher told me. 'I said I don't much care what anyone says about me. They can say anything, but to accuse me of murdering those boys, my own staff, was beyond the pale … Casey was right in what he said. "They haven't got a brass farthing, so suing them is not going to do any good." I said it's not the money … Then I thought, if this is all I've got to put up with, its nothing compared with the families who are going through hell. So I just decided to cop it sweet.'

Throughout the entire ordeal Maher claimed his first concerns were always for the victim's families. No one fought as hard as he in securing financial compensation from the HWT, a settlement made in private. No one fought to suppress the private gossip surrounding Greg's personal life more than he. Several weeks before Shackleton left for Timor, he made no secret of his intention to leave his wife Shirley. While the Federal Government was involved in a cover-up over Timor, Maher was also attempting to cover-up Greg's personal affairs.

'For the sake of his family,' he said. 'I did. I mean it was awful, but Greg told me his marriage was finished. I think he had actually left Shirley and was living in a caravan at the time.'

Throughout the funerals and memorial services the Federal Government maintained its official line:

DESPITE INTENSIVE INQUIRIES WE REGRET VERY MUCH THAT WE DO NOT HAVE A

SATISFACTORY ACCOUNT OF THE DEATHS OF THE FIVE JOURNALISTS. TAKING INTO CONSIDERATION THE FAMILIES' DISTRESS AND IN SYMPATHY WITH THEIR WISHES THE MATTER SHOULD NOT BE PURSUED ANY FURTHER.

A week after the funeral in Jakarta, Foreign Affairs rang Channel Seven to inform us that the personal belongings of the dead newsmen were waiting to be picked up at their office in the city. I volunteered to collect them and send them on to their families. As I drove back to the newsroom with the package of damaged gear and water stained notebooks, I managed to read Greg's diary. His final entry (in part) read:

Balibo, October 15th

We have just received our first food supply in days. Fretlin members brought us some potato chips and coke. The first chips and drinks we've had since our final night in Melbourne at the Musicians Club with Mal and it is really going down well.

As I read that note and looked at the date, I suddenly realised the entry was written the night Greg's mother rang me saying that her son had already been killed. Olwyn Shackleton was wrong. Her son Greg was very much alive when I took her call. He was killed the following morning. It was not a mother's intuition as she had insisted; it was a mother's terrible premonition.

Throughout the following decades of anguish, frustration and tears, the families of the Balibo Five have all dealt with the tragedy in different ways. Some campaigned more than others but it took the efforts of one woman from Bristol in England to finally turn the so-called Balibo folklore into fact. Maureen Tolfree, the sister of British born Channel Nine cameraman Brian Peters convinced the NSW coroner to conduct an inquest into his death on the grounds he had been a resident of NSW in 1975.

On Friday, 16 November 2007, NSW Deputy State Coroner Dorelle Pinch handed down an official finding into the death of Brian Peters. She outlined in the beginning, '... to investigate the death of one of the Balibo Five was to investigate the deaths of all.'

The inquest was able to uncover facts that five previous investigations, including two Government inquiries, failed to do. It confirmed the cover-up engaged by successive Australian Governments, which had maintained the Indonesian stand '... they had all died in crossfire'.

Witnesses from opposing sides to the Balibo attack travelled to Sydney to give evidence on oath and in open court. Some from UDT and Apodeti had fought alongside Indonesian Special Forces, together with former Fretlin fighters who were the last to see the journalists alive.

The inquest found the five Australian-based journalists known as the Balibo Five were deliberately killed to prevent them from exposing Indonesia's 1975 invasion of East Timor. They died on 16 October, 1975 from wounds sustained when (they) were shot or stabbed deliberately and not in the heat of battle, by members of Indonesia's Special Forces including (Commander) Christoforus

Da Silva and Captain Yunus Yosfia. There was strong circumstantial evidence those orders came from Special Forces Major General Benny Murdani. Witnesses said Captain Yosfia led the charge into the Balibo town square and was first to open fire despite attempts by the journalists to surrender. Australian Commonwealth officials agreed they had seen an intercepted Indonesian radio message that read:

As directed and in accordance with your instructions the five Australian journalists have been located and shot.

This message dated October 16 has never been seen again. Deputy Corner Dorelle Finch found the deaths constituted a war crime and referred the matter to the Commonwealth Attorney-General. Yunus Yosfiah, one of the men accused, was contacted by phone in Indonesia. He refused to comment and hung up. Family members wept once more, this time though, because the truth had finally come out.

'Hopefully,' said the Coroner, 'this inquest will demonstrate that the truth is never too young to be told, nor too old.'

Greg's wife Shirley found unique support in a friendship with Greg's former girlfriend Madeleine. Shirley's son Evan, who was eight at the time of his father's death, became a successful barrister in Western Australia. Unbeknown to anyone of his colleagues, cameraman Gary Cunningham had a brief but passionate affair with a young nurse just before he died, producing a son. By the time his son reached his mid-thirties, John Milkins also began searching for the truth into the death of the father he never knew. Several years after Greg was killed his mother Olwyn committed suicide. It was not the murders that destroyed her. It was, according to Shirley Shackleton, a combination of official indifference, the Jakarta Lobby's eagerness to blame the Balibo Five for their own fate, and the behaviour of Australian government officials. No war crimes charges were ever laid.

It's the saddest legacy in my life as a journalist. I have tried to forgive the Whitlam Government and all successive governments since, but the bottom line is they have all put politics above their people. I may one day forgive. But I will never forget.

CHAPTER 8

LEGACIES OF THE '70s

1976

HEADLINES

The Great Bookie Robbery nets 1.5 million
Chairman Mao dies
Jimmy Carter elected US President
Sir John Kerr faces angry protests
Eloise Worledge disappears from her family home

HITS

Fernando – ABBA
Dancing Queen – ABBA
Let's Stick Together – Bryan Ferry

MONDAY, 12 JANUARY 1976 – 7.30 A.M.

The slightly built four-year-old boy padded barefoot down the hallway into his parents' bedroom, as he did most mornings. He slipped between their sheets and as he curled up between them, Blake Worledge uttered the six short words that would trigger his parents' worst nightmare, 'Ella is not in her bed.' His sister, eight-year-old Eloise Worledge, had been abducted from her home in the middle of the night and despite the state's biggest missing persons search and a $10,000 reward she was never found.

MONDAY, 19 JANUARY 1976 – 10.30 A.M.

One week after Eloise Worledge was reported missing I was sent to their family home in the Melbourne Bayside suburb of Beaumaris in the hope of filming the first one-on-one interview with her devastated mother Patsy. John Maher was convinced it was a domestic dispute.

'Daughters don't just disappear. Get inside that house. Use your bloody charm,' he said without a hint of compassion. 'Find out what happened.'

The damp smell of tea tree hung in the air from the light morning drizzle as I walked the short path to the front door. An overturned tricycle on the front lawn lay as a symbol of happy family times but added to the impending moment of intrusion I was about to impose on the parents; the moment most journalists dread.

I knocked. I waited. A moment later the door suddenly swung open. 'I am so terribly sorry to intrude …'

'I know who you are, Mal. Please come in.' Within minutes Patsy

Worledge was fussing around in her kitchen, organising coffee for the crew who had now joined me in the lounge and were re-arranging furniture and chairs for the interview. I sat taking notes, drawing comparisons to her last appearance on television news several nights earlier as she appealed with her husband Lindsay for information that could help police. Now seeing her in person conveyed another image. She appeared more composed on the surface but as I noted: 'while her bright blue-grey eyes sparkled with a glimmer of hope they were etched by red rims and dark circles drawn from a mother's worst fear.'

Two chairs were placed facing each other in the centre of the room. The lounge was comfortably furnished with dozens of prints and paintings, including her own work of art. There was also a large family photo including, eight-year-old Eloise, six-year-old sister Anna, four-year-old brother Blake, and her proud parents Patsy and Lindsay all smiling down on us. Lindsay was not present and Patsy made no apology. In fact, I felt some relief as his rather brusque and somewhat defensive nature had reportedly intimidated some senior police who had placed him as the main suspect.

Police who received the initial phone call recorded Lindsay Worledge telling them in an unemotional and almost off-hand tone that there had been a break-in at his house and '... the only thing missing is my eight-year-old daughter.'

I didn't have to ask too many questions as Patsy Worledge used the interview in much the same way a traumatised patient would use therapy. Her softly spoken voice was almost devoid of emotion as she relived the initial shock of discovering her daughter was missing. Panic-stricken, she rang her sister and then ran across the road to a neighbour. I then asked if she suspected anyone without specifically naming her husband. But she replied no, and then quickly followed up saying she fully believed that

Eloise would soon be returned. This supported the initial theory that her husband may have been involved as retribution to their impending separation and that after a brief period Eloise would be returned. That theory could also be attributed to the glimmer of hope I saw in her eyes. Patsy also elaborated on how the fly wire screen had been cut from inside the home and how police had discovered traces of tan bark on the bedroom floor from the garden bed below the open window.

Our interview suddenly took on an edge as Patsy voiced frustration that police had not taken the abduction seriously at first, treating it as a domestic. She accused junior police who initially responded to their call as incompetent in that they had trampled over vital evidence beneath Eloise's bedroom window. She then spoke of the huge support from senior police who had formed a special task force within days, headed by Detective Superintendent Fred Warnock. I sat listening and preparing for a flood of tears that never came. We stopped at one point to change film reels but then continued as if it had been a commercial break on live television. I also took copious notes concentrating on names Patsy referred to including her close friend Pauline. It was Pauline who was among the first to support the family on hearing of Eloise's disappearance. It was Pauline who she had shared her initial grief and suspicions. Pauline, I noted, would become someone to contact later should this interview become the basis of an extended program. The story of Eloise Worledge was lead story for many nights on all networks and most of the viewers it seemed were turning to Seven for the details. It was a made for-television mystery. Not since the Beaumont children – Jane, Arnna and Grant – had disappeared without a trace from a beach near Adelaide in 1966 had there been such public reaction and like the missing Beaumonts, interest in this case was also being led by female viewers.

The abduction of Eloise Worledge coincided with one of the most profound periods of assessment in the television news industry. For the first time, networks were spending vast amounts of money on research – and that research would set the blueprint for the way TV news would be viewed well into the next millennium. One of the most significant aspects of that research was the impact women were having on television news. As Maher would continually espouse, 'Women are the key to the success of a television news bulletin … Aim for the western suburbs and particularly the women.'

The Worledge case reaffirmed his theory.

ATV Channel 0 (Network Ten) had commissioned Frank N Magid Associates from Marion, Iowa to conduct research into television news in Melbourne. Their research found Melbourne was recording the highest news figures in the country with 70 per cent of people watching news five nights a week at 6.30 p.m. Of those, 83 per cent were in the low socio-economic bracket with 76 per cent being women.

INFLUENCE OF THE NEWS ANCHOR

Another finding revealed the influence of the "News Anchor". Apart from clearly identifying the personality-related dimensions of Seven's news service it also identified the one person responsible for Seven's success. The key man in the mix was clearly the newsreader Brian Naylor. This fact was not lost on the Nine Network who also had commissioned private research. In many respects viewers felt the same about Channel Nine's main reader Eric Pearce as they did about Channel Seven's Brian Naylor. Surveys revealed that Pearce was seen as 'an exceptional communicator using precise diction, presenting in a comfortable yet interesting pace and above all was seen to be trusted'. At the same time, many participants in the survey were aware that Pearce was approaching retirement. They felt he 'had been on-air a long time and was looking a little tired', a fact that GTV9 was also very much aware of. Not surprisingly, the research revealed that most viewers of Channel 2's news tuned in because there were 'no commercials or interruptions' but their viewers were mostly from a select group in the higher socio-economic market and thus were in the minority. Channel 2's newsreader Geoff Raymond was mentioned specifically by 9 per cent of respondents but Raymond was seen as 'a professional news presenter' rather than a personality. Finally, Channel ATV0 was generally seen to have a distinctive news identity, but apart from the station's one-hour format, it was not always a positive one. From a personality perspective, presenter Bruce Mansfield was mentioned by name but many viewers remembered Mansfield from his earlier days on children's television and felt his past 'hindered his chance to establish some form of credibility in the news area'.

At the time of the Eloise Worledge abduction, rumours began circulating within the industry that GTV9 had been trying to poach Naylor from HSV7. They hadn't at that stage. It was purely a provocative rumour circulated by their news director to test the waters. However, the seed was sown during a corporate dinner later in the year at Melbourne's Southern Cross Hotel.

Seated at the same table, with Maher and Naylor, was Maher's nemesis at GTV9 and his one-time journalist colleague at the Melbourne *Herald*, John Sorell.

During the dinner, Sorell casually leant across the table and in a loud provocative voice asked Naylor when his contract was due to expire. The table conversations came to an abrupt halt and caused almost apoplexy for Maher when Naylor replied, 'I'm not under any contract ... it's just a gentlemen's agreement.'

The seed began to take root.

The following morning Maher was in the general manager's office demanding Ron Casey draw up a contract immediately or risk losing the station's key presenter. Howard Gardner, the station's sales manager, was also present, hammering Casey with facts and figures outlining the financial cost to Seven if they lost Naylor to Nine. Casey was from the old school of thought. He had evolved from "office boy" to Station Manager within the Herald organisation and believed a gentlemen's agreement was better than any written contract. However, he relented to the pressure from his senior executives and had a 12-month contract drawn up which Naylor signed. Very few knew of its duration. The headlines simply read: *Naylor re-signs with Seven.*

Six months later Tom Worland, one of Seven's senior reporters, also received an offer from Nine. His deal meant a little more money than he was already being paid at Seven but it included a car parking provision. Seven matched the financial offer but not the car parking facility so Worland accepted the job at Nine and left. The issue of car parking was about to cost Seven dearly.

Casey had taken delivery of a new car and because of its size was finding it difficult to park. He decided to take over Naylor's more convenient number one spot in the laneway close to the front door of Seven's studio complex in South Melbourne. This infuriated Naylor and was just another irritant following the contract fiasco. A few months later Worland rang Naylor and set up a meeting with Sorell in a bid to coax him over to Nine. This time Naylor was far more receptive.

By mid 1976 police were still no closer to solving the disappearance of Eloise Worledge and the special taskforce was disbanded and the file sent to Moorabbin CIB. Both Patsy and Lindsay attempted to keep up public interest by conducting separate interviews in the media in the hope that Eloise was still alive. Sadly, that hope was fading with every passing day. Patsy and Lindsay officially separated in June that year.

Around this time John Maher appointed a new secretary, a unit manager who would virtually run the news department's management structure. She was classy and efficient, did not suffer fools gladly and, above all, had a great sense of humour. These were the ingredients needed to work alongside Maher in a roomful of hedonistic male egos and females battling for equal rights. She walked straight up to me on her first day in the office, held out her hand and introduced herself. 'I'm Pauline, friend of Patsy's.' Her name was Pauline Durham and I immediately realised she was "the" Pauline, mentioned so many times during my interview with Patsy Worledge. What I didn't know at the time was that Pauline had not only become my boss's secretary but would also become my wife and Patsy Worledge would become godmother to our daughter Sarah.

FRIDAY, 23 SEPTEMBER 1977 – 10.30 A.M.

3DB's Denis Scanlon, interrupted his radio program with a newsflash:

> *The biggest news story on Melbourne television in a decade. Brian Naylor has announced his resignation from HSV7 and is to head up National Nine News on GTV.*

I was home at the time preparing breakfast. It was towards the end of the September school holidays and I was fulfilling my duties as backup reader for Naylor who had taken a three-week break. I was also counting down the days for his return eager to get back on the road as a reporter. This newsflash could not have come as a bigger shock however, nothing could have prepared me for the next part which would change my life forever.

In a statement from Channel Seven, General Manager Ron Casey has confirmed the decision by Naylor and announced that Mal Walden will take his place.

There was no warning, no discussion and no one more stunned than me.

'Well, we're fucked in the ratings now' was the only comment I heard as I walked into the newsroom half an hour later. The station's publicity boss Eileen O'Shea burst in grabbed my arm and ushered me into her office.

'We have the *Herald* newspaper on line one, the *Age* on line two and Robert Fidgeon from *TV Scene* also wants to talk to you. The radio stations will just have to wait,' she gushed. 'This is Veronica Ridge,' she said, handing me the phone. 'Just repeat the questions so I can steer you in the right direction.'

As I ended the interview Program Manager Gary Fenton (Channel Seven) arrived. Draping an arm around my shoulder there was no word of congratulations.

'Well, Mal pal, who cuts your hair? Casey has booked you into the "Wellington Boot" in East Melbourne; in the meantime he wants to see you so let's go.'

Casey was sitting at his office desk.

'Congratulations,' he said as he stood to shake my hand. 'We are all thrilled that you have been appointed…'

'No, I'm sorry,' I cut in. 'I don't want the job, I'm sorry.'

There was a stunned silence.

'Why not?'

'Well, it's just not enough for me to read the news. Coming in at 4 o'clock every afternoon and leaving at 7.00 p.m., it's just not enough to occupy my time.'

'Well,' he replied, 'why don't we send you back to university?'

'I never went to university in the first place.'

'How about we join you up with a golf club somewhere?'

That was the most ridiculous offer I had ever heard. He obviously didn't know the standard of my golf! With that offer rejected he then called in Finance Manager Gerry Carrington who began talking about pay rises. Starting at $60,000 a year, he said we could increase it on a yearly basis.

'It's not the money,' I tried to explain. Although $60,000 was sounding pretty good compared with the $120 a week I was now earning as a reporter. Fenton returned, this time clutching a pamphlet.

'Mal pal,' he said, 'look at this.' It was a brochure on the soon-to-be released Mazda RX7. 'Take the job and this is yours.'

I paused for a moment. *Everyone has a price,* I thought. 'If you want me to read, then let me report as well.'

There was another long pause. 'We will agree to that,' Casey said, 'but only special news reports and not the day-to-day stories.'

I agreed.

We all shook hands, a contract was drawn up and a week later I took delivery of the first Mazda RX7 in Australia. The RX7 lasted two weeks before a hit–run driver slammed into it one dark wet night while I was reading the late news – it was a right off. I was terrified the short life of my car would replicate the life of my new career.

The police were most sympathetic and promised they would

track down the driver who had fled the scene. They did, two years later, charging him with an indecent offence in a notorious toilet block at Albert Park. The police constable then made an obscene link to slamming into the back of my car.

Meanwhile, I had become "Melbourne's first working journalist to be appointed a newsreader" – a trend that would soon be adopted throughout the television industry. Now came the task of marketing the image. For a start they decided to elevate my age by two years to create some maturity. The joke at the time was: 'Newsreaders should wear black for maturity, have glasses for authority and haemorrhoids for a look of concern.'

Casey's concern was my hair. He believed it was too red and created a distraction. So I began having it sprayed each night. The problem was each night it was a different shade. Cartoonist Robert Fidgeon noticed this and the process ceased immediately. The age discrepancy would continue throughout my career. By the time I reached my fifties however, station publicity suddenly had me several years younger and yet only one observer ever questioned this discrepancy.

'Some people use Botox to maintain their youth,' he said, 'Walden uses biogs.'

By the end of 1977 my life was centred on publicity and promotion while Patsy Worledge was doing her level best to avoid the limelight. In the weeks after Eloise's disappearance Patsy held on to hope, supported by friends, counsellors and the Reverend Dr Francis Macnab from Melbourne's Collins Street Uniting Church. Inevitably, she was forced to accept the fact that Eloise was gone and it was "time to move on". The media however, were more reluctant to let go and pigeon-holed her as a victim, turning to her for interviews on anniversaries of Eloise's disappearance or whenever another abduction took place.

Thirteen years later, on the day Eloise would have turned 21, *New Idea* magazine published a story that included a computer-enhanced picture of how Eloise would probably have looked as a young woman. In a bid to support Patsy and shield her from further media scrutiny a small group of friends took Patsy out to dinner.

The out-of-town restaurant was busy and at times noisy. Towards the end of the evening an acquaintance of one of the guests joined our table. She was pleasant and chatty and soon began revealing why she had recently given up her highly paid job in the publishing industry.

'You know,' she said, raising her voice above the sounds of the restaurant, 'the type of stories they are now covering like that bleeding heart woman who lost her daughter all those years ago and is living in the blind hope she may still be alive. God knows why?'

There was a deathly silence at the table before Patsy's voice broke through loud and clear, 'I think you are referring to me, I'm Patsy Worledge.'

The woman was clearly shocked. 'Oh my dear, what can I say?' Tears welled up in her eyes and she visibly paled. Patsy simply told her to think before she opened her mouth in future at which the woman stood up and quietly walked into the ladies room. Several minutes passed before someone went and checked, but she was no longer there.

Sadly, tragedy does not discriminate. Like a black cloud it tends to hover over some more than others and years later it would strike the Worledge family again. There is never a good time to receive bad news and the worst time must be in the middle of the night. My wife Pauline fumbled to answer as the phone broke our sleep. There was a pause. Then a deep throated primal cry. Throughout the sobbing and the shock that must accompany news of every road fatality came the words 'Blake is dead'. This time Patsy Worledge had lost her son. Pauline had lost her godson.

On that cold and wet winter's night in August 1997, 26-year-old Blake Worledge left a party and stepped out on to Whitehorse Road in Nunawading straight into the path of an oncoming car. Blake was killed instantly, devastating his surviving family and his wide circle of friends. In the early hours of that terrible morning we gathered around Patsy to offer what support and comfort we could. At the funeral I embraced Blake's father Lindsay and felt his body shudder in inconsolable grief. At the time of Eloise's disappearance, Detective Superintendent Warnock told a cynical media that he believed Lindsay Worledge had been unfairly judged.

'I think he has been seen in a bad light. A lot of people believe he has acted callously … He's not the kind of person who wears his heart on his sleeve. Deep down, he cares about his children and he is very distressed.'

As we stood in that cold damp morning at the Springvale Crematorium I looked into the eyes of a father who had now lost his second child and like his former wife Patsy, their grief was overwhelming.

Twenty-seven years after Eloise Worledge was snatched from her bed in the dead of night a new investigation was conducted by the Victoria Police Cold Case Unit. Detective Senior Constable Robert Nazaretian told the Melbourne Coroner's Court that despite Eloise's father Lindsay being the prime suspect at the time of her disappearance, the investigation found no new evidence to implicate either of Eloise's parents. Convicted sex offenders interviewed when the case was reopened included a teacher and a librarian at Beaumaris Primary School, as well as a man who coached at the Beaumaris Junior Soccer Club, but police failed to link them to Eloise's disappearance or uncover any evidence linking sex killer Raymond "Mr Stinky" Edmunds to the crime.

Handing down an open finding, Coroner Frank Hender said Eloise Worledge was a shy girl who would not have voluntarily left her home with a stranger. He said significant information given to police included a neighbour's account of hearing a child cry out and a car door slam at 2 a.m. on the night of the disappearance. He ruled it impossible to identify who was responsible for Eloise's disappearance.

Outside court, Patsy told reporters that the family had been 'devoted to learning from our experiences, to healing and accepting the mystery and now we don't actually need to know'. Patsy said the family had found its own form of closure years earlier. The case had a lasting impact on my life, but there were other legacies of the '70s that would also shape my life as a newsman.

You're not worth a pinch of shit until you've been sacked or sued.
– Veteran journalist, 1976

I was sued in 1978 and sacked in 1987. I silently hoped that senior journalist would eventually concede I had well and truly earned my stripes. At the time he uttered those prophetic words I had just been issued with my first writ so I presumed he meant them as encouragement. However, this was not just a simple libel case. This was a massive $8 million writ for damages, which included the cost of a missing Rembrandt. Although his first attempt to sue me failed, the plaintiff, who couldn't afford or find appropriate legal representation, reissued the writs three years later. At the age of 68, the plaintiff, Leslie Albert Wallman, enrolled in a crash course of legal studies at university and then returned to fight the case himself.

My offending news report was recorded two days before Christmas 1975, when a group of elderly tenants were forcibly evicted from their South Melbourne boarding house. They made a pathetic sight for our cameras sitting on the nature strip outside the double story tenement where they had lived for many years. Suitcases lay scattered around with personal objects spilling out from where they had been thrown. I conducted a series of quick interviews and recorded two pieces to camera. The first piece I realised was far too subjective:

After refusing to leave the building their landlord then had the gall to threaten them.

I repeated the stand-up, deleting "had the gall" threat and replaced it with 'leaving them homeless just before Christmas'. I completed the story, returned to the newsroom and made several unsuccessful attempts to phone the landlord for his side of the story. I was then sent out on another assignment leaving a producer to edit my story. Needless to say the wrong, and arguably defamatory, piece went to air on the 6.30 news.

The plaintive was claiming that he had been identified by the story that night and had been viciously attacked in the street leaving him with serious injuries. The writ also claimed that several weeks after the report went to air his home in the outer suburb of Eltham was destroyed by a mystery fire and the first people to arrive at the scene was a news cameraman from HSV7. The cameraman just happened to live nearby but the plaintiff interpreted his presence as part of a vicious plot by the network of "intimidation" and "victimisation". He also claimed that within the house at the time of the fire was a priceless Rembrandt painting which had been destroyed – a family inheritance that was too expensive to insure. To support his claim of ownership, he possessed an ABC documentary on the Rembrandt that he said had been produced several years earlier. His total writ for damages exceeded $8 million including medical expenses, mental anxiety, damage from the fire and the loss of the priceless painting.

After a week of intense cross-examination it went down to the wire. Throughout the case our fear was that the jury would cast a sympathy vote seeing it as a David and Goliath struggle; an aged pensioner battling the HWT media monolith. Our legal team headed by a leading QC and a team of barristers and Melbourne solicitors from Corr and Corr found themselves at a complete disadvantage due to the plaintiff's lack of language skills and knowledge of the legal system. Every attempt to approach him was seen by him as a sign we were on the back foot. Therefore there was no opportunity to reach a settlement. However, in the end, it all came down to one word – malice. Did Walden deliberately set out to defame the plaintiff?

It was a tragic costly story all round. The jury found in my favour and awarded costs against the plaintiff. There was no appeal because he died a short time later. From that moment on I always checked my stories before they went to air. If I felt in any doubt, then the legal department would become involved. Seven's legal department became an integral part of the television newsroom system. My only concern was that legal brains inevitably leant towards conservatism. However, that week under cross-examination in the Supreme Court was an invaluable lesson in both jurisprudence and journalism. Some stories, I believe, are simply not worth the risk. So there I was, I had been sued and eventually I would be sacked. But that is another chapter.

TELEVISION NEWS IN THE '70s

As the '70s began to draw to a close we were leaving behind one of the most defining decades in news and the news industry.

The decade began with the Vietnam moratoriums, the gunning down of Pat Shannon during the Painters and Dockers war and Gough Whitlam becoming Prime Minister of Australia. Internationally, Cambodia fell to the communists, followed by Saigon. The Ayatollah Khomeini forced the Shah of Iran into exile, Idi Amin fled Uganda and Margaret Thatcher became the first female Prime Minister in Britain. To be here in Australia as a cadet journalist, nothing was as exciting as witnessing Whitlam's ascent to power in 1972. Then again, no journalist or scriptwriter could have foreseen the sacking of Deputy PM Jim Cairns and the destructive influence of the Khemlani affair, which culminated in the constitutional crisis and sacking of the Whitlam Government.

By the end of the '70s, the television networks were also preparing to move on. The battle for news supremacy was neck-and-neck between Seven and Nine in Melbourne, although research indicated that Nine might have captured part of the vital female demographic. Their lead-in program, the teen-oriented medical drama *The Young Doctors*, was also helping them. Now with Brian Naylor at the helm, their news was beginning to enjoy that little extra lift, Seven countered by sending me on assignments to reinforce the promotion that a journalist had more credibility than just a presenter.

Privately, this infuriated Naylor who rightly argued that communication was just as important. Nine then launched a most successful soapie style jingle *Brian Told Me* and very soon the news battle in Melbourne tightened. If women were seen to be the driving force behind a successful news service then management believed there was only one thing more they loved to watch on television – and that was a wedding. Pauline and I were married in a three-camera coverage, which led the evening news and filled the front page of the Sunday papers. But even a wedding only wins ratings for a short period.

We entered the new decade of the '80s with new hope. In 1981 the scars from Balibo had all but healed, so it was incomprehensible to imagine that just around the corner was another tragedy, one that would claim the lives of four more of our news colleagues. According to the philosophy of Patsy Worledge, 'you never get over tragedy; you have to go through it'. And to the best of our ability, that's exactly what we would have to do – together.

CHAPTER 9

HANDLING A CRISIS –
CHOPPER DOWN

1982

HEADLINES

Chamberlains stand trial
Argentina invades and captures the Falkland
The bottom of the harbour tax scam exposed
Lindy Chamberlain gets life in prison
Greenies blockade Tasmania's Franklin River

HITS

Eye of the Tiger – Survivor
Don't You Want Me – The Human League
Physical – Olivia Newton-John

THURSDAY, 7 JANUARY 1982
MELBOURNE

The day began with a freak 45-minute summer storm. It swept through from the western suburbs before dawn, cutting a swathe of damage and leaving power-cuts and flash flooding in its wake. The worst hit suburb, leafy well-heeled East Melbourne, was left counting the cost of damaged roofs, fallen power lines and downed trees. It had all the potential to be our lead story and by its very timing became the first story chalked up on the newsroom blackboard and the first story fully edited. In fact, it set an unusual precedent that day with most stories fully completed by early afternoon. A precedent and a blessing, for any story that happened to break after 2 p.m. could never have been covered due to the state of traumatised staff.

Reporter Mike Smithson had been assigned to cover a snap strike by security guards at the Turana correctional centre; Nick McCallum had been dispatched to the Melbourne Show Grounds for a colour piece on the six-day rodeo but had already radioed in that it was turning into a huge flop; Alistair Patterson was preparing to cover the announcement proclaiming actor Frank Thring the King of Moomba; Police reporter Dermot O'Brien was putting the finishing touches to a piece on a former South Australian rogue cop – Collin Creed – believed to be in Melbourne and wanted for rape and armed robbery. Meanwhile cameraman Blake Hobart had earlier rung in to say he was running late. It was a slight annoyance to producer Bill Ramsey but was easily overcome with a freelancer.

Now 27 and married with a young baby, Blake Hobart was showing promising signs of maturity. Battling peak-hour traffic Hobart had suddenly noticed the baby stroller on the back seat of his news car. Alisha was now 19 months and he knew how much his wife Jenny loved taking her for long walks. He waited a moment before doing a u-turn and headed back home where he dropped off the pram and quickly phoned the office to tell them he would be running late.

Ramsey had now moved across to the blackboard of assignments, wiped off Hobart's name alongside Jona's Press Conference and replaced it with freelancer Michael Briggs. Then he wiped Briggs from the "Land rumpus" assignment and replaced it with Hobart. Briggs would remember that moment for the rest of his life.

Blake Hobart's fate had been sealed.

Across town, 23-year-old Brigitte Best had set out for her city office. She was on time but not feeling well. It was just an uneasy discomfort that friends would later recount, but by then of course they too would be suffering. Her identical twin sister Nicky had already arrived at her place of work, just as eager and as excited as she was on her first day. She was one of 45 youngsters who enrolled in the 1977 journalism intake at RMIT and in May 1980 went on to beat 300 applicants for the position of cadet journalist at HSV7.

Now approaching her third year as a junior reporter, Nicky had accepted her assignment that morning with the same enthusiasm she had always shown. The office had already booked the single engine Jet Ranger helicopter from Jayro while veteran pilot Doug Hogg was approving the necessary flight details. Flinders Island in Westernport Bay once housed a minimum-security prison-farm, which had since been closed down, and the land was being sold off. For the purpose of her story Nicky located land developer and real estate agent George Samargis who would join them for the short flight to the Island to explain the type of development that could take place.

Shortly after 9.30 a.m. Blake Hobart arrived in the newsroom, red-faced and apologetic. Together with 21-year-old freelance assistant Paul Sullivan they loaded the car with the extra equipment needed for aerial footage then all four headed off to the helipad on the Yarra River. It took less than 20 minutes to reach their destination on French Island and by 1 p.m. they had completed filming. The story included an interview with George Samargis and stand-up (piece to camera) footage – as well as various ground and aerial shots.

At around 1.30 p.m., as they were preparing to take off on their return flight, they received a radio message to divert from their course and head towards the South Gippsland Highway near Lang Lang where there were reports of a fatal car smash and traffic chaos. They soon reached the highway and followed the ribbon of road until flashing lights and traffic indicated the scene of the accident below them.

Having dropped to several hundred feet, Blake grabbed the camera gear and strapped himself into the safety harness. He then slid open the door in a bid to film the scene from above. It was not easy in the cramped conditions and made much harder by the buffeting from the crosswinds. As they hovered slightly to one side of the crash site, pilot Doug Hogg was attempting to counter the effect of the crosswinds, which were now causing the rear rotor to vibrate. The chopper was bouncing as the engine changed pitch. Inside the cabin there would have been a few anxious seconds as Blake withdrew his camera unable to focus with the movement.

Suddenly, without warning, the chopper lurched to one side. Then, as its engines increased pitch, it quickly descended into a horrifying death spin plunging to the ground. The impact created a dull thud as the engine cut out. However, the blades were still spinning – *whoomp… whoomp… whoomp* – sending dust, dirt and clods of earth high into the air.

Inside the cabin, pilot Doug Hogg was calling to his passengers, 'Wait… wait… wait!' Then there was a moment of silence, just a nanosecond in time. They had all survived. But before he could call,

'Go… go… go,' and before they could even think of unbuckling seat belts or make any attempt to get out, there was a sudden roar as the entire chopper erupted into a huge ball of flame.

Senior Constable Larry Oakley, who was directing traffic around the highway crash site, immediately began running across the paddock towards the scene of the helicopter crash when a man suddenly emerged from the flames and smoke. It was the pilot Doug Hogg. He had survived the impact and escaped.

'He was on fire and yelling out,' said Oakley. 'We tried to calm him down and put the flames out but he kept saying there were four others inside … We managed to grab him and smother the flames but he was in a very bad way.' However, Constable Oakley conceded there was 'no way' they could have reached the others.

Back in the Seven newsroom police reporter Dermot O'Brien received a phone call at his desk. It was his close friend and contact at D24, homicide detective Jack Jacobs.

'Listen mate sorry to have to tell you this but there has been a chopper crash involving the Seven helicopter and… I'm sorry… it doesn't look good.'

O'Brien hung up, rushed out of the newsroom and ran down the passage towards the office of General Manager Ron Casey.

I was at home raking up leaves from the early summer storm when I heard the phone ringing.

'Mal, it's Pauline. Drop what you are doing and come straight into work.' There was a certain edge to her voice so I immediately asked what was wrong.

'Please just come in; there has been a terrible accident with the chopper.' Then she added, 'Please don't listen to the radio, just come straight into work.'

Needless to say, I switched on the car radio as I drove to the station and the first sound I heard was a newsreader reporting the tragedy but with no names being mentioned. As Pauline had warned, switching on the radio was the worst thing I could have done. The words from that news report roared through the closed confines of my car ending in a sound that echoed with an unexplainable whoosh. My senses momentarily lost complete control and my emotions swirled from one extreme to another as I drove through a fog of tears.

As I rushed into the newsroom several of the reporters were just sitting at their desks with their heads in their hands. And there was the silence. It was Timor all over again. Before I could even ask who was in the chopper, acting news editor Col Patterson grabbed me by the arm.

'I'm sorry mate,' he said, 'It's Nicky, Blake, Paul and a real estate guy. Doug has survived but he is in a critical condition ... Look, you're just going to pull yourself together ... We have a news service to get to air and you are just bloody well going to have to read it. I'm going to get you to write the story as well.'

I think I must have agreed because Patterson led me to a typewriter in John Maher's empty office then shut the door leaving me alone. Maher had called the newsroom earlier that morning saying he was unwell and would not be coming in.

A short time later, Jack Jacobs rang O'Brien again. The deaths had been confirmed and police needed details and addresses of next of kin. It would be left to O'Brien and senior management to drive out to their homes and break the tragic news personally. But the most terrible task of indentifying the bodies was left to one of our cameramen. Most families were already aware to expect the worst.

Around mid-afternoon John Maher rang O'Brien and asked, 'Is it true?'

'Yes it's terrible,' O'Brien replied.

Maher broke down sobbing. He then asked, 'Have you got everything under control? You don't need me do you?'

'Yes, we do need you. The staff is in crisis, it's bloody terrible, and you need to be here.' O'Brien's voice was raised almost to the level of a shout. 'You bloody need to be here. Do you fucking understand? You need to be with us.' He then slammed the phone down, believing he had over stepped his mark.

Several technicians and cameramen arrived and stood, silent and red-eyed against the assignment blackboard. One of the more senior technicians then lamented the sad loss of the newly acquired TK 76 and its costly recorder pack. He was immediately grabbed around the throat by one of the cameramen who slammed him off his feet and pinned him to the wall. The action coincided with the arrival of station manager Ron Casey who had quietly walked in. Turning to the technician he just calmly but firmly said, 'Get out, now!'

Maher arrived an hour or so later threw his arms around O'Brien and burst into tears. There was nothing that could be said that would make it easier. We still had a bulletin to get to air. There would be no point-scoring this night. No thought of ratings, just an incredible feeling of loss, despair and a growing doubt that I could even read the news.

The other networks provided us with vision while I spent the afternoon writing the fundamental details. I was fed the biographies of my colleagues and between inconsolable sobs I attempted to piece together the details of the crash as was being described by radio reports from eyewitnesses. However, by 6 p.m., just half an hour before the news, I was having severe doubts I could even read it.

Finally, it was decided we would record the news up to the first commercial break. At 6.25 I had made three attempts and on each take I had broken down. On the fourth and final take I succeeded without tears.

We completed the bulletin, emotionally drained and teary-eyed, but we did it as a tribute to those we lost and the families of those victims. Sadly, it didn't end with the closing theme of the hardest news bulletin I would ever have to read. Like the Timor tragedy, there was no official counselling offered to help overcome our grief. We all adjourned to our local pub and self-medicated.

Several months later, Coroner Kevin Mason summed up his inquest: 'I feel I can come to no positive finding as to the totality of this incident.' He then handed down an open finding. What was never revealed was that at precisely the time of impact Nicole's identical twin Brigitte was said to have been violently and unexplainably ill. In another horrifying twist one wonders whether cameraman Blake Hobart recognised the car he was filming in that fatal accident. It would have been familiar as it belonged to his neighbour, 67-year-old Sidney Victor Harris, who lay dead in the crumpled wreckage after colliding with a semi-trailer. The families would probably never recover and similiar to my experience with Timor, they most certainly will never forget.

In 2006 during a radio interview on 3AW to mark a milestone in my career, I was asked my most difficult bulletin. I replied without hesitation, 'The night the news chopper crashed.' Within a week I received a letter from Blake Hobart's widow Jenny who had been listening. I had not heard from Jenny since the funeral. She said she was thrilled that I hadn't forgotten and went on to explain how difficult life had been without a husband and father to help bring up a young daughter who had just celebrated her twenty-first birthday. In 2009, the *Pakenham-Berwick Gazette*, which was commemorating 100 years of community news, included the story concerning the chopper crash. The story was centred on Blake's daughter:

Gazette: November 2009

Alisha Hobart always gets told she is a carbon copy of her dad. Her nose, her laugh, and her sense of humour are just some of the similar features she shares, as family members often remind her at Christmas and family get-togethers. Last week, for the first time visiting the site where her father died, Ms Hobart, from Frankston, said she would do anything to spend five minutes with him. 'I get told I'm exactly like him, except for the red hair, so not to have him my whole life has been difficult. He would have been my best friend,' Ms Hobart said.

Alisha's mother does not talk about the crash much because of the painful memories, so after the *Gazette's* centenary story Alisha says she became interested in finding out for herself more about the father she never got to know.

'I knew what happened but I was too young to comprehend it. I don't know what his smile looked like. I don't know anything about him.'

In a strange twist to the tragedy, Alisha's mum told Blake not to go to work the day of the crash – something she rarely did.

'The last thing she remembers saying to my dad when he walked out of the bedroom was "I love you". You just never know when someone's not going to come back.'

CHAPTER 10

ANOTHER CRISIS –
ASH WEDNESDAY

1983

HEADLINES

Franklin Dam showdown
Bob Hawke wins snap poll
Cliff Young wins the Sydney to Melbourne Marathon
Australia wins the America's Cup
Ash Wednesday

HITS

Karma Chameleon – Culture Club
Uptown Girl – Billy Joel
Every Breath You Take – The Police

WEDNESDAY, 16 FEBRUARY 1983

The day began with PM Malcolm Fraser preparing his Liberal Party policy launch at the Malvern Town Hall. Two months earlier Fraser had opted for an early double dissolution. On the day he called the election however, the ALP replaced its leader Bill Hayden with ACTU secretary Bob Hawke. The whole political spectrum was thrown wide open. Hayden then claimed that a "drover's dog" could lead the ALP to victory. The drover's dog was now barking and the mood was as dark as the sky had been over Melbourne one week earlier when a huge dust storm swept in.

It was 10.58 a.m. – just two minutes to a radio news service. Traffic was still heavy on Melbourne's Queens Road as intimidating trucks sped by on the inside lane belching out volumes of black exhaust. The air was already thick and I thought of mentioning truck pollution as a possible story if I ever made it to Channel Seven through this chaos. I was on my way to meet Maher for lunch.

By now we had both formed a mutual respect for each other, which had extended into my personal life. Maher had been a tower of strength throughout a personal crisis with my father suffering terminal cancer and he had encouraged me in the purchase of my first home, a single-fronted weatherboard in Malvern. This also became a regular stopover on his way home whenever he needed a drink, which was all too often. I was also appreciating his eccentricity, albeit in small doses, so lunch would be brief. Besides, he now had a new whipping boy in his police reporter Dermot O'Brien.

'You're not a journalist bootlace', came the familiar bark – but of course he was. In the years ahead O'Brien would become a protégé of Maher as a news director in his own right.

On this day there was no shortage of good news stories. And the biggest was about to break. Since the dust storm and several bushfires around the state, a smoky haze had lingered in the air, a haze that appeared to be increasing with all this traffic and truck pollution. To make matters worse, the day had dawned unexpectedly hot. As we left for lunch the CFA appeared to have been taken by surprise and suddenly announced a total fire ban. Lunch was peppered with small talk until Maher suddenly announced, 'I have been diagnosed with what's called Meniere's syndrome.'

I immediately assumed this was why he had appeared tense and fidgety throughout his meal. He also kept looking out the window to the sky. He explained very briefly that it was a debilitating illness of the inner ear, which affected his balance. It was a very poignant moment for me. For years we had all sniggered behind his back whenever he had stumbled, believing it to be the legacy of a long lunch. Now I was bearing the guilt of being a party to his detractors. But as I had been told in confidence, there was little I could say in his defence. Meanwhile, he continued fidgeting and looking at the sky. Maher had a sixth sense when it came to news. I had seen it many times.

By the time we left the restaurant at 2.30 p.m. the sky had completely lost its dirty haze. The temperature had risen dramatically to 39 degrees. The car radio also reported the humidity had fallen to an incredibly low 7 per cent. There was already an ominous feeling in the air. Walking back into the newsroom Maher immediately adopted his edgy attitude demanding to know, 'What's happening?'

'Unlike South Australia, there are no bushfires burning in Victoria,' the producer defensively replied. The main story at this stage was still the Liberal Party policy speech by Malcolm Fraser, although that depended on South Australia.

By 3 p.m. the fire situation around Adelaide had worsened and was highlighted on radio by 5DN news reporter Murray Nichol giving a graphic and emotional account of watching his own home being destroyed by fire. A short time later we began receiving reports of spot fires around Victoria but again nothing abnormally large considering the weather conditions.

At 3.55 p.m. the temperature reached 43 degrees, the humidity was now down to 6 per cent and CFA headquarters in Malvern was reporting a fire at Belgrave. Shortly after 4 p.m. the CFA confirmed the fire was "now out of control" and we immediately re-directed a news crew, which had been sent into the area a little earlier. Meanwhile, similar reports were coming into ATV Channel Ten's newsroom. They were closer to the Dandenong ranges at Nunawading. Senior cameraman Ron Ashmore had been dispatched to the docks for a story on an old sea captain. It was a light fluffy story, which on a normal night would sit comfortably at the end of a one-hour format. But as he tried to locate "the old salt" he continued to monitor the radio communications between the reporters and his chief of staff. After 15 minutes he decided to cancel the story and return to the station to prepare for a worst-case scenario. 'Call it gut feeling', he would later say.

By now reports were filtering into all newsrooms of a sizeable dust storm approaching the city, which if it proved as big as the previous weeks dust storm then it would play havoc with helicopter transfers so close to our bulletin. We had already dispatched the news chopper to cover a fire at Macedon; now we were forced to find another chopper to send to a fire in the Otway Ranges to the south east. Reporter Malcolm Gray dispatched with a live eye crew to Belgrave had orders to get what he could and file it back in time for the fast approaching news at 6.30 p.m.

At 5.45 p.m., I had written a news update with what information I had on the Victorian fires but the only pictures I had were being supplied from South Australia, where the situation was horrific with many reported killed and hundreds of homes destroyed. We were now facing a real dilemma with our local coverage. Another check with the CFA revealed the Belgrave fire was reaching major proportions and heading towards Narre Warren, east of Melbourne. Fires were also burning in Cockatoo and in the Otways to the south east and further west towards Warrnambool. The problem was we didn't have any pictures and we were only half an hour from news time at 6.30 p.m. Suddenly the monitors on the newsroom wall tuned to *Ten News at 6 p.m.* Ten were showing live crosses, huge flames and graphic accounts of rescues from Victorian homes being destroyed. They were already on air and half an hour before our scheduled news. Maher was now chain-smoking and pacing the floor but remaining unusually silent.

At 6.05 p.m. a shout suddenly echoed from one of the editing suites, 'We have pics coming in!' A unified sigh of relief swept through the room. Our first report came in from Belgrave containing footage of an evacuation of residents. Then... that was it. There was nothing more. It faded to black. From the link van a panicky voice suddenly radioed, 'We are unable to pass police roadblocks. They won't let us through and we can't find a suitable point to feed out fire pics.'

The frustration was building again. We knew Channel Nine had also received their pictures, which we had seen in their news updates. Their news was also at 6.30. Now we were just 15 minutes from going to air and still had no vision of Victorian fires. At that moment I left the newsroom chaos for a brief silent moment of respite in the makeup department. Priority, I believed, would be given to the Adelaide fires (where at least we could see some flames).

With just two minutes to go, I rushed into the studio (still unaware of the lead story). Flustered, I quickly sat behind the news desk. Then, panic took over. No scripts, no pictures and no advice of what to do.

One minute to go. The producer burst in through the heavy soundproof doors and ran across the studio floor, thrusting a handful of papers at me. The floor manager had already begun the final countdown calling '5... 4... 3... 2... 1'. The theme began as I heard, 'Mal, read the top one. Read the top one.'

'Cue, Mal.'

'Good evening...' Just a few minutes earlier, the link van had begun feeding footage of the Belgrave fire into the ENG communication centre where editors were frantically cutting and editing as we went to air. Meanwhile, confusion continued in the studio. As I was reading the lead story, other news staff were rushing in handing me updates. Fire updates were now pouring in; one fire was out of control and heading towards Upper Beaconsfield. As the first footage from the Otway's fire arrived, there were reports of more serious outbreaks. It had to happen. I became lost in the mountain of reports. The first film story suddenly ended, cutting back to me at the desk sorting through piles of scripts and phoning for advice.

'Forgive me for a moment,' I said as I shuffled the sheets, 'the news reports are coming in faster than I can read them.' I suppose it added to the drama but it did nothing to ease the tension. There was now no disguising the awful truth. The viewers could only surmise the state was in the grip of an awesome crisis, second only to the one that was unfolding in Seven's studios. At the end of the bulletin I headed back to the newsroom for a debriefing and post mortem. While Nine had done exceptionally well and Seven was said to have been adequate, there was unanimous opinion that Channel Ten scooped the pool with its footage, eyewitness accounts and dramatic live crosses. The youngest network on the block had finally come of age.

As I walked into the newsroom immediately after the bulletin,

I was met with equally despondent looks. John Maher was on the warpath, blaming producers. Producers were blaming reporters and reporters were blaming the chief of staff for sending them into wrong areas in the first place. However, the story was not over and according to Maher's rally to the troops, 'We can still catch up. Don't dwell on it, just lift your game and get on with it.' And we did with success.

As the hazy sun rose over the city the following morning, Melbourne awoke in a state of shock. No one was untouched. Cinders had fallen on the city and towns had been completely destroyed. Seventy-two people died in that 24-hour period. The Victorian towns of Gisborne, Upper Beaconsfield, Framlingham, Naringal, Narre Warren, Cockatoo and Macedon were extensively damaged. While fires formed a semi-circle around Melbourne, others fires raged through the heavily populated coastal areas west to Warrnambool. In one of the worst incidents, 12 fire fighters at Beaconsfield became trapped and perished in their tanker. In the same area, police found one man dead in his farmhouse still clutching a hose across his chest. His wife lay dead two metres away. The tragedy was made worse by reports that some of the fires were deliberately lit.

At 6.30 a.m. that Thursday we were back again at Seven with an "Ash Wednesday Roundup" – a one-hour early morning special edition that again I thought was just average. Our lead story was late and missed its time slot, meaning we had to lead with a story of the aftermath. We began with farmers shooting cattle and a colour piece on historic homesteads around Macedon many of which had been destroyed. We eventfully covered in detail every aspect of Ash Wednesday even if the order was a little skewed.

On Thursday evening all networks threw their entire recourses into their coverage of the fires, many of which were still burning.

ATV10 sent their main presenters David Johnston and Jo Pearson into the worst hit areas of the Dandenong's. Shedding their reading attire, they began their main evening bulletin looking wind-blown and worthy with flames as a backdrop of tragic proportions. They presented an image of authoritative journalists and compassionate presenters – appropriate for such an occasion.

GTV9 sent Brian Naylor into the fire zone that destroyed the town of Cockatoo but with his image as a well-established desk anchor, critics described him as "looking totally out of place". His normally immaculate hair continually blew across his face and at times he appeared flustered as he grappled with his folder of scripts.

HSV7 maintained its tradition of a single desk anchor as I crossed live to reporters in the field who were all trying to control their emotions after seeing the horror of one of the state's biggest disasters. Personally, I felt a little miffed that as Melbourne's first appointed journalist/newsreader I wasn't sent into the field but was confined to my desk. However, I avoided the risk of those critics who suggested Nine's attempt to send their reader "had backfired". There is a very fine line in the competitive field of journalism between point scoring and covering a tragedy of such proportions as Ash Wednesday. However, it's the nature of the beast to out-manoeuvre our competitors the best we can. If that is point scoring, then so be it. There is no question from the critics who unanimously praised Channel Ten, describing it as "a turning point in their long struggle for news credibility".

In 1984, boosted by the success of their lead in program *Perfect Match*, Ten's news went on to become the top rating service in Melbourne and the fifth most watched program on television. Of course in 1984 I had no idea within three years I would be joining this winning team.

If maturity comes from age and experience, then my experience came from poor judgements and mistakes.

CHAPTER 11

PRINCES OF DARKNESS

1987

Chamberlains pardoned over Azaria death
Sir Billy Sneddon dies
Christopher Skase buys the Seven Network
Hoddle Street massacre
Stock market crash

HITS

Never Gonna Give You Up – Ricky Astley
China in Your Hand – T'Pau
Walk Like an Egyptian – Bangles

There is a famous and frequently used quote attributed to American journalist Hunter S Thompson:

> *The TV business is uglier than most things. It is normally perceived as some kind of cruel and shallow money trench through the heart of the journalism industry, a long plastic hallway where thieves and pimps run free and good men die like dogs, for no good reason.*

I am unsure of its authenticity, and some will question its accuracy, but experience tells me it may contain an element of truth.

MONDAY, 9 MARCH 1987

It was described by the Victorian Premier John Cain as 'one of the darkest days in the history of Australian television'. The $312 million takeover of Melbourne's Channel Seven was as swift as it was savage. The ink had barely dried on the agreement before the new Fairfax owners arrived from Sydney in a bid to reap the spoils of corporate greed and to widen the chasm of inter-city rivalry.

From my position as senior anchor at Seven they appeared as an "apparition of the apocalypse" – four horsemen in the guise of senior executives hell-bent on creating as much brutal chaos as their biblical namesakes. Their initial intention was to assess the value of our inventory, our people, our programs and our technology. Once assessed, their agenda became one of elimination (retrenchment) and plunder (reassignment). Within a week they had packaged-up newly acquired studio equipment in Melbourne and freighted it back to their head office in Sydney. Someone likened them to Hitler's storm troopers but very soon they simply became known as "The Princes of Darkness".

The winds of change began to stir in 1985 when Australian media tycoon Rupert Murdoch took out American citizenship. Two years later Murdoch announced he was pulling out as owner of Network Ten and buying into his late father's Melbourne newspaper the *Herald*. We knew under new media legislation the HWT would be forced to divest its television interest in Seven but the speculation centred on Perth based entrepreneur Robert Holmes à Court as our new owner.

FRIDAY, 27 FEBRUARY 1987

Two weeks before the takeover I received a surprise phone call at home from the secretary of General Manager Ron Casey.

'Case would like you to join him for lunch,' she said. 'He has some news he would like to share with you.' Elaine Cairns was being most circumspect on the phone however she did convey a feeling that the news he was going to impart would be "good news" and I was among those he wished to share it with.

We met at a local Chinese restaurant on the corner of Park Street and St Kilda Road, a two-minute walk from the Seven studios. Also present at the lunch was News Editor John Maher, Program Manager Gary Fenton, Sales Manager Howard Gardner and Finance Manager Gerry Carrington. I felt honoured at having been invited to join these most senior executives. There was much banter and "boys club" talk about football and ratings before the second course of the Chinese banquet was served and Casey brought us to order.

'Robert **Holmes à Court**,' he said, 'is taking over the Seven Network and I am to be appointed network boss.'

There was no preamble or warning. It was typical Casey. Straight to the point and greeted by a unified sigh of relief as it ended months of speculation. For the last 12 months budgets had tightened, promotion had been cut and ratings had plunged due to the uncertainty of our future. Now it was official. The banter and one-liners resumed with vigour as "chairman elect" and Casey revelled in his newfound elevation. It was also made abundantly clear that some details had still to be hammered out but an in-principal agreement had been reached.

As the courses of the banquet continued to be delivered, Ron Casey was openly planning the moment when he would deal the *coup-de-gras* to his Sydney counter-part Ted Thomas.

The relationship between ATN7 Sydney and HSV7 Melbourne had reached rock bottom since Sydney pulled its financial support for the Melbourne produced network soapie *Neighbours*. Casey was not a man to hold grudges but there was no mistaking the feeling at that luncheon. The days of Ted Thomas calling the shots from Sydney were numbered and he couldn't wait to be the one to tell him. But a weekend is a long time in television. By Monday morning the Holmes à Court deal had fallen through and Fairfax had suddenly emerged in control. This was the same Fairfax who controlled ATN7.

It was a body blow to Melbourne executives who feared Sydney would exact a revenge for the years of frustration between the two stations that had co-existed in a de facto network relationship. However no one in Melbourne suspected the extent of brutality the Sydney executives would inflict. Casey's door remained shut and he was not seen for that entire week.

It wasn't until Wednesday when I arrived in the newsroom and scanned the rundown for our nightly news that the full impact hit me. Fourth story down read, CASEY QUITS. Even as I read the news story subtitle, I didn't realise initially it was Ron Casey. I would be reading a story in tonight's news about Ron Casey. Our Casey? Going? A memo was eventually issued confirming Ron's decision to retire and inviting staff to his farewell. It apparently followed a very intense few days for Casey, negotiating a "golden handshake" settlement with the *Herald* before the Fairfax Company took full control.

Friday soon arrived and we all gathered in a vast new studio complex in Dorcas Street South Melbourne sipping beer and nibbling on meat pies. The atmosphere was subdued and tense, as no one quite knew what was to come. Ron Casey began his speech reminiscing the past. It was tinged with humour but one suspected he was fighting to overcome a tidal wave of emotion. After 15 minutes he began to wind up: 'The future of television is on the brink of change and no more so than here at HSV7. Some will survive, some will decide to move on, others may not be so fortunate and a decision may be made for them. Throughout it all though, television will continue. It may not continue in its present form, but it will continue and grow. I wish all those who are dedicated to the industry, sincere best wishes for the future.'

No one knew just how prophetic his words would be. It was the end of an era in television and like all great empires in history the Casey era was not only to crumble – but also be wiped from the slate.

The following Monday as Fairfax/ATN executives arrived I stood among a small group of colleagues in the Melbourne newsroom to welcome our newly appointed network news boss. Phil Davies was a genial, confident if not slightly arrogant head of Sydney news but had never been a match for the sharp mind and acerbic tongue of Melbourne's John Maher. Sydney had lost many battles to Maher over the years, particularly in funding and overseas assignments. However, Maher was now on extended medical leave and his replacement, Warren Wilton, while adequately experienced in running the day-to-day news was not as equipped to handle a situation like this.

Davies swaggered in with an exaggerated air of arrogance and walked right through the middle of our welcome party that parted in a pitying scene of acquiescence. He headed directly into Maher's vacant office and slammed the door behind him. Moments later he emerged with a wry smirk to announce in an abnormally loud voice for such a small group, 'Well guys I am running this show now and if you don't like what I am about to do you can pack your bloody bags and leave.' He appeared to laugh at his newly inherited bravado before heading for the door. 'I am going out to lunch now with some of your prospective replacements.' Then, in a very poor Arnold Schwarzenegger imitation, he called out, 'But I'll be back!'

Similar ruthless and totally unacceptable breaches of corporate governance were taking place throughout the building but no one officially complained because everyone feared for their own jobs. It wouldn't have mattered anyway. By the end of the first week more than 70 staff had been sacked. Australian Rules Football, which was not just a sport but also a way of life in Melbourne, was cancelled – just one week before the season began. The *World of Sport* program, a Sunday morning institution since the early 1960s, was dumped along with our Sunday night family tradition, *Disneyland*. Melbourne's popular night time current affair host was replaced with little known Sydney identity Terry Willesee, immediately raising speculation as to the future of Melbourne's newsreader.

Speculation heightened during the second week of the takeover when Melbourne's leading talk back radio host Derryn Hinch announced, 'I can confirm Mal Walden's future is on the line because I personally have been approached to replace him.' I was listening at that moment and would be lying if I said those words didn't hurt. I felt a deep-seated combination of betrayal and bitter disappointment. I was also reminded of the words of a former news presenter who once said, 'In a storm it's always an anchor that is tossed over the side first.' And this storm was intensifying by the day.

FRIDAY, 27 MARCH 1987

Three weeks after the takeover, I was called up to the fifth floor office of our former finance manager Gerry Carrington who earlier in the day had been elevated to acting general manager. I was thrilled for Gerry and relieved at the appointment, which I hoped would add some stability in the midst of the current turmoil. Gerry and I had worked together for 17 years and while we were not close friends we had shared many good times and a huge success at Seven. My particular memory of Carrington had taken place during my last contract renewal in which the cash component he said was non-negotiable. So I asked for a new television set, 'Like the 23 inch Phillips you have in your office.' Two days later he had his office television sent to my home and then ordered a brand new one for himself.

As I walked into his office this time, I immediately sensed the tension. I had a premonition of what was coming. Carrington sat behind his desk flanked by the four senior Sydney executives including Phil Davies. They remained seated and all looking at their feet. Only Carrington looked me in the eye and I felt immense embarrassment and sadness at the situation he faced.

'I am so sorry Mal,' he began, 'Many hard decisions are being made and this is the hardest for me.'

I knew exactly the words he was struggling to find but I had no intention of making it easier for any of them.

'So we have decided to take a new direction and I am so sorry to say Mal you are not part of that plan.'

I glanced around at the Princes of Darkness but they were still looking at their feet.

'No that's fine Gerry,' I said, 'just call my lawyer and I hope you and I will remain friends.' A huge relief lifted from my shoulders as I left that office, just as I felt a similar relief by those I had left behind. There had been no dramatic scene or vitriolic tantrums.

It was 3.05 when the elevator stopped one floor short of my level. Head of Sport Gordon Bennett stepped in. Bennet was usually softly spoken and sensitive-natured. On this day however, his look defied his nature and his voice had developed an edge of concern. 'Is it true? Have you just been dropped? It was on the 3 o'clock radio news. Christ mate, I can't believe it.' But he obviously did.

Apparently my successor, Greg Pearce, a well-known and very popular news anchor in Perth, had announced his resignation and appointment to Seven Melbourne. The national wire service had carried the story, which broke at precisely the moment I was being sacked. Had I not arrived early to work that day I would have heard it first on radio.

By the time I reached my office and rang my lawyer Brian Ward it felt as if the entire world had known judging by the number of condolences being offered. My lawyer told me to sit tight. 'Don't talk to anyone and I will ring you back on Gordon Bennett's phone.' He was also Bennett's lawyer and a close associate of Seven. Bennett then became my go-between, avoiding the many calls that I would attend to later. By the end of the day he had handed me his phone three times. The first call came from the Victorian Opposition Leader Jeff Kennett who expressed his disappointment and his outrage. The second call came from the opposition news director at Channel Nine John Sorell offering me an immediate job. Then finally, Ward rang back having reached a termination agreement, on one condition.

'Mal, they want you to read your final bulletin tonight,' then added his personal caveat 'But I suggest you don't pour shit on them.'

I prepared for the news, as I had for the past nine years and headed to the studio. The bulletin proceeded without a hitch and I didn't give much thought to its significance. However, immediately following the weather, I launched into my adlib farewell.

'As you may well be aware there have been a number of changes made here at Channel Seven over the last few weeks, the latest change involves me.'

I then heard a stifled sob from a member of the floor crew.

'Management has decided to head in a new direction and I am not part of that move, so tonight is my last night as newsreader here at Seven.'

There was another audible sob, this time from the sports presenter sitting right alongside me. This sob shook me to the core.

'There is little more to say other than to thank you for your loyalty over the past 17 years,' my voice began to break, 'particularly the last nine years here. Take care.' I turned away from camera as I said my final "good night".

At that moment John Maher was lying in St Vincent's hospital recovering from eye surgery. One of the sisters on duty had seen my sign off. She immediately ran through the ward to consult with her patient.

'That was one of the most humiliating times of my career,' he said. 'Without any warning she said, "Have you heard about Mal Walden?" I was simply stunned when she told me they had sacked you … On the Monday morning I discharged myself from hospital and took a cab straight into Seven … I called the staff together and told them it's not the end, it's just a hiccup … I said the Fairfax Company is an honourable family media organisation and everything will be all right … But boy, oh boy, was I wrong … That's when I decided it was time for me to retire.'

My friends and colleagues constantly reminded me, 'Mal, you are too bloody naïve.' It was naïve of me to think my departure at Seven was any different from the other 70 staff members who had been sacked. It was naïve of me to be surprised at the number of press photographers waiting for me to leave the building or the protestors outside with their hastily drawn up placards denouncing the takeover. I had been with Seven for 17 years, the first year as host of the network game show *Jeopardy*. I had risen from journalist to anchor. In 1983 I married Pauline in a five-camera coverage that led the nightly news and filled the next morning's papers. Two years later I ended the news with the words, '… and if you detected an added smile tonight, a short time ago I discovered I am to be a father of twins'. Perhaps I became a little more aware of the impact of that last news service later that same night when Pauline and I discovered we had run out of nappies for our 18-month-old twins, Sarah and James.

I drove to the nearest 7-Eleven to find a group of people gathered in earnest conversation around the till. Two elderly women were crying. Suspecting there had been a hold-up I was about to leave when one suddenly sobbed, 'And he has two young babies' and I realised they were talking about me.

Within 24 hours the impact of the $312 million Fairfax takeover was not only making headlines around the country but was fuelling a long simmering inter-city rivalry between Melbourne and Sydney. The charge was led at the highest level with Victoria's Premier John Cain damning the takeover in Parliament the following week.

'It isn't just the Melbourne-Sydney rivalry,' he tried to explain. 'It's much deeper than that. Why should we, a city of three million people have a situation where almost entirely all our TV is directed by Sydney?'

MONDAY, 20 APRIL 1987

Melbourne is a very conservative city. She is proud of her own and most protective of her brood. She is also slow to anger but once roused she can be very unforgiving.

My replacement at Seven had arrived from Perth. The affable Greg Pearce stepped from the plane at Melbourne airport and immediately hailed a cab. He threw his luggage in the back and sat next to the driver who asked for his destination. When he replied 'Channel Seven' the cabbie immediately raised his eyes and asked, 'You work there do you mate?'

'I'm about to start,' he replied. 'I'm the new anchor.'

The cab immediately slowed down and pulled to the side. 'Well, you can bloody well get out here because for sure as hell I ain't driving you.'

Within two weeks of Pearce starting at Seven their news rating plunged to an unprecedented zero, or equal to *Mr Squiggle* on the ABC. Melbourne viewers boycotted the channel in a mass protest never seen in the history of television. Then to add to the HSV7 crisis the surviving staff went on strike, banging on the studio doors as Pearce attempted to read his new extended one-hour news. Shortly after his children arrived from Perth it was reported that they were being bullied and ridiculed at school while his wife Jenny was being persecuted while trying to establish her business in Melbourne. According to Pearce this was the hardest time of his life.

'We can all be brilliant tacticians with hindsight,' he told the Age newspaper. 'I'd been offered the greatest job in my career and I came here to find the station had no viewers because of industrial action.'

When asked if he knew what the rating figures translated to, he replied whimsically, 'Do you mean do I know my viewers by their first names?' Then he lashed out claiming, 'The only people who are being hurt are the staff and the people of Melbourne have themselves to blame for that.'

The story soon became a national event, with *60 Minutes* attempting to investigate both sides. Host Jana Wendt explained, 'Whatever the fact of the matter, Sydney painfully extracted the "Melbourne" from the most Melbourne station of them all.' In her interview with Phil Davies, the news boss conceded, 'We are the Princes of Darkness shaking up an institution which is Melbourne and that's what they don't like.' When pushed further Davies replied with another smirk, 'Well a man's got to do what a man's got to do.' As for Mal Walden, the report continued, 'They simply threw the baby out with the bathwater.'

Fairfax held Channel Seven for three months and one day. It became a $312 million corporate disaster and within 12 months Fairfax imploded under the steerage of Warwick Fairfax Junior. One of the first to speak after Fairfax withdrew from Seven was Gerry Carrington. 'Sydney had been waiting so long to take control and become the dominant force in the Network that when they finally got it they over-reacted to a terrible degree, they just over-reacted.' Carrington was boosted in the knowledge that after the Princes of Darkness had left, a great white saviour had arrived. Queensland media mogul and television tycoon Christopher Skase salvaged the Seven Network and as titular head during the brief Fairfax regime Carrington continued on in an executive role. Sadly, Pearce was perceived as part of that sordid period and was forced to pack up and return with his family to Perth.

CHAPTER 12

A PROTECTED SPECIES

1987

HEADLINES

Black Monday Stock Market crash
Hoddle Street Massacre
Queen Street Massacre

HITS

Locomotion – Kylie Minogue
La Bamba – Los Lobos
I Wanna Dance With Somebody – Whitney Houston

Following an unprecedented publish backlash over his sacking at HSV7 in 1987, Mal Walden was deemed never to be sacked again. According to one news editor he had become a rare "protected" species.

– TV critic Robert Fidgeon

MONDAY, 27 APRIL 1987

You can't get the sack under any circumstances and not feel some form of rejection. It was three weeks since my contract had been terminated at HSV7 following the Fairfax takeover. The first week was spent in a vague state of emotions ranging from confusion to anger and then some relief gained from unprecedented support from Victorian viewers.

The second week ended with a visit to my lawyer. Brian Ward was a high-flying media and sport celebrity lawyer who I had used during most of my contract negotiations in previous years. As Pauline and I walked into his plush carpeted office in the outer suburb of Burwood, he offered his familiar warm welcome. He then pulled out two modern chairs and immediately referred to three neat piles of papers on the matching chrome and glass-top desk.

'Mal, you have three offers on the table,' he said. He paused as we sat looking at the three neat packages. 'The first is from Seven,' he said, which totally stunned me. 'They want you back, but given the treatment and their behaviour, I suggest we dismiss that offer immediately.' He then slid it to one side in a theatrical gesture. 'The second offer is from Nine and their news boss John Sorrell has just informed me that his offer will expire at 2 p.m. this afternoon.'

We had just over two hours to decide. I had spent an evening with Sorell in the boardroom at GTV9 a week before but with so much alcohol consumed I could no longer remember the details of the offer. Now it was officially on the table as senior reporter but with no news reading duties.

'And this,' he said while placing his hand on the third pile, 'is an offer from Network Ten and the one I suggest you consider most closely.'

Ten's offer was for less money but with a provision to read their news as a backup to presenter David Johnston. Ward then firmly suggested that we put pressure on Ten to match the money. For the next two hours I sat with Pauline as unseen forces through the latest technology called a "facsimile machine" played out my future. Finally at 1.45 p.m. the machine spat out a letter of agreement sent by Ten's news director and former colleague David Johnston. The letter confirmed that Ten had matched Nine's offer.

Once I had signed the paper and we faxed it back to Johnston I then rang Sorrell at his local pub to thank him for the offer and to tell him I had accepted a position at Ten. Against a noisy background from the Richmond beer garden I could only just hear his reply, 'You win some and you lose some.' He then hung up. The "win some" was a reference to GTV9 signing up another Seven victim of the Fairfax takeover, football legend and comments man Lou Richards, the week before.

Three weeks after my sacking, as Seven was being savaged in the news ratings, I drove towards a new start at Network Ten. If a rainbow is the promise of a new beginning, then the one hanging above Blackburn Road on my way to Nunawading should have been the sign I was looking for. But it failed to offer any reassurance. I was nervous, unsettled and clinging to the possibility that the Fairfax takeover of Channel Seven would prove to be a huge disaster and former manager Ron Casey would be reinstated and invite me back. According to everyone I listened to, "Fairfax couldn't run a bath". However, the sun was shining brightly by the time I arrived at Channel Ten's Nunawading studio complex. I drove through the security boom gate and up the sweeping drive past manicured lawns and into the number 3 car parking spot, which had already been allocated to me. The station's news editor Neil Miller and network news boss David Johnston met me in the foyer. It was Johnston, former HSV7 colleague and good friend, who had tossed me this lifeline.

As they walked me into the open sunlit newsroom with panoramic views across to the nearby Dandenong ranges, familiar faces offered words of welcome, many of whom I had worked with over the years at Seven. It was more like changing offices than changing stations. Then, emerging with a smile and a warm handshake, stepped in senior cameraman Morrie Pilens. With his soft European accent he whispered, 'Welcome from the dark side.' Remembering what I'd heard of Pilen's past, my Princes of Darkness paled against his. Reputedly, Morrie Pilens had been conscripted into the SS as a cameraman for the Nazis in the Second World War.

We adjourned into Miller's office where my duties were outlined.

'Given the enormous public backlash over your sacking, we have decided to capitalise on the situation by highlighting the "Melbourne" influence of *Ten News*,' said Miller. 'The segment we want you to host from the news desk each night will be called *Mal's Melbourne*.'

At that moment my buttocks tightened in cringe. 'What about something with a little more gravitas like *Walden Report* or – '

'No, we have researched this and we know it will work.'

End of story. In fact, it was the start of a series of stories; Melbourne related stories about unsung heroes and events that were shaping our city. Not necessarily in the traditional news sense but rather personalised character based colour stories. My final instruction: 'Be subjective rather than objective. Make it your segment, make it *Mal's* Melbourne.'

And I did.

CHAPTER 13

THE RISE AND FALL
OF NETWORK TEN:
1964 – 1987

introduces a big,
new one hour
news service
'EYEWITNESS
NEWSHOUR'

Anchorman Bruce Mansfield leads
the Eyewitness Newshour team of
top professional reporters who
probe the world, the nation
and the city to bring you more
news than ever. It's gutsy,
accurate and fast.

It's FIRST
at 6 p.m.

1964

*US Surgeon General releases report concluding
that cigarette smoking causes lung cancer
GI Joe debuts as an action figure toy
Cassius Clay defeats Sonny Liston in Miami
Dr Martin Luther King Jr. wins the Nobel Peace Prize*

HITS

*Can't Buy Me Love – The Beatles
My Boy Lollipop – Millie Small
The Shoop Shoop Song – Betty Everett*

TUESDAY, 4 AUGUST 1964 – 9.15 A.M.

The first news service on ATV Channel 0 went to air on 2 August 1964. It commenced at 6.15 p.m. and ran for 45 minutes, as opposed to the more traditional 6.30 p.m. half-hour services on the other channels. Its duration would alter several times over the next 12 months before reverting to a one-hour format at 6 p.m.

I was 21 and working in Launceston with Radio 7EX at the time. On Tuesday 4 August I was in the office overlooking the Punch Bowl region and gazing out to the snow-capped Mount Ben Lomond beyond. I had just completed my breakfast shift and was still dressed in pyjama top, jeans, desert boots and duffle coat. Sipping coffee and staring out at this magnificent view, I was thinking of nothing in particular when the phone rang. It was Geoff Smith, the news director of TNT Channel Nine, calling from the far end of our joint media complex.

'Mal, come down to my office. I have something to show you.'

Smith was an A-typical journalist – stocky, loud and confident. On the other hand, I saw warmth and humour that others quickly dismissed. Although, if I were to be perfectly honest, our friendship was flimsily based around the same brand of menthol cigarettes we shared.

I wandered down the long narrow passage, through the central foyer and into TNT Channel Nine News Department. On a small black and white monitor he and several news staff were watching a "kine" of the opening night of ATV0. Kinescopes (a system by which they filmed the vision from a monitor) were the only practical way to record live television prior to the introduction of videotape. Smith had received a copy of ATV0's gala opening night program *This Is It*, which was hosted by their newly appointed newsreader Barry McQueen. The program featured a galaxy of singers, dancers and national stars. Smith, however, was more interested in the style of their host. With a BBC background in broadcasting McQueen had been lured from GTV9 as Channel 0's first newsreader. The kine also included ATV0's first news service, but McQueen did not read it.

'Look at this. Just look at this for Christ sake, they are supposed to be presenting their first news bulletin.' Smith was referring to the station's executive-producer Brian Wright who was reading while standing at a podium. Smith (who was from the old school of journalism) then folded into uncontrollable laughter, calling their news a joke. 'Standing up, for God's sake what are they thinking of? Can't afford chairs?'

As we stood watching these black and white grainy images from their opening night, McQueen introduced the Chairman of Austarama and owner of ATV0, Reg Ansett. Ansett only added to Smith's frustration as he stuttered and stammered through his speech, looking, sounding and probably wishing he was anywhere else than standing in front of the latest camera technology on his newly acquired television station.

Smith took another deep breath of frustration then simply announced, 'Shut the fucking machine off.' We were all dismissed. There was a certain irony several years later when Smith became the director of news at ATV0 Melbourne and was given the chance to put his own imprimatur on the same bulletin he had been so quick to criticise after their opening night. Sadly, he became one of many who would fail.

ATV0's failure in news was not entirely due to the decisions of news directors, of which there were many; nor was it the staff they were hiring. Being the new station in town and broadcasting on a low frequency, ATV0 struggled from the start to attract a decent audience causing their costs to spiral out of control. For the first few years they recorded a massive loss not helped by the high cost of its news. However, news still remained a priority and in its first eight years Barry McQueen remained the front man. To help lift their news profile further, the station then introduced its first serious current affair program *Dateline,* hosted by McQueen. Others in the team were experienced high profile reporters, such as Phil De Montigne and Andrew Carroll. Later additions included Jonathon King and Jocelyn Terry. However, not even high profiles could lift its flagging ratings and the program subsequently folded. Management remained determined that news would succeed whatever the cost and whoever the presenter.

1967

This was the year McQueen established his credentials and became the first presenter to break the news of our missing PM Harold Holt. However, as he and his colleagues were soon to discover, one scoop was not enough.

The following year when news came through of a chopper crash on the Bass Strait oilrig, a feeling of euphoria swept through the ATV0 news staff. Their senior cameraman Morrie Pilens had not only survived but had captured the tragedy in a camera scoop.

FRIDAY, 22 MARCH 1968 – 1.58 P.M.

I was sitting in the basement studio of Melbourne's 3DB conducting the afternoon radio shift when a red light above the door began flashing. This was my signal that the 2 p.m. news scripts had landed. "Landed" was the operative word as the scripts had been encased in a metal capsule and sent via an air pressure chute from the *Herald* script room several floors above me. I had less than two minutes to race out and retrieve the scripts from the holding box just outside the studio door and get back before my record finished. As I sat back behind the console and injected the news theme into the cartridge machine my phone suddenly flashed. The voice of cadet journalist Norm Beaman simply said, 'Sorry mate for the late delivery there has been a chopper crash ... it's your lead story.'

News Script: *Emergency teams are rushing to a Bass Strait oilrig following a fatal helicopter crash. It's believed up to a dozen press people have been injured or killed. Several have already been airlifted to hospital at Sale. Television cameraman Morrie Pilens who was on board the helicopter at the time of the crash, survived.*

Voice of Ten cameraman Morrie Pilens: *As we hit, the chopper twisted. Then, as it twisted, we veered sideways and started to bounce. My immediate thought was to just sit tight and wait for the bouncing to stop and I would get out. The pilot started screaming, 'Stay put, stay put! Don't move, there's a blade still spinning!' I was filming all this from inside. It was chaotic. There were bodies and blood flowing everywhere.*

It wasn't until an hour or so after the injured had been evacuated that the full impact of the incident emerged. Two journalists were dead and eight injured, three critically. Another would die from his injuries a short time later. But Morrie Pilens survived and the legend of the man who had appeared from the dark side of German history would continue to grow.

MONDAY, 24 MARCH 1968

The Bass Strait helicopter crash succeeded in raising the profile of
ATV0's struggling news by little more than a blip on the ratings
radar. By the end of the weekend the blip had plunged off the
radar like the chopper itself. It reminded us all that one story was
simply not enough to change viewers' habits. There had to be
consistency. Seven had it. So too did Nine. The only constant at
ATV0 appeared to be Pilens.

Cameramen were described as the eyes of a generation, the
driving force of visual news in the '50s and '60s and the most
experienced cine cameramen had made the transition from
the big screen of Movietone Newsreels to the small screens of
television. Journalists, or TV news reporters, were adopting skills
honed by these movie trained news gatherers who knew the
power of pictures. Each network had its senior cameramen but
none had anyone quite like Pilens. And judging from all reports,
no one wanted him anyway. He was cantankerous, caustic and
controversial, but all his colleagues reluctantly agreed he was
"bloody good at what he did".

Reading the radio news story of the "Oilrig" tragedy was the
first time I had been made aware of the man who many would
later call "the great survivor". I was also reminded of the first time
I had been made aware of his fledgling television station, ATV0,
and the news department he had been personally charged with
setting up.

1969

I watched in almost bemused indifference as ATVO launched a bold
bid to attract more viewers. To encourage Melbourne television

viewers to modify their TV antennas to pick up the 0 frequency, Reg Ansett underwrote a world title fight. He personally signed up Australian titleholder Lionel Rose and Britain's Alan Rudkin for the world bantamweight title to be staged at Melbourne's Kooyong Tennis Centre. It was an $80,000 gamble that paid off attracting a record rating of 72 per cent of the television audience. It was a TV ratings record that stood for more than three decades until the opening ceremony of the Sydney Olympics in 2000, which reached a 77.6 per cent share in Melbourne. However, it was not enough to keep their audience.

LPT Channel 0 and Australia sun) July/Aug 1969.

1971

Former HSV7 newsreader Geoff Raymond, had returned to Melbourne after enduring a rather unsuccessful period on Sydney talkback radio. He replaced Barry McQueen as newsreader on ATV0 and launched the first *Eyewitness News* at 6 p.m. He also hosted his own Sunday night current affair program *The Raymond Report* with reporters Tim Skinner, Tom Jones and Wayne Tragaskis.

However, while ATV0 proved there *was* an audience to be had, the viewers were not persuaded to stay – particularly with the news service that now boasted some of the most experienced journalists and presenters in town.

1972

By 1972 I had commenced my news cadetship at HSV7, which was now boasting unprecedented success under John Maher and with Brian Naylor at the helm. I watched with a mixture of personal satisfaction and concern at how tenuous life could be in television news, particularly at ATV0. Newsreader Geoff Raymond suddenly left of his own accord to seek a more secure and rewarding future at the ABC where he continued until 1984. However his departure highlighted the crisis and insecurity in the ATV0 newsroom.

In the four-year period between 1972 and 1976, five news directors and up to 100 journalists and reporters passed through, what critics had dubbed "the revolving door". Among the news editors were Ian McFarling, Geoff Smith and former press officer to Malcolm Fraser, Eddie Dean. Clearly ATV0 was seen as "Australia's most troubled newsroom" with the media attacking not only the management but also Sir Reg Ansett himself.

Journalists have always had a stock of horror yarns from their newsroom but ATV0 must surely be the graveyard of them all ... In the latest saga they are calling for the sacking of news director Eddie Dean. But Mr Dean is only part of the problem ... Channel 0's management is a joke around the industry but if the flying Sir Reg thinks it's funny then it's a tragedy ... The doyenne of Melbourne's TV News bosses is the eccentric Irishman John Joseph Peter Patrick Maher of HSV7.'

– Barry Doyle

It was quite magical (if not arrogantly disturbing) to be among the winning team across at HSV7. Trouble however was not confined to ATV0. Over at GTV9 newsreader Eric Pearce was temporarily sidelined in 1971 when news editor Michael Schildberger took control. Senior Nine newsman Ian Haigh confided that tension existed between Schildberger and Pearce.

'Pearce was a gentleman but slightly dictatorial in that he would change what was written for him if he didn't approve. He was easily offended so there was much personal interference by Eric.'

This led to heated clashes with Schildberger who was keen to put his own stamp on the product. Schildberger finally got his way when Eric was replaced by John Bailey. But that didn't work for long either. Nine would be further damaged in 1976 by an ill-fated attempt at a national bulletin called *News Centre Nine*. This attempt by network news boss Gerald Stone was aimed at linking up Sydney, Melbourne and Canberra in a half-hour bulletin. It failed badly, handing a further bulk of the audience to Seven.

Meanwhile, Geoff Raymond's departure from ATV0 triggered another brief succession of readers, including Ron Alderton and Ralph Neil, until Bruce Mansfield arrived with weather presenter actress Briony Behets.

1973

In June 1973 ATV0 signed veteran newsman Mike Willesee to run their news department.

Willesee was seen to be the "great white hope" in building-up the stations ailing news and current affairs. His mega-dollar appointment as news boss included the five nights a week current affairs program *24 Hours*.

The program was produced by Willesee's company Trans Media and hosted by former GTV9 Deputy News Editor John Bailey. Alongside Bailey were Claudia Wright (3AW), Michael Carlton, Vincent Smith (formerly of ABC's *This Day Tonight*) and Kay Stammers (formerly of GTV9's *No Man's Land*).

Sadly, *24 Hours* lasted only a little longer than the name implied and John Bailey ended up hosting a game show *Who, What, or Where?* One year later, the press issued its critique on Willesee.

Willesee Crisis

The great expensive Willesee gamble has flopped. Mike Willesee, hailed as the 'messiah' by Channel 0, hasn't delivered the goods. His 7 p.m. – much ballyhooed '24 Hours' - is also being thrashed by its opposition. The station is in a state of shock and disbelief over his failure. 'We gave him the world,' lamented one executive.

1974

Willesee's demise was believed to have been sealed after an internal dispute involving senior cameraman Morrie Pilens.

Just one day after receiving his gold pen for ten years of loyal service, Willesee sacked Pilens. It was said to have been on the basis Pilens was too old, but regardless of the reason the decision sent shock waves through the newsroom and triggered threats of union intervention. It was Willesee who was terminated and Pilens was reinstated. Morrie Pilens had survived another battle.

1975

By the mid '70s Pilens had become somewhat of an industry icon. I had watched him operate during frequent encounters on the road as a reporter but continually found him slightly intimidating so kept my distance. However, his colleagues were quite open in their critique of his brittle nature but always quick to defend his professionalism and creativity. An example of his volatility followed an ongoing campaign against the use of radio microphone signs. They had proliferated to such point they were dominating camera shots at all-in press conferences. Pilens obsession flared into an angry clash with 3AW reporter Les Morley. At one all-in press briefing he suddenly grabbed the radio mike, ripped the sign from its mount and smashed in on the ground. He inadvertently cut his hand in the process and then wiped the blood on Morley's shirt. This led to 3AW calling for an apology and threatening to take legal action for assault. Other networks joined in support of Pilens and the signs were subsequently removed or reduced in size.

On Sunday, 5 May 1975, I had my first encounter with this legendary figure. This was not just any Sunday – this was "May Day".

On this day in 1856 stonemasons from Melbourne University marched on Parliament house to push for an eight-hour working day. Each year Unions put aside this day to commemorate workers rights. I had drawn the short straw at HSV7 to work the Sunday shift and it ended with blood on the streets of Carlton and blood on my hands through naïve stupidity. About a dozen young Jewish students had gathered at Melbourne airport to protest the arrival of two Arab students.

Eddie Zananiri and Samir Chiekh, both Palestinian, were invited to Melbourne by the Australian Union of Students to speak at their union headquarters in Carlton. It was the timing of their visit more than anything else that triggered hostilities. Tensions were still simmering from the Munich Games massacre of Israeli athletes by PLO terrorists in 1972. I arrived at Melbourne airport with a camera crew just as the protest was getting underway. We were met with sounds of chanting and yelling, 'Go home! Go home!'

The Jewish students were swinging their anti PLO banners, not only at the two student visitors but also the delegation of local left wing students who had invited them. It was a noisy protest but non-violent as the two Palestinians were quickly escorted past our cameras and out to a waiting Kombi van before being driven away. The Jewish students had made their point and had achieved their moment of glory, which would be replayed on prime time television that night.

As the van with the Palestinian visitors swept out of view, several Jewish students returned to ask if I knew their destination. In what was my most regretful breach of impartiality, I blurted out the address, 'The Union Student Offices in Carlton.' As they turned and ran to their cars, the van carrying the visiting Palestinian students was already driving out of the Melbourne Airport.

I arrived for the press conference that afternoon as the throng of media was being ushered upstairs. The small group of Jewish students stood outside with their placards. Several called out, 'Thanks, Mal!' As ATVO reporter Kay Stammers walked in with me she leant across and asked, 'What was all that about?'

'No idea,' I replied and then asked where her cameraman was.

'Morrie Pilens,' she said with a laugh. 'He hates press conferences. We will get interviews later so he is staying in his car.'

As the two Palestinian students addressed the Melbourne media, sounds of a disturbance could be faintly heard. We assumed it was just the Jewish protest continuing.

Immediately following the press conference, we wandered casually down the stairs and out into the Drummond Street, Carlton. The horrifying scene that greeted us resembled a mini war zone.

Jewish students lay bleeding, ambulance and police lights were flashing and broken glass littered the road with remnants of May Day banners. Dozens of left wing Unionists from the traditional May Day March in Melbourne had broken ranks and converged on the Jewish students totally outnumbering them and attacking without warning.

Standing there at the centre of the chaos was ATVO cameraman Morrie Pilens, nursing a bleeding head but grinning with pride. He had filmed the entire clash, exclusively. He called me aside and simply said, 'Thanks, Mal. I owe you one.' The following year Pilens won the Thorn Award for his scoop and became "Cameraman of the Year".

Sometimes being a novice reporter had its advantages, although rarely for me. Former colleague Bill Edmonds had only recently made his transition from radio 3DB to begin a television career at ATV Channel 0 Nunawading.

It was Fathers Day 1974 and PM Gough Whitlam was due to open a public library in suburban Collingwood. Unaware we were all about to witness the story of the day, I stood among a throng of journalists waiting at the door for a quick sound grab. I explained to Edmonds that Gough never gave curbside interviews. It was just an unwritten understanding.

As the limo arrived we watched from some distance as the towering figure of Gough Whitlam struggled to emerge. Suddenly, to our disbelief, Bill Edmonds ran forward, thrust a microphone in his face and wished the PM a happy Father's Day.

Before Gough could even respond to this breach of journalist protocol Edmonds then followed by asking his view on Queensland Premier Jo Bjelke Peterson's appointment of an anti Whitlam labor man Albert Field to the Senate. Gough immediately roared, 'That Bible Bashing Bastard.'

There was an immediate stampede as dozens of journalists rushed the PM in an attempt to get him to repeat the line but he just strode silently and purposefully into the building. An historic constitutional crisis had just moved a step closer. Being a novice paid off for Edmonds but as far as I was concerned any further curbside etiquette was over.

However, while ATV0 news was certainly getting the scoops, it was just not reaping the rating rewards.

Bruce Mansfield had been teamed up with Australia's first commercial female newsreader, Gail Jervis, but Jervis failed to impress and was soon replaced by an attractive brunette from Queensland, Annette Allison.

In 1977 management then hired former *Herald* man Max Grant and former Seven producer Jeremy Cornford. They formed the first private company to out-source a commercial television news service in Australia.

Less than one year later, on 6 March 1978 the headlines said it all again:

ATV0 gears up for news revolution
A major newsroom shuffle for its one-hour news service. The moves follow a split between Max Grant and Jeremy Cornford, ending a year long partnership. Anchorman Bruce Mansfield will continue reading the news and incorporating product and facilities from the current affairs show "Firing Line", which will end on Sunday.

Then just days after that announcement came another headline:

ATV0 NEWS CHIEF QUITS
Channel 0's news chief Max Grant resigned today after a row with station executives.

The TV news industry is a small family, connected in many ways by its members who float from station to station in search of minor promotions. That is the nature of the beast.

We all have friends in opposition and we all feel for each other's frustrations, this is despite a collective desire to win. But now the industry was offering advice on what direction ATV0 should take. Many were simply saying, 'Go tabloid, go sensational'. And they did.

NEW YEAR'S EVE 1978

Word quickly spread that Channel 0 had secured a news scoop. It was a story we were told would become "the most sensational story of the century – if not all time". At Seven we were left curious and a little concerned. Had they captured "the coming of Christ?" The story did in fact shake the news industry albeit rather briefly. It certainly captured the viewer's curiosity. UFO stories have a tendency to do that. On the surface it was a reporter's dream, in this case it became a reporter's nightmare. The reporter was ATV0 journalist Quentin Fogarty, who happened to be on holidays with his family in New Zealand when the story unfolded.

A few days earlier, a series of radar and visual sightings in New Zealand had been reported from a pilot of an Argosy cargo plane. He had tracked a series of unidentified lights for several minutes before they disappeared then reappeared in a different area. The objects also appeared on Wellington radar and were sighted by hundreds of people on the ground 45 miles north of Kaikoura. Channel 0 in Melbourne caught the interest of these sightings on the wire service and knowing Fogarty was in the area on holiday they called him up.

Interest in UFOs had already been heightened in Melbourne. In October that year, 20-year-old Frederick Valentich disappeared in his light plane after reporting a UFO while flying over Bass Strait. He was never seen or heard from again. The news director requested Fogarty reconstruct the NZ flight in the hope of making similar sightings.

SATURDAY, 30 DECEMBER 1978 – 11:50 P.M.

An Argosy with Fogarty and a freelance cameraman on board crossed Cook Strait in excellent clear weather. Within 150 miles from Christchurch, the objects returned. Again the sightings were confirmed by ground radar but this time they were also being filmed by Fogarty's news crew.

After landing in New Zealand with the film, Fogarty immediately went into hiding. He requested the station get him back to Melbourne immediately as he was afraid the film would be confiscated before he could return. Concern at ATV0 began to mount. It was New Year's Eve and almost all airline seats had been sold out. Luckily, they managed to get him a first-class ticket on an Air New Zealand flight into Melbourne. Quentin arrived as we were all preparing to celebrate New Year's Eve.

Shortly after midnight, Melbourne producers stood with Quentin in a darkened editing room at Nunawading as a film editor began spooling through the footage. No one slept that night as they worked into New Year's Day, trying to pull together an international release of a news story they believed would be "the scoop of all scoops". But unlike other news stories, they had absolutely no reference points for this one. Most cynical journalists having previously believed UFO sightings were akin to spotting "hobgoblins down the back of the garden".

Meanwhile, telephone calls were coming from all over the world. The BBC asked to feed them the story and at one point producer Leonard Lee received a call from Walter Cronkite himself from CBS News, offering to pay US$5000 for the film. Throughout New Year's Day ATV0's publicity machine went to work drumming up viewers for that night's news. Rival stations watched with interest and envy, then with great amusement and relief when the news finally went to air. The report showed only small spots of light dancing across the screen. There were no little green men and no shiny flying saucers. The pictures simply didn't meet the expectation of the hype and the reaction from viewers, sceptics and scientists left little imagination as to how they felt.

Lee was horrified. 'They began with accusations we had filmed Venus, Mars, Jupiter, squid boat lights, mating mutton-birds – everything except UFOs.' Lee felt the media had also turned on them, insinuating they had somehow hoaxed the whole thing. In fact, one senior cameraman told me of their attempts to doctor the film with pinpricks of light to enhance the image, but rejected the new images amid fears it would be discovered. Lee then decided the footage needed to be examined scientifically, so a judgment could be made as to what the objects were, or weren't, and perhaps salvage some credibility. Handcuffing his briefcase containing the film to his wrist, much to the amusement of his colleagues, he flew to the United States where he gave the film to Bruce Maccabee, an optical physicist who specialised in laser technology for the US Navy. He also persuaded ATV0 to spend some of the proceeds of the story on flying Dr Maccabee to New Zealand to interview witnesses, check radar equipment and review other material concerning the sightings. Maccabee also came to Melbourne to interview Quentin Fogarty who by then was suffering an enormous backlash from disbelievers.

Dr Maccabee returned to the US, releasing his preliminary findings a couple of months later. He disputed all the various theories put up by the so-called experts, although he later wryly agreed the lights were generated by an unknown source and as such fulfilled the UFO criteria: "unidentifiable, flying solid objects". Further scientific research on the sightings was shut down in April 1979 and no further mention was made by ATV0.

Fogarty subsequently quit the network and went on the speaking circuit to defend the story. He eventually wrote a book titled *Let's Hope They're Friendly* – unlike his critics. No one disputed that Quentin Fogarty saw something but by the very nature of the subject matter and the way in which the station handled the publicity surrounding it, they were left with no way to turn. The sceptics won, the channel lost and Fogarty's life was left in almost as much turmoil as ATV0's news.

According to one cynical journalist back then, Nunawading was an Aboriginal word meaning no ratings.

SATURDAY, 27 OCTOBER 1979

Another deal was struck – this time with Nine's Michael Schildberger. More changes were implemented and presenter Bruce Mansfield was axed.

'To be quite frank, I'm very disappointed that a reputation and credibility built up over six years appears to be lost in a day.' Mansfield and co-reader Annette Allison were told after Thursday night's bulletin that they would be replaced. ATV0 news would be read by news director Michael Schildberger and News Producer Peter Hanrahan.

Then, 15 years after ATV0 first went to air, came the turning point.

In 1979, Rupert Murdoch's News Corporation acquired a controlling interest in Channel Ten Sydney through investments in Ansett Transport Industries, including a 50 per cent interest in ATV0 Melbourne. Their total investment was $120 million. In January 1980, Channel 0 became Channel Ten and Murdoch set his sights and his management team on reviving the station's flagging news services. The next month Schildberger was dumped, followed by Peter Hanrahan. Out of all this upheaval, reporter Mark Bishop became the newsreader with perhaps the shortest career ever. Seconds before his first weekend bulletin, he had an attack of the nerves calling out, 'Abort, abort! I can't go on.' He did, but it was his first and last bulletin.

The following weekend, the newly-appointed news director John O'Loan tried out a young, fresh-faced female cadet and Jana Wendt went on to become a household name.

1980

In 1980 ATV0 joined the Ten Network – becoming part of an extended family, with bigger budgets, which finally led to ultimate success. Jana's appointment as co-anchor to *Ten News* was the next piece of the jigsaw that led to the revival. Several weeks later, former HSV7 reporter and presenter David Johnston remembers a similar offer by O'Loan while he was working at his Elsternwick newsagency. It was an offer he "couldn't refuse".

The first I heard of his appointment was when HSV7 Program Manager Gary Fenton stood waiting outside the news studio at the end of our nightly bulletin at 6.30.

'Got some news, Mal pal,' he said with a smile. 'You're going to be up against your old mate DJ. He's teaming up with Jana Wendt.'

'Oh shit!' was my first reaction – and so it became a three-horse news race in Melbourne. Johnston's appointment to the new on-air news team added credibility to Jana's youth and appeal. Very soon Jana would prove she had ability well beyond her visual attraction as their ratings continued to improve.

In 1982, another fresh-faced cadet reporter joined the news team. Eddie McGuire was just 14 when he began his media career as a football statistician with the *Herald* newspaper. He joined Australian Associated press (AAP) as a cricket writer and continued reporting with them until 1982 when he joined Ten as a sports reporter for *Eyewitness News*. He began cutting his teeth alongside colleagues Bruce McAvaney and Stephen Quartermaine in a nightly football segment *Doing the Rounds.*

Just when the jigsaw pieces were coming together Channel Nine did what they did to Seven with Brian Naylor. They bought Jana Wendt from Ten to join their flagship current affair show *60 Minutes.* They simply removed the threat. Into the breach at Ten stepped Jo Pearson, a young Queensland journalist with a blonde bob hairstyle and a youthful exuberance. Brian Courtis of the *Age* announced her arrival with some doubt but the viewers soon took Jo to heart as did weather presenter Rob Gell. Within two years they married in what was billed as "the wedding of the year". The team was now established. *Perfect Match* was the perfect lead-in to the News at 6 p.m. as David Johnston and Jo Pearson established a winning combination through the '80s.

WEDNESDAY, 16 FEBRUARY 1983

That long sought after element of credibility finally fell into place. And while one wonders if anything constructive could possibly emerge from such a holocaust as Ash Wednesday, television observers watched in fascination as Channel Ten's coverage provided a legacy of becoming the most watched news service on Australian television. Then success simply bred more success.

The only yardstick for success is winning. However, being a winner in television news is, more often than not, the result of simply being at the right place at the right time and as I watched from my position at HSV7 all I could do was wince in frustration.

THURSDAY, 27 MARCH 1986
RUSSELL STREET MELBOURNE

Shortly before 1 p.m. on the day before Good Friday 1986, several news crews arrived at Channel Ten's city office – affectionately called the "Lodge". It was purely coincidence that they all arrived around the same time.

The Lodge, run by Morrie Pilens, was part of a solid brick, double story building circa 1870 situated in McKenzie Street directly behind the Russell Street police complex. The annex adjoining the heritage horticulture building was used as a transfer centre for late breaking city stories and a base for reporters waiting to be helicoptered back to the studios at Nunawading after their assignments. The occasional live interview was also conducted from this venue.

The crews arrived in their news cars, drove to the rear of the building and parked in the small gravel enclosure next to the live-eye truck. Cameramen Barry Pullen, Peter Farragher and Mark Dickensen, together with live eye technician Richard Glenny and reporters Jennifer Hansen and Brian Shrowder, climbed the narrow wooden staircase winding up to the musty smelling first floor rooms, earmarked for studio, editing and general office use. Pullen began recharging batteries and cleaning tapes while Hansen and Shrowder were preparing to grab some lunch from the nearby sandwich shop in McKenzie Street.

Suddenly, the large antiquated wall clock in the general office, which was just about to reach the top of the hour at 1 p.m., flew across the room and crashed to the floor. The huge blast that left the clock face frozen in time also blew in the main window shattering the glass in a sickening thump that shook the building to its very foundations. The force of the explosion was felt across the city. Those closer to the centre of the blast were slammed with a solid vortex of air, which caused momentary deafness, severe chest pains and shear panic. Inside the Lodge loud screams and expletives were followed by sudden silence and distant sounds of sirens.

Cameraman Barry Pullen's first thought was the live eye truck parked outside had been blown up. Seconds later they all recovered from the initial shock and reacted instinctively. Morrie Pilens attempted to ring the studio and newsroom at Nunawading but the lines were down. Each cameraman grabbed his gear while one of the reporters raced to the car and radioed the newsroom. The rest bolted from the building and ran in the direction of a large black plume of smoke that was now billowing above the police complex. Rounding the corner of McKenzie Street into Russell Street they were confronted by a scenelolly of burning chaos. Just as Pullen hoisted his camera to his shoulder, he was hit by a second blast. As he continued to move forward, he suddenly realised he was deaf. He described it as 'if an audio operator had turned down the sound'. His other faculties appeared intact so he continued moving forward. 'The only thing I could hear was a feeble alarm from a nearby building … To my right I could see a woman crying hysterically while being comforted by several people, but I couldn't hear.' Pullen moved slowly through the scattered debris and thick smoke until he spotted a number of men working on another victim lying on the other side of a burning car. This would turn out to be 21-year-old Constable Angela Taylor who was crossing the road to get lunch when a vehicle exploded sending a huge fireball towards her. She survived the blast but died from her injuries 24 days later. She became the first Australian policewoman to be killed in the line of duty. A further 21 people were injured.

As Pullen moved forward there was a third blast, not as big as the first but bigger than the second.

'I captured it right in front of me and all along I kept wondering if there would be another … I don't know what drove me on but I just kept filming.' A Walkley or a Logie award was the last thing on his mind. They would follow, as would details of a stolen Commodore, which had been loaded with 50 to 60 sticks of gelignite, some detonators and a timing device. The vehicle had been parked outside the Russell Street police station by a group of armed robbers with a pathological hatred for police. The massive explosion blew in every window of the building and most windows in the nearby Magistrates' Courts. For Pullen and the others it seemed an eternity but in fact it was just two and a half minutes before police moved in and sealed off the area as a crime scene. By then Pullen's hearing appeared to be restored.

'There was shouting and screaming with sirens wailing and police yelling orders to clear the area … I knew we would only have two minutes before that would happen because we had all been instructed of that in our "Operational Disaster Plan".'

After Ash Wednesday in 1983, David Johnston and his chief of staff David Phelps had produced an Emergency Disaster Plan, an operational manual that sat on the production desk. It was described as the "Bible of Procedure" in the event of a major news story. It laid out instructions for producers, reporters, editors and cameramen directing them through an operational newsroom command centre in order that no one doubled up and everyone knew their role. It was the last time it was ever used. No one knows where it ended up or why it was never revived. Another lesson lost!

Within three minutes of the blast the three cameramen had spread out to cover strategic points. The reporters each grabbed eyewitness accounts of what had happened and the live eye truck had parked across the nearest intersection to beam back live pictures to the studio at Nunawading. Nothing was left to chance. A short time after police ordered them to leave the crime scene, they set up a studio centre on the top floor of the nearby Rockman's Regency Hotel, where they stayed.

'We couldn't leave even if we wanted to,' said Pullen. 'The entire city was gridlocked. We were at the centre of the action and we had captured it all on camera.' Melbourne's *Eyewitness News* eventually won a Logie Award and a Television Society Penguin award for Best News Story of the Year. A Thorn Award for Best Cameraman of the Year proved to be the trifecta.

While many exclusive moments in news are attributed to being at the right place at the right time, the other element worthy of recognition is confined to those who create research and produce special stories. *Ten News* was on a winning roll and its success spawned more success.

In 1987 a special *Ten News* team of Iain Gillespie and Terry Carlyon produced a Walkley award-winning documentary *Suzie's Story.* It concerned the last few months in the life of Suzie, an American woman living in Melbourne with AIDS. Her husband, the manager of Australian rock group *The Divinyls*, had left his job to care for his wife who in 1985 (shortly after their marriage) was diagnosed with the AIDS virus. Their baby son also was infected. Suzi consented to having the events prior to her death, filmed for this documentary.

While the *Ten News* turnaround may well have begun with Ash Wednesday the team that was in place was able to maintain the momentum. However, life is cyclical and nothing lasts forever – particularly in television.

1987

In February, David Gonsky – the managing director of Frank Lowy's Westfield Capital Corporation – bought the Ten Television Network from Rupert Murdoch. The deal earned News Corp $840 million. Acquisitions and changes that followed included the frequency swap between Seven and Ten in Adelaide, resulting in a five-station network. Gonsky was reported to have said, 'We have been looking for a cash-flow business and there is good cash-flow in television.'

He was right about one thing. Cash was certainly flowing freely at Ten – straight out the door.

MONDAY, 27 APRIL 1987

When I accepted the offer from my former Channel Seven colleague David Johnston to join Channel Ten I followed my friends from the *Neighbour's* cast who had also been rejected by Seven. And while we left behind the shambles of the Fairfax takeover at Channel Seven, the TV dramas continued on Ten with *The Henderson Kids, Bangkok Hilton, Vietnam* and *Dirtwater Dynasty.*

They told me when I first arrived at Channel Ten that I was

joining a special family. Such was the feeling of friendship and belonging that had been proudly nurtured from its very beginning. It is said that last-born siblings have been known to show a tendency to be free spirited, slightly vulnerable and prepared to take risks. ATV0 was the youngest of its commercial rivals and from the word go was prepared to take risks in order to survive. Some of those risks paid off, some didn't but they continued to challenge the existing boundaries of television.

MAL'S MELBOURNE

One of my first stories concerned Melbourne's oldest woman, 106-year-old Monte Punshon.

It was April 1987 when I tracked down the sprightly centenarian to her home in Glen Huntley Road, Malvern. I sat in awe as she spoke lucidly and philosophically of years I could only read about in history books.

She was 11 years old when Henry Ford invented the car and 19 years old when Australia became an independent nation on 1 January 1901. She had just turned 21 when Orville and Wilber Wright flew the first plane. Since then she had witnessed space flight and seen the introduction of the telephone, radio, television, computers and the Internet. So what, in her mind, was the greatest moment in time? Without a moment's hesitation she replied, 'The electric light.'

Monte Punshon helped establish *Mal's Melbourne* and with an average weekly audience in excess of three million viewers her story struck a chord among a new generation of Australians – and particularly other journalists who became eager to expand on her memories. Google Monte Puncheon today and her legacy also includes "the world's oldest lesbian". But in April 1987, had I even known of her sexuality, I doubt it would have been raised on *Mal's Melbourne*.

FORGOTTEN SAMARITAN

There was Baden–Powell Pretoria Walpole, or "George" as he was known by his West Ivanhoe neighbours.

He was one of those senior citizens who couldn't do enough to help others. George would weed the gardens of those who had become too incapacitated. He would shop for those too ill. He would do odd jobs for those beyond his own 70 years and was the lollipop man at the local school. But George couldn't look after himself and was too proud to ask for help. His home had fallen into disrepair, his garden had become an eyesore, he couldn't cook and could barely cope living alone.

When a neighbour wrote to *Mal's Melbourne* we responded with a sympathetic report highlighting his plight. Within weeks a local building company repaired and repainted his house, a local nursery removed a mountain of rubbish and landscaped his garden. The local council stepped in with a regular delivery of Meals on Wheels. Maybe it was helped by the slow-mo pics and appropriate music but the final result was described as "a miracle for a forgotten Samaritan" and the reputation of our segment began to grow.

NURSING MUMS

Later that year, Mary Paton wrote with a plea for help. Mary confided she had difficulty breastfeeding her first-born child and had turned to five other young mums facing similar problems.

Doctors and nurses were not trained to handle breastfeeding

problems and there were only a few older women to turn to for advice. Together these mums formed the Nursing Mothers' Association but all attempts for State Government funding had been rejected so they appealed for some pressure on politicians through *Mal's Melbourne*. Within weeks they received a $1 million grant. The association has since morphed into The Australian Breast Feeding Association and is now supported by health authorities and specialists in infant and child health care. This triggered another surge of story suggestions from those who were facing similar bureaucratic brick walls.

PENSIONERS APART

The following year I heard about Clyde and Silvia Coats. They had been married for more than 60 years and other than the war years, had never spent a night apart. Now in poor health, they were being forced to live in care. However, former returned serviceman Clyde had been located to an RSL private residential unit in Camberwell while Silvia was allocated a bed at Kinkora in Hawthorn. Both in their eighties, they were devastated at the thought of living their last years apart. But that was the rule in 1988. Within 24 hours of our story going to air, the RSL President Bruce Ruxton stepped in and not only sent Silvia to live with Clyde at the RSL unit but changed the system to ensure this could never happen again.

MELBOURNE'S LANEWAYS

Mal's Melbourne met up with a young couple, Diana and Roger Norswood. They had leased part of an old warehouse in a disused city laneway in a bid to open a coffee shop for city office workers but they hit a hurdle with the City Council by-laws officers who deemed it a health risk area. Despite the graffiti plastered walls we found the restored area, down several blue stone steps, provided a clean unique environment for a small café operation with plans for an occasional folk singer in the evenings.

We set up for a midday shoot and invited a local councillor for an official comment. The lease was subsequently granted which became part of the catalyst of change to revitalise Melbourne's inner city alleys and laneways.

MELBOURNE'S UNDERGROUND

Then there was the frustrated miner who had carved out metres of tunnelling beneath his quarter acre-housing block in North Balwyn. Dropping below his kitchen floor on a primitive hydraulic lift, we descended into another world of underground living. Rooms leading off passageways all excavated illegally but professionally, despite the concerns of his wife. Initially it was intended to be a personal nuclear shelter but Frank Szanto just couldn't stop excavating. I suspect the tunnels and rooms still exist today whether the current owners are aware or not.

However, I soon discovered there are a limited number of these extreme characters in Melbourne and gradually, without any immediate awareness, a new sub-culture slowly began to take over *Mal's Melbourne*. Blind carpenters, handicapped hairdressers, deaf mute performers and survivors of almost every conceivable illness found their way onto prime time television. And while many may have been very worthy, it all began to become rather wearing. No one questioned my direction because the segment continued to be such a success. The success not only boosted Ten's news ratings but soon began spawning other segments.

Within 12 months we had *Mal's Melbourne, Science and*

Technology and an extended segment on Victorian personalities titled *Travelling Man*. We introduced *Money Matters* with Robert Gottliebsen and *Arts and Entertainment* with man-about-town, Roland Rocchiccioli.

A short time later *Herald Sun* journalist Peter Costigan joined the team providing news and social commentary in *Costigan's Comments*. *Ten News* gradually morphed into a "feature news" service that some viewers found unacceptable. It was then GTV9's aggressive news director John Sorrell seized the moment. Responding to the threat Ten was posing, he did what Nine had succeeded to do with Brian Naylor and Jana Wendt – he pounced on the opposing team by buying the talent.

THURSDAY, 20 AUGUST 1987

David Johnston rang me at home.

'Mal,' he said, 'how would you like to read the news with me?' Co-newsreader Jo Pearson and her husband, weather presenter Rob Gell had just informed him they had accepted an offer from Nine. Gell would be presenting the weather and Pearson would be co-hosting a program, which was still on the drawing boards but would later involve shows including *Coast-to-Coast, Live at Five* and *Body and Soul*.

The deal was reported to be worth $1 million for Pearson and Gell. They were both taken off-air immediately and held under contract by Ten until cleared to fulfil their new obligations at Nine in the New Year. Johnston was proposing that he and I read together as a double-headed male combination – but I knew if viewers indicated they preferred a female reader then we would be forced to find one and revert to the more traditional team.

Once again, the ratings held firm and within weeks it

became clear the combination was working. Meanwhile senior management flew up to Brisbane where they competed with Nine in a bitter chequebook war and hired a young, attractive weekend newsreader by the name of Tracy Curro. It became a double source of celebration to sign her up, beating Nine at their own "cheque book" game.

By the end of 1987 *Ten News* in Melbourne had clearly left the opposition behind, attracting three million viewers a week ($600,000 a night) and the billboard and full page ads said it all. But new storm clouds were threatening the start of the 1988 ratings year. Ten now had three readers – Johnston, Walden and Curro.

1988

The year began with a news campaign, which ran for several weeks before Curro arrived and the viewers were immediately divided.

'*Eyewitness News* with David Johnston and Tracy Curro *with* Mal Walden.' The Walden supporters who had come across from Seven were convinced I was "being shunted sideways", so Ten revamped the promos.

'*Eyewitness News* with David Johnston, Mal Walden and Tracy Curro.' Curro was furious. She rightly felt that she had been brought to Melbourne under false pretences. She wanted equal billing with Johnston. So the billing changed again.

'*Eyewitness News* with David Johnston and Tracy Curro *and with* Mal Walden' (greater vocal emphasis on *and with*). No one was really happy, but the *Mal's Melbourne* segment seemed to appease the Walden supporters. However, the experiment of three readers appeared doomed from the start leaving Ten with little room to move. In fact, there was no room at all, particularly on the news desk, which became obvious during the closing credits.

David Johnston, Tracy Curro, Mal Walden, sports presenter Bruce McAvaney, weather presenter Julie Foster and right at the end of the desk sat Peter Costigan. We all missed the humour of that until it featured in a comedy sketch on the *Steve Vizard Show* in a parody of Seven's Good Friday hospital appeal panel.

Meanwhile, another management shake-up was emerging with the appointment of Sydney based network news director Tom Barnett. His first edict was, 'Get rid of the three readers and put Walden on weekends.' In a bid to appease any concerns I may have had working weekends, Ten offered to fly me back and forth from our holiday house at Blairgowrie on the Mornington Peninsular. It was indeed the crazy '80s and while most departments had exceeded their budgets, the news department kept running on empty. The warning lights had been flashing but all attempts to stem the financial haemorrhage had failed.

The '80s was described as the decade when "greed was good" and there was no question television was leading the way. Large sums of money had been splashed around on expensive productions, huge pay packets, improved technology and increased production values. Finally, even bigger sums of money began changing hands as networks began changing ownership.

1989

In September, no one was more aware of Ten's fragile financial position than its owner Frank Lowy who had put his son Peter in charge. They may have known how to run shopping centres but neither knew the television industry. More importantly, the people they entrusted to run the network had also failed.

In one of many desperate attempts to stem the decline, they were reported to have approached veteran TV pioneer and former

Nine boss Bruce Gyngell to run the network. Gyngell was said to have turned the job down but recommended an American by the name of Bob Shanks. Rumour had it, that Gyngell actually mentioned someone else and that Ten approached the wrong man. The bottom line was the Texan accepted the offer. Under instructions to cut costs, he arrived with a product of downmarket programming – including his notorious *Doubledare Green Slime Game Show*. Eventually, after realising he was not the great white saviour, his contract was terminated. This resulted in a legal writ, which saw him walk away with a golden handshake. Everyone was making money, with the exception of Ten. In the end, the Lowy's capitulated. Having paid $840 million for a three-station network, before adding Canberra, Adelaide and Perth, it was now a total disaster. Lowy later described owning Ten as like trying to 'hold onto a fish. The tighter we gripped, the more it slipped out of our hands. However,' he conceded, 'if I hadn't taken risks in business I'd still be a delicatessen owner.'

SATURDAY, 2 SEPTEMBER 1989

Former broadcaster Steve Cosser and his production house Broadcom Australia took control of the network. By the Monday, Cosser was preparing to shut down Nunawading and move operations to his Broadcom offices in South Melbourne and Sydney. The plans stunned us all. The unions were notified and we all prepared for an industrial showdown. Broadcom had acquired the Melbourne and Sydney stations when Cosser tied up a deal to buy 19.9 per cent of Northern Star Holdings for just $30 million. It was an incredible deal leaving Cosser with little to lose. The decision to move from Nunawading was put on-hold as expenses were trimmed and programming cuts were made. However, the life expectancy at Ten seemed terminal and in the midst of this latest storm Channel Nine threw me a possible lifeline.

TUESDAY, 3 OCTOBER 1989 – 8 P.M.

Nine's news director John Sorell rang me at home offering me a way out. Admittedly, Sorell sounded a little tired and emotional again but I immediately showed interest. He responded by saying he would ring back tomorrow night when his head was a little clearer. He did and it was much clearer for both of us.

The offer was to read the 11.30 a.m. *National Nine News* out of Melbourne leading into the *Ray Martin Midday Show*. I would be replacing Tracy Grimshaw who was moving to *The Today Show*. For two days a week I would also be required to report for *National Nine News* in Melbourne and as a sweetener there was the guarantee of no weekend work. The salary was in excess of $200,000. Sorell concluded that the deal would be sealed at a lunch with network chiefs David Leckie and Ian Johnston in the next few days. I thanked him, hung up and Pauline and I opened a bottle of champagne to celebrate. My only concern was how to tell my good friend and colleague David Johnston the following day. It was Johnston who had thrown me a lifeline from HSV7 in '87 – I needn't have worried.

WEDNESDAY, 4 OCTOBER 1989

The following morning news headlines put paid to any new contracts or agreements at Nine:

It was announced that Alan Bond, who purchased the Nine Network from Kerry Packer in 1987 for $1,055 million, has sold

it back to Kerry Packer for just $200 million. According to Packer,
"You only get one Alan Bond in your lifetime, and I've had mine."

The story continued...

In cost cutting measures Packer has announced a series of axings
including Nine's 11.30 a.m. news.

I never heard back from Sorell and continued reading at
weekends on Ten and producing segments for Mal's Melbourne.

1990

One year later in September, having endured 12 months of budget
restraints under Broadcom, I received my first overseas assignment
at Ten.

I was sent to cover the Melbourne Olympic bid in Tokyo,
which ended not only in disappointment for Melbourne but for
hundreds of staff at Network Ten around Australia.

On the night of the announcement, as I was live on-air, our
small team scooped all our competitors as PM Bob Hawke and
the entire Olympic Bid Committee walked into our Tokyo studio.
It was only hours from the announcement and they all conveyed
overwhelming confidence that Melbourne would win the bid.

Several hours later the name "Atlanta" dashed all our hopes, but
not as much as the following morning in the form of a fax from
our Melbourne newsroom, which simply read: *Network Ten in
receivership, find your own way home.* It was a sad attempt at humour
and within two months there was even less to smile about.

Morrie Pilens was among the first to surrender to the
administrators of Network Ten and on his final day muttered
how the battles in television paled against his wartime experience
under Hitler's notorious SS. He accepted a redundancy and finally

retired with his wry sense of humour intact and a set of standards in news coverage that continue to this day.

MONDAY, 26 NOVEMBER 1990

Network Ten announced the sacking of more than a quarter of its staff, over 700 people in Melbourne, Sydney and Brisbane. The measures were aimed at cutting costs in excess of $100 million over 12 months. It came just one week after Broadcom Chief Steve Cosser was removed and replaced by former GTV9 boss Gary Rice. That same week the Seven Network, also in receivership, announced the sacking of another 100 of their employees and a freezing of all salaries. The television industry was in total turmoil.

On the Monday morning as I drove the 30 minute journey to work, I began planning a life outside of television. I felt I could not endure another moment of insecurity caused by events totally out of my control. Not even during the Fairfax fiasco at Seven had I felt so completely bereft of morale. Fearing administrators would seize all assets including vehicles. I decided to park my car at the nearby carpark at the Kegg restaurant. Every executive within the network appeared to be driving BMWs but no one could explain how they had been acquired. The receivers would soon discover an entire fleet of missing BMWs, which would never be accounted for. While my vehicle was a recently updated Mazda RX7, I was not prepared to risk having it impounded even though I was paying for it.

On arrival in the newsroom, I was met by that familiar sinister sound of silence. It followed an announcement that our new chief executive Gary Rice would be making a video statement from Sydney headquarters to all staff at around 2 p.m. I couldn't wait until 2 p.m. so I approached our news editor Neil Miller to ask, 'How safe am I?'

'Mate,' he said, 'after what happened to you at Seven I have been informed you are the safest of us all. You are the last on the list. You have become a protected species.'

It would apply for the rest of my career.

There was some personal relief but that didn't protect me from the tears and the emotions my colleagues were enduring. As they gathered around the several newsroom monitors in preparation for Gary Rice to deliver his *coup de gras*, I took Miller's advice and went home. I was a union member so couldn't appear on camera that night anyway. David Johnston was not a member so he was left to read alone.

Rice began by outlining plans to further reduced staff. Of the 56 retrenchments in Melbourne most would come from the news department. In a slow soft monotone voice, Rice continued by claiming the retrenchments were necessary for the network's long-term health. 'The action,' he said, 'gives us no pleasure but is one of several responsible decisions by the current management and the receivers to revive the network and to provide a basis for its financial recovery.'

Similar words would echo throughout the history of Network Ten.

Delivering his message from Sydney he couldn't possibly see the tears or hear the cries of pain and frustration from staff members who had dedicated their lives to the industry they loved. The newsroom, normally a happy supportive group of colleagues, was now in a state of absolute shock and disbelief. We had already survived one round of retrenchments 12 months earlier. A terrible time during which each Friday the names of those selected for retrenchments were read out over the PA system. Someone coined the phrase "Flick Friday" as one by one they would walk to the management section adjoining the foyer, receive their slips and depart in tears. There was nothing private about the sackings.

History was now repeating – it was utterly incomprehensible. We were all so deeply affected, even those of us who had survived. While some immediately packed their belongings and left, others adjourned across to the nearby bar at the Kegg where members of the press came to film and take pictures of them. They were the latest victims of a sad chapter in Australian corporate history in the '80s. As they grouped together for comfort, support and to drown their sorrows, there was a certain irony that they were not reporting the news that night – they *were* the news.

Gary Rice was right. Time heals in television … or so it seems. While in the hands of the Westpac Bank and under the steerage of the former GTV9 boss, the network emerged from that period of sackings and cost cutting with a glimmer of hope, particularly for the troubled newsroom. Westpac was now desperate. There were few buyers for the "worst house on the street" until Canadian billionaire Izzy Asper appeared on the scene. His lawyers created a structure that allowed him to get around the law restricting foreign ownership.

In 1992, under a complex group of Australian syndicates, the Canadian media company CanWest emerged with 57 per cent economic interest in the syndicates, but only 15 per cent voting shares. The studios moved from the outer suburb of Nunawading to the inner suburb of South Yarra and our new home at the Como shopping centre.

From there Ten rose from the ashes like the Phoenix to become one of the early '90s corporate tales of success. What is not generally known is that the network had come to within 24 hours of closing down. According to former company CFO Gerry Carrington even the cheques had been counter-signed in preparation for the licence to be handed back to the Government. Gary Rice was left with little product and few staff, but within a very short space of time Ten discovered the programs they had left were attracting a very young audience. *Melrose Place, The Simpsons, M★A★S★H* and *Seinfeld* were all attracting young viewers with the exception of its news at 6 p.m.

With so few staff left to service our one-hour news at 6 p.m. management was forced to reduce it to 30 minutes. It was almost incomprehensible that just a few years previously we were boasting the most watched news on Australian television. How the mighty fall! Ten News was now being soundly thrashed by all the opposition at 6 p.m.

Totally frustrated and terribly disappointed, Johnston says he was aware of the American trend of afternoon bulletins so arranged some private research in Melbourne. Amazed at the response and the size of the potential audience at 5 p.m. he then commissioned a further two more surveys, each supporting the first. Finally with news director Neil Miller they arranged to meet Gary Rice at a Camberwell restaurant where they privately convinced the CEO that *Ten News - First at Five* would work, not just in Melbourne but around the Network.

And it did to varying degrees.

Within a short period Ten became the envy of its competitors. *Ten News - First at 5*, was born out of a necessity to survive. We had become a boutique television station, small in comparison to our competitors comprising three office floors and three small studios with a staff of 120. A further 100 staff remained at Nunawading to provide broadcast facilities from Studio Centre productions, which would later be renamed Global.

MONDAY, SEPTEMBER 28 1992

At 5 p.m. we produced our first live program from our new home. David Johnston and Jo Pearson, who had returned to Ten, read the one-hour news. Pearson had recently replaced Tracy Curro who had become embroiled in a legal stoush over contract duties and had left the network under a cloud. However, the clouds were beginning to clear.

At 7 p.m. on our first night at Como controversial broadcaster Derryn Hinch launched his 180 program with Network Ten. Thirty-six weeks earlier he and his long serving executive producer Dermot O'Brien had been lured from HSV7 by Ten's CEO Gary Rice to continue an "in your face" style of current affairs. The ratings gamble further paid off when he and O'Brien negotiated an exclusive interview with fugitive businessman Christopher Skase, their former employer at HSV7. They were the first Australian journalists to get the full entrée to his self-imposed exile in Spain resulting in two-hour news special.

However, what Hinch and O'Brien were not aware of was the imminent appointment of a network news and current affairs boss who would have them in her sights right from her start. Nor would we be aware of more obstacles along the way including "a bloody iceberg" that very nearly sunk us all. And this time we had no one to blame but ourselves.

Timing is everything in television and as we were struggling to restore some form of credibility to a news service reduced in staff numbers and battered by low morale, "Operation Iceberg" could not have come at a worse time in our recovery period. Like the passengers on the Titanic, very few of us in the newsroom had any idea of this impending disaster. Only a select few were involved in an investigative news story called Operation Iceberg and those involved were all sworn to secrecy – even the cameramen. The entire five-day shoot and editing of this report was out-sourced, such was the sensitivity of its contents.

It was only hours before the story went to air that there was any hint of something special in the wind and again, an ominous silence enveloped the newsroom. Doors were locked, meetings were in progress, lawyers wandered in and out of the room with clipboards, briefcases and grim faces. The always-affable Director of News Neil Miller was looking concerned as was newsreader and former director David Johnston. The only ones with confidence and an air of "I know something you don't know" were investigative freelance journalist Iain Gillespie and the network's former chief of staff and police reporter Rick Willis.

Mid-afternoon we were all informed of a "bombshell of a story" – a story which would have serious implications for the Government, major banks and the police force. I stood listening as Miller outlined the briefest details which implied wide spread corruption involving police at the highest level. The same details were also given to talk back radio and newspapers in the hope of getting the widest possible coverage and indeed promotion for this night.

At 5 p.m. the news began with David Johnston and Jo Pearson teasing the upcoming story before throwing to investigative reporter Iain Gillespie. Against a background of deep emotive music, Gillespie began with a piece to camera holding the so-called secret "Iceberg report" in his hand:

This is the result of two years of work by a special task force working within the Victoria police internal security unit. The contents are explosive. So explosive in fact, only a few top police have been allowed to read it and the only full copy has been delivered under *guard to the Governor of Victoria. ... According to the report more than $3 billion was plundered from Government bodies, VEDC, State Bank and Tri-Continental, by a network of corporate crooks that infiltrated the Government the Police Force and the Banking system ... Operation Iceberg was never intended to be made public but now that it has been, the Kirner Government and the Police Force have a lot of explaining to do.*

Standing outside a building described as the ISU (Police Internal Security Unit), reporter Rick Willis then took over with the second part of the story:

This was the building where police investigate their own and their own Government and where the Iceberg report had been written in strict secrecy for more than two years.

He then began quoting passages from the report:

The report paints a horrific picture of bank officials forging documents for million dollar loans ... three past and present ministers paid off ... police conspiring to murder other police and innocent people deliberately sent to jail ... It even exposes a deal between police and Israel's secret service, Mossad. But above all, it traces the plundering of billions of dollars from Victorian taxpayers. Several members of the Operation Iceberg task force have spoken to 'Ten Eyewitness News' but for their own protection their identity will not be revealed.

Reaction was spontaneous, but not what *Ten News* had hoped for. One of the first callers identified himself as the owner of the building that had just been identified as the ISU Internal Security Unit. He said he was a confectionary manufacturer and that particular building had been making candy for the past 20 years.

A reporter from the *Age* rang explaining why they had rejected the story several weeks earlier on the basis that the source was "nothing more than a con". It was down-hill from the very first night. As *Ten News* desperately attempted to salvage some credibility, the stories we continued to run only served to discredit the man at the centre of the report further and of course discredit our news. The source variously known as Stuart Gill or Anthony Adam Zoccoli had been dubbed as "Mr Fixit". He was described as a self-styled computer expert who had once formed a link between corrupt police and criminals. It would later be revealed he used these links to make a profit for himself as a paid police informer, eventually becoming involved with members of the ISU. After falling out with some of his former police contacts it then became a personal vendetta to get even by approaching the media to reveal details of corruption he said existed in the force... or at least his former friends. He failed to sell his story to the *Age* so had then turned to Ten.

THE FALLOUT

Following reports on *Ten News*, police held a high level press conference in which they denied all allegations labelling it a hoax.

I was asked to attend as a representative of *Ten News*. Apparently no one else volunteered. I had no choice and it was one of the most embarrassing moments of my career. I sat among hostile police and smug media colleagues listening to the allegations by senior police directing their wrath at *Ten News*. It progressively worsened as they systematically pulled apart all our allegations piece by piece revealing what they described as a giant hoax.

Gill later responded to the "hoax claim", saying it was a reply by police to cover their own mistakes. He said police had set him up to discredit the investigation. But no one was listening to Gill. Even political leaders who had campaigned on police corruption were backing off.

Initially, Deputy Opposition Leader and Shadow Police spokesman Pat McNamara had promised a judicial inquiry into police corruption if his party was elected to government. However, after Jeff Kennett was elected to office on 3 October 1992, it was not surprising this was perhaps the first pre-election promise the Kennett government dropped.

Several police officers faced disciplinary action for leaking information. *Ten News* quietly dropped all further reference to the stories and the threatened legal writs from senior police against the network never eventuated. We could not blame anyone else but ourselves.

The ghost of Operation Iceberg never completely left the Melbourne newsroom. The report remained under lock and key in the news editor's office with orders "never to be shown". I am told it is still there today.

Gary Rice did not survive under the CanWest management team and became the holder of the dubious distinction of a CEO who had received a "golden handshake" termination from all three commercial networks.

CFO Gerry Thorley immediately took direct control over news budgets and editorial content. ATV10 didn't venture into investigative reporting again. Operation Iceberg was only mentioned when the issue of "anonymous news sources" was raised, as all future anonymous sources were unofficially directed to be revealed to management first in a bid to avoid any journalist from being manipulated or bringing the network into disrepute.

However, trouble at Ten was far from over.

TUESDAY, 22 JUNE 1993

They say a moon always shines brighter after a storm. Nine months after the Operation Iceberg fiasco we welcomed the appointment of network news director Carmel Travers. It was hoped this former producer and host with the "Beyond" organisation would bring a wealth of production values and much needed reassurance for our future. Many even accepted the sexist view that her appointment would also bring a healing and perhaps a softer more feminine side to a male dominated management structure of the past.

In fact, it would be revealed CanWest deliberately chose a female for the executive news position in a bid to be seen as more liberal thinking in the eyes of those who may have been critical of their foreign ownership of Ten.

Whatever the reason for her appointment, the positives never materialised. We never saw the healing or the "learning curve" she so often referred to. What we did see were her endorsements and appearance in "Physical Milk" advertisements on prime time commercial networks on a nightly basis, despite a standard edict that no news staff could be aligned with any outside commercial enterprise.

More significantly, we witnessed another massive drain of high profile experienced news staff. They left either due to their inability to work under her brief or directly by her authoritarian rule of termination.

Carmel Travers flew to Melbourne to meet and greet her staff and to outline her news agenda. About a dozen or so journalists, producers, reporters and presenters gathered in the Como newsroom immediately after the 5 p.m. news.

We were eager for some direction and hoping above all, any

changes would be minimal. On first impressions she won me immediately. I was not only impressed by her confidence but found her mellifluent voice quite intoxicating as she purred with a seductive quality of sincerity and warmth. She began by admitting she was "on a learning curve" but was determined not to change direction.

However after about 20 minutes, during which time she had captivated 98 per cent of her audience, she began a series of contradictions. Within 25 minutes huge cracks began to emerge as she outlined "total changes" in direction and style.

When questioned about these contradictions, her replies came in more lengthy waves of clichés and hyperbole.

Eventually, after more than 40 minutes, Travers wrapped up by singling out the nation's leading newsreaders, Brian Henderson in Sydney and Brian Naylor in Melbourne, describing them as 'dinosaurs who have overstayed their time'.

No one questioned that her so-called "dinosaurs" were responsible for bringing in top ratings and subsequent revenue. But it was her final comment that convinced us we were in trouble when she described our very own *Current Affair* host Derryn Hinch as a "loose cannon".

There were shuffles and throat clearing as one senior producer whispered, 'We have a problem Houston,' as he popped open a bottle of red. He would be the first to be sacked.

And so began another round of resignations, sackings and uncertainty involving some of the most experienced and high profile news staff who had already survived the painful period of receivership.

Arguably, her biggest decision was the sacking of current affairs host Derryn Hinch who was replaced by controversial Sydney radio shock-jock Alan Jones. If, as she frequently claimed, Derryn Hinch was a loose cannon then Alan Jones soon became a nuclear nightmare. He lasted just 13 weeks (64 programs) before network management interceded and he was pulled from air due to poor ratings. Never had the network been so decimated of on-air talent in such a short time, yet still Carmel Travers continued to run the News and Current Affairs division for more than two years.

WEDNESDAY, 18 OCTOBER 1995

The rumour mill had been working overtime with reports that newsreader David Johnston and news editor Neil Miller had been approached by former CEO Gary Rice who was now running Seven. Rice had defected to Seven after a disagreement with CanWest Management over the future direction of Network Ten.

At 12.30 p.m. I received a phone call in my office from Carmel Travers in Sydney. 'Mal, would you place yourself on standby to read tonight's news?' she purred in that seductive way. When asked why, she just replied, 'I can't say. I'll call you back.'

At 12.35 p.m. Miller called me into his office. 'I want you to know I have just resigned after being appointed director of news at Seven,' he said. 'Carmel Travers was putting pressure on David Johnston to make a decision as he too had been offered a job.'

It was a package deal.

At 12 45 p.m. I walked into Johnston's office and simply said, 'Is it true?'

'Yes,' he replied, 'I have decided to go —' He was then cut short mid-sentence by an incoming phone call from Travers. She was demanding Johnston's resignation and informing him that he was no longer a staff member and was to remove himself from the premises immediately. As she was ringing from Sydney, Johnston simply rolled his eyes and hung up without comment.

Seconds later my phone began ringing next door. It was Carmel Travers.

'I suppose you have heard the news?' she purred.

I explained I had and she then asked if I was okay to read tonight's news. I said I was but then inquired, given the changes, would this become permanent?

'As far as I am concerned you will continue reading the news at Ten,' she said, then added, 'I will be flying down to Melbourne in 48 hours after dealing with a certain problem here in Sydney.'

The problem apparently concerned Sydney newsreader Juanita Phillips who had been escorted from the Ten studios. According to press reports she was quoted as "being upset" after being told she would not be replacing network newsreader Anne Fulward who had resigned to go to ATN7. Travers had appointed Sandra Sully instead. Phillips was said to have "thrown a wobbly", resigned and was promptly escorted from the premises. It was another staff crisis involving Carmel Travers. More were to leave during her reign including sports host Eddie McGuire, sports reporter Peter Donigan, and newsreader Jo Pearson.

THURSDAY, 19 OCTOBER 1995

The day began with calls of congratulations from friends and colleagues responding to the assumption and unofficial reports I had been appointed newsreader. I then received another call from Travers.

'How are you coping?' she asked.

'I'm fine,' I replied, 'but can you confirm that this situation is permanent?'

'Absolutely,' she said. 'There is no other person more qualified to take over from Johnston. You have my unequivocal support.' I recorded the comment for the record and assumed it was confirmation. For several years I had been waiting in the wings with no sign of a senior reading position. Now, with David Johnston moving to Seven at his own instigation, my future seemed assured. Yet I still had a nagging gut feeling about it all. We had a saying at Ten that "assumption is the mother of all stuff-ups".

FRIDAY, 20 OCTOBER 1995

On my arrival at 9 a.m. I was met at the lift on the fourth floor by acting news director Mike Tancred.

'Osmo (ATV0 station manager Robert Osmotherly) wants to see you in his office immediately.' Both were smiling as I entered and both offered their congratulations on my appointment. All that remained, they said, was to negotiate a salary package.

'I assume then I will negotiate with Carmel Travers?'

There was a long pause and the atmosphere perceptibly changed.

'Not so,' Osmo continued. 'You will negotiate directly with us. Travers is about to depart the network. But for the time being say nothing to no one about her position.' The deal was confirmed and I returned to my office just as my phone was ringing. A male voice identified himself as Shane Dannet, a television newsreader with Channel 2 in Adelaide.

'Mal,' he said. 'I am calling to say how much I am looking forward to working with you in Melbourne.'

'In what capacity?' I asked.

'I have just signed a contract with Carmel Travers to read the nightly news at Ten in Melbourne.'

I sat stunned by his reply.

Dannet filled the silence. 'I asked Travers about you and was told you didn't want the job and that you were going to read the morning network news.'

I was unable to tell him Travers was no longer in charge so I wished him well and we hung up. Apparently after her visit to Adelaide, Travers returned to Sydney where she attempted to push the Dannet contract through the department of human recourses. However, they refused to accept it pending the return from overseas of CEO Peter Viner. Ten was preparing to launch a public float Instability was the last thing the network needed at this time. Friday afternoon Viner arrived back from Canada and called a meeting with Carmel Travers.

At 5.20 p.m. during the news, the studio phone buzzed. The producer's voice simply said, 'Travers has gone.' Her official statement read:

The past two years have been intense, often rewarding but also consuming. I look forward to spending more time with my children and returning to my roots as a program maker.

At the end of the bulletin we all gathered in the newsroom for a farewell to Miller and Johnston. It was a bittersweet moment for us all.

The following morning, Robert Fidgeon of the *Herald Sun* wrote:

Word of Carmel Travers' resignation hit Channel Ten's newsroom not long before local news boss Neil Miller and reader David Johnston bade their farewells. Colleagues couldn't help thinking there was a certain irony in the announcement. A belief reinforced when Johnston in his speech made passing reference to the fact that if the news had come earlier, he and Miller may not have been standing there saying goodbye. The same applied to Anne Fulwood, who quit a week earlier. All three had left primarily because of disenchantment with the situation and within its news. Travers remarked to Sydney colleagues after Friday's announcement that she was the sacrificial lamb.

It was a bittersweet moment for me on a personal level. I was losing a colleague and friend I had respected and admired since our days together in radio. In all my years in broadcast media there was non other I held in such high regard as David Johnston.

Johnston and Miller both went to Seven. Miller later moved to *GTV9 News* as senior producer and Johnston remained with Seven as a specialist reporter until he introduced a mid–afternoon network news at 4.30 p.m. which he hosted out of Melbourne until his retirement in September 2005. Johnston claims to this day that those few years at 4.30 p.m. were the most satisfying of his career, they were certainly a game changer. Shane Dannet, who resigned from Channel 2 in Adelaide after signing an agreement with Travers, was not reinstated and eventually left Australia to continue his television career in Europe.

By year's end, former Hinch producer Dermot O'Brien replaced Miller as Ten's News Director/Manager in Melbourne. Jennifer Hansen joined me as co–reader, Mike Larkan arrived from Canberra as our weather presenter and Stephen Quartermaine presented sport.

If former news director and newsreader David Johnston brought the highest success in terms of ratings in the '80s, then Dermot O'Brien established the longest period of stability to Ten's once troubled newsroom from the '90s. We became the longest-serving news team on Melbourne television. While most of that success was shared with my co–reader Jennifer Hansen I also had the pleasure of beginning a partnership with Marie Louise Theille and ending with Helen Kapalos.

Melbourne's *First at Five* news became the most watched service on the network, and many nights it was the most watched program on the entire schedule. Ten had once again proved to be a pioneer – first with the hour, first at 6 p.m. then first at 5.

Yes, there were challenges, changes and disappointments but the stability between 1995 and 2010 was unprecedented for the Ten Network. The irony was our success in news paved the way for others to follow and eventually the 24-hour news cycle would combine to fragment our viewers and threaten the very success we had achieved. But that is another story.

CHAPTER 14

SERENDIPITY

*The New Oxford Dictionary of English defines 'serendipity'
as the occurrence and development of events by chance in a
satisfactory or beneficial way.
My father Hugh Lawrence Walden defined his moment of
serendipity by an event in which I saved his life during the D-day
invasion of Europe.*

WEDNESDAY, 6 JUNE 1945
NORMANDY

The day bore all the signs of becoming the last day of his life. Two by two the small detachment of British forces leapt into the cold grey waters of a beach on Normandy. Weighed down with a backpack of radio equipment and holding his 303 Enfield rifle waist high, my father fought desperately to maintain his balance as he began wading ashore towards his destination – a beach codenamed 'Sword'. He was tall, of slim build with fine wispy hair and a moustache, which he had proudly maintained since his late teens. He spoke with a soft slightly cultured voice born out of Essex and cultivated in a Northern English boarding school. He had an endearing shyness and the manners of a gentleman. Recently married with a baby son he was anything but a soldier.

Just several metres from shore his foot stumbled against a sunken object. The force of the strike dislodged it and a body suddenly appeared. A mixture of seasickness, adrenalin and fear overcame him and the bile rose from his stomach like the body in the surf. He retched, yelled and stumbled up the stony beach to his designated assembly point. The Royal British Signal Corp had landed and their immediate priority was to establish radio, telephone and messenger communications to the Beach Command. Several groups immediately headed inland, ahead of the infantry to observe and correct battleship gunfire on enemy positions. Many of those would become the first casualties of the allied invasion.

Back on the beach my father's immediate task was to lay down telephone lines, install switchboards and open up radio frequencies. Lance Corporal Tommy Turner from Chipping Norton – a market town in the Cotswold Hills of Oxfordshire – teamed up with him and called him "Hughie". Together they ran through the dunes laying down rolls of wire through the troughs and across the mounds that separated the beach from bombed out houses along the coast road. Several other members of the signal group followed up by connecting the wires as each roll ran out. There was little chat between the men as they concentrated on the purpose of extending communications from one landing site to the next.

Shortly after reaching the adjoining beach a jeep pulled up and they were ordered back to rejoin the rest of their group. A large canvas covered truck with its camouflage markings was waiting in line to move out. Both men ran to their designated vehicle as hands came out to haul them on board. Tommy leapt up then grabbed Hughie who was now breathless and eased him onto the wooden seating next to him.

'Are you okay Hughie?' Tommy asked noticing the shortness of breath and dripping perspiration.

'Yes,' Hughie gasped. But he knew he wasn't. Through a gap in the canvas tail cover Hughie looked back down to the beach and saw two soldiers drag the body he had encountered from the water. The sight of the limp lifeless corpse being carried across the beach heightened fears that he would perhaps never see his wife or baby son again. Tears blurred his vision as the truck suddenly lurched forward at the start of the long hard journey with the liberating forces across Europe.

Hughie looked around inside the truck and recognised several of the dozen men each about his age, some he had trained with but all remained silent in their personal world of thoughts.

Tommy Turner was the most extroverted character in the group and while out ranked by Sergeant Angus Witherspoon from Middlesex it took little more than an hour before Tommy had gradually broken down the barriers and by mid-afternoon even had them all singing the anti-Hitler song:

'Hitler has only got one ball,
Göring two but very small,
Himmler is somewhat sim'lar,
But poor Goebbels has no balls at all.'

This ended in high-spirited laughter until Witherspoon brought them back to order. Each man again sat in silence assessing their roles of communication that would include relaying dispatches and reporting back to HQ on the advances and set backs of the invasion.

Communication, particularly radio, had always fascinated Hughie – how voices and music could travel unseen and emerge from inside Bakelite headphones and more recently speaker systems. He also admired BBC War correspondent Richard Dimbleby. Now here was Hughie also reporting the progress of the war and while he was specifically reporting for military purposes he privately hoped after his information had been declassified it would make its way to the civilian sector and perhaps become the basis of public news – just like Dimbleby. It was this interest in communication that led him to work for British Post but it was another form of communication where he had become a leading expert, the emerging technology of teleprinters, which had developed into a crucial advantage during this vital stage of the war.

Several days into the journey his health became a serious matter of concern. There was no question in his mind he had a high temperature. The continual perspiration was testament to that, now it was compounded by a sudden itching. A rash had also broken out on his forehead and behind his ears, a rash very similar to the one he had noticed on his son several weeks earlier on his last visit home before the invasion. Measles for a toddler is a two-week inconvenience but for an adult it can be far more serious and even life threatening if not treated. For a soldier in a war situation and living in close contact with fellow troops, contagious diseases such as measles can be catastrophic. Next to direct injuries, illness accounts for the second level of troop hours lost on battlefields. Eventually Hughie reported to his sergeant and was immediately sent to quarantine.

As his colleagues drove off through France, Hughie was virtually carried into a military field hospital where he would be confined for at least the next ten days. The fever had taken a firm hold. He lay on a stretcher in a tent not knowing where he was or for that matter not even caring. He drifted in and out of a fitful sleep and the noise and smell of antiseptic drifted in and out of his dreams; vivid dreams of his wife and baby son and of holidays spent in Wales. Dreams broken by cries of injured men waiting for repatriation back home. Dreams interrupted by the sound of trucks arriving and departing and the hushed spoken words of medics as they moved in earnest from one tent to the next.

Towards the end of Hughie's first week in quarantine the tent flap parted and a young official-looking staff sergeant entered and dragged a collapsible chair to the foot of his bed.

'You're looking better now private.' He remained standing but leant on the back of the chair as he paused while searching for his next words. 'You are about to be discharged and returned to duty … you will remain attached to the 30th Royal Signal Corp but assigned to a new unit.' There was another pause as he cleared his throat. 'I am sorry to say your original unit is no more … they were killed in action four days ago.'

Hughie lay there trying to absorb what was being said just catching snippets of his departing words.

'Details of your new unit will be made clear in the next 48 hours. I am sorry, good luck.' He then stood and swept the tent flap to one side and disappeared. A German Panzer Mark IV tank had fired a single shell through the canvas covered signals truck with initial reports claiming "no survivors". Hughie lay on his camp stretcher trying to remember what he could of his colleagues particularly Lance Corporal Tommy Turner from Chipping Norton whom he had grown most fond of.

Forty-eight hours later he was discharged to continue his contribution to the liberation of Europe. He was driven by military jeep into South Eastern Belgium where eventually he caught up with his new unit being billeted in a small village where they had established a communication centre. Hughie loaded his gear onto his back and slung his rifle across his shoulder. While feeling anything but healthy he struggled towards a truck parked alongside the local Post Office. As he approached the vehicle a familiar figure emerged. Short in build, swarthy in complexion, a smile to break a woman's heart and with arms outstretched to greet a friend.

'Tommy fuckin' Turner,' whispered Hughie – and Hughie never swore.

Tommy hugged him while Hughie wept at how wonderful fate could be in a time of war. Tommy's gregarious personality had apparently worn thin with Sergeant Angus Witherspoon from Middlesex who recommended he be transferred to another unit. Hughie again called it serendipity, which sealed their friendship for the next stage of their war.

THURSDAY, 18 OCTOBER 1999 – 2.30 P.M.

I had been invited to speak to a group of former executives of the Herald and Weekly Times as a guest of their "44 Club" which derived its name from the former address of the *Herald* building – 44 Flinders Street, Melbourne. The theme of my talk was Serendipity or the importance of being at the "right place at the right time". It seems we all have similar stories to tell.

After my talk I returned to sit next to Ron Casey (former

general manager and mentor from HSV7). He then turned to face me saying he too had *his* moment of serendipity. Obviously eager to tell me I grabbed a paper napkin to take notes. Casey rarely ever opened up about his private thoughts until now it seemed...

It was in June 1972, the Australian Council of Trade Union's had just placed a ban on all French shipping as a protest against French nuclear testing in the Pacific. ACTU President Bob Hawke was also facing intense pressure to ban the forthcoming Springbok Rugby tour in protest against apartheid. That week the West Australian Transport Workers Union and Hotel Industry workers voted to accept the Rugby players in Perth opening the way for their controversial tour. There were also early rumours suggesting Bob Hawke was considering entering politics and possibly running for leadership of the Labor Party. However, reports of his heavy drinking and womanizing, were not only running counter to his political aspirations but were placing considerable strain on his family life.

Against this background of breaking news and the growing public interest in Bob Hawke, HSV7 Melbourne invited him onto its Sunday night current affair show *This Week*. The program was loosely based around the traditional *Meet The Press* format hosted by newsreader Brian Naylor and featuring a panel of staff reporters and journalists from the Melbourne *Herald* interviewing newsmakers of the week.

I remembered the show well. Every Sunday night we gathered in the boardroom around 7 o'clock, fed ourselves from several plates of sandwiches and prepared to ply our guests with a modicum of drink from the bar fridge. It was a traditional Sunday night routine. However, on this particular night we found the fridge had been locked by Ron Casey who feared a repeat of a previous incident where all the liquor had been consumed – mainly by the news staff. It took an enterprising journalist who removed the hinges and opened the fridge paving the way for a remarkable series of events. The program was scheduled to be recorded around 8 o'clock and then replayed after the Sunday night movie, which varied from 10.30 onward, depending on the length of the movie.

Bob Hawke arrived accompanied by his wife Hazel. He was already quite primed for the occasion. This was a man who had earned an entry in the Guinness Book of Records for the time it took to skol a yard of ale. On his arrival he appeared to have just competed in another attempt at that record. The last thing he needed was another drink but it was the first thing he was offered despite a protest from his wife Hazel. This immediately brought a strong rebuke by Hawke who snapped in a withering tirade, immediately reducing Hazel to tears. Humiliated in front of us all she left and was driven back to their Sandringham home by one of our cameramen.

As tension mounted Hawke was led to the studio and a short time later, still on schedule, the opening theme began and Brian Naylor introduced his guest and the panel of interviewers. Throughout the program it was a vintage Hawke, cutting down each questioner in much the same way John Maher would regularly swipe at me:

'What sort of question is that? I would expect more from you... You call yourself a journalist... you're not a journalist's bootlace!' And that was just for openers!

However, the program never made it to air and now, 28 years later, Ron Casey who was station manager at the time was prepared to reveal what had happened. How he may have helped save the political career of Bob Hawke and ironically cemented his own future as a legend of television. He began...

'*It was Sunday, 4 June, 1972… I was sitting at home that night when a call came through around 9.30 from the producer of* This Week, *Sandra Fitzell. She simply said, "Ron, I have a problem. The program is complete but our guest Mr Hawke is pissed and he has slandered and slurred his way through the show and I don't know what to do? Naylor is demanding we run it, but I have my doubts," she said.*

Casey knew it would be good television, but fearing the implications for the station and for Bob Hawke himself, he made a decision and ordered the program be destroyed and arranged for a movie to replace it.

The following day Casey received a phone call from a very contrite Bob Hawke.

'*Ron,' he said. 'I want to apologise for my behaviour last night and thank you for the action you took. I owe you one, I really do.*'

Three months later, Ron Casey left for Munich. The Seven Network had agreed to shared rights (pool-shoot) of the Munich Olympics in Australia, which would be a ground-breaking television event. Millions of dollars had been invested and sponsors were paying record prices, as this was the first Olympic Games to be streamed around the world in vivid colour. Colour had not yet been launched in Australia but special arrangements had been made at the HSV7 studios in South Melbourne to accommodate sponsors and media buyers to witness this historic live colour feed before it was re-transmitted in black and white.

However, a short time before the Olympic athletes began to file out into the stadium, Melbourne's postal technicians went on strike and the video link from Munich was shut down. There was total panic from the master control centre in Melbourne to the

Olympic broadcast centre in Munich. The only man to remain calm was Ron Casey.

'I simply picked up the phone in Munich and called Bob Hawke at his home in Melbourne. "Bob," I said, "I have a problem… and you owe me a favour." According to Casey, Hawke slammed the phone down, jumped into his car and drove directly into the city. He was seen bursting into the telecommunication centre where he physically pushed the plug into the socket himself. That action connected the Olympic studios in Munich to the television studios in South Melbourne with just minutes to spare. HSV7 did not lose one second of the opening coverage or one dollar of sponsors' fees.

In Munich, Ron Casey was not alone in breathing a sigh of relief. Judy Patching, the Olympic *chef de mission* and Victoria's Olympic team boss was so impressed with Casey's calm reaction and the smooth coverage of the opening ceremony he responded by giving him his personal phone number.

'Judy scribbled a number on the back of a business card and literally stuffed it in the top pocket of my reefer jacket. "Call me," he said. "Any time. It's the direct number to my room." But then I forgot all about it.'

Two nights later Casey says he was woken by the phone in his hotel room. It was news producer Sandra Fitzell back in Melbourne.

'First thing she said was, "What can you tell me of the Olympic massacre?" The fact is I knew nothing about the events that had unfolded near my hotel. Events that would change my life.'

Tuesday, 5 September, shortly after 4 a.m., eight heavily armed members of Black September, a faction of the PLO, scaled the perimeter fence and ran towards the building housing Israeli games officials.

A short time later they stormed their apartment, capturing a number of Israeli athletes. When several athletes fought back the Palestinians then opened fire.

'I sat there stunned as she told me that Arab terrorists had killed several Israeli athletes and others were being held hostage. I told her I would call her back, and then hung up. I was out of bed in a shot and fumbling for that business card Judy Patching had pushed into my pocket. I then called his number and he responded almost immediately. "Come straight round to my room, I have the sole eyewitness with me.'"

British silver medallist swimmer, David Wilke and two of his swimming teammates had been returning to the Olympic Village after celebrating a night on the town. They witnessed two people in tracksuits climbing over the perimeter fence and assumed they were athletes. It was the start of the attack.

Another eyewitness Israeli survivor Shaul Ladany described how his roommate woke him claiming that Weinberg had been shot and killed. Ladany dressed and left the room, "I was half expecting to see a war zone outside our apartment. The first person I spotted was a member of the terror squad wearing what I thought was an Australian hat ... he was talking to four of the unarmed village guards and a lady who was pleading, "You must let the Red Cross in; be humane," she said. The terrorists simply replied, "The Jews are not humane.'"

These eyewitness quotes were exactly what hundreds of international and local reporters covering the 1972 Olympics were seeking.

Meanwhile in negotiations that followed, the terrorists demanded the release of 230 Palestinians jailed in Israel and Germany. In a failed rescue bid, nine Israeli hostages died along with five terrorists and one West German policeman. The Black September assault and subsequent failed rescue attempt was played out on television around the world becoming the first terrorist attack reported in real time. However, the behind the scenes hunt for those exclusive eyewitness scoops was won by Melbourne based sports commentator and HSV7 station manager Ron Casey. He assumed the duties of a journalist by acquiring the first eyewitness accounts.

From that moment on Casey says he never looked back. He cemented his reputation as an Olympic commentator not just in Australia but also on the world stage. Recognised by IOC delegates as a media player with clout, he not only went on to cover nine more Olympic Games but also became part of the official team that lobbied strongly for the Melbourne Olympic bid in Tokyo. He became President of the North Melbourne Football Club and served three terms as chair on the Board of the Federation of Commercial Television stations and was awarded an MBE.

After returning from Munich in 1972 he was promoted from Station Manager to General Manager of HSV7. However, in summing up his extraordinary story, he simply laughed.

'In all probability it would never have happened had Bob Hawke not got pissed.'

According to former HSV7 program manager Gary Fenton, there was one other act Casey performed in Munich that virtually sealed his television future as titular head of the Seven Network. It was his decision to broadcast the Munich Memorial service the night after the massacre – a decision rejected by his counterpart at ATN7 in Sydney. Ted Thomas argued the service would never rate and made the personal decision to dump the memorial service from their schedule and replace it with the feature movie *Sons of Katie Elder*.

In Melbourne, the Munich Memorial became the highest rating program of the year while in Sydney the movie was a total disaster. According to Fenton, 'It was a decision Casey never let Ted Thomas forget.' Ron Casey's success in covering the Olympics stood for ten years. While Munich may have helped establish him as the Network Olympic presenter, it was his role over the controversial Moscow Olympics that cemented his reputation as a tough corporate leader…

MOSCOW OLYMPICS

Three days before New Year's Eve 1979, Russian tanks and troops rolled into Afghanistan. So began a fateful incursion that would cost over two million lives and embroil the Soviet Union in a ten-year war, a war they wouldn't win. The repercussions were felt worldwide and nowhere would the situation be more resolutely tested than at the studios of HSV7 in Melbourne.

The US branded the invasion as the greatest threat to world peace since the Second World War. The Western world was united in its condemnation and leading the charge was Australia's PM Malcolm Fraser. The looming Olympics in Moscow suddenly became a political issue. Pressure was being applied on local Olympic Federations to boycott the Moscow Games. The US, Canada, West Germany and Japan bowed to the pressure and announced they would not be sending teams.

The Australian Olympic Federation was split down the middle. Some were angry at what they perceived was the PM's meddling in sport. Others believed it was morally wrong to recognise so prominently, a nation that was so brutally invading another. The community was polarised. Even the athletes became involved with Olympic veteran Herb Elliott urging Australia to boycott while swimming legend Dawn Fraser warned a boycott would destroy the Olympic movement. Eventually it came down to a vote.

Olympic chiefs would meet to make a final decision on whether Australian athletes would attend the Moscow Games.

The day arrived and nowhere was the tension greater than it was at HSV7 in Melbourne. Ron Casey paced the corridors. His face flushed, he scratched his already inflamed and blotchy skin. He nervously checked teleprinter reports, constantly accompanied by the equally nervous executives Howard Gardner and Gary Fenton. Casey had more to lose than most as he personally had negotiated an exclusive rights deal; the first exclusive rights for the Seven network to broadcast an Olympic Games. It was an agreement secured in a hitherto unreported deal and a secret tip off by an unknown member of the Australian Olympic Committee. Casey had received word that Kerry Packer was about to fly to Moscow in a bid to secure an exclusive deal for the Nine network. Within hours of being tipped off Casey flew to Moscow out-manoeuvring Packer at the last moment. Such was the intensity and interest in the decision for Australia to compete in the Moscow Olympics that the vote was to be broadcast live on the ABC. Millions of dollars in network sponsorship was at stake. Millions of dollars in technology had been assembled. The nation may have been divided, but Channel Seven was totally in support of the Games going ahead. Never had so much interest been concentrated on a single radio broadcast. Then as the vote was finally announced, there was an almighty scream from Casey's office, followed by pandemonium and celebrations among the staff. The decision was made 6–5 to go to Moscow.

Within days, Ron Casey received a deputation from PM Malcolm Fraser. The PM arrived at the Station in Dorcas Street, South Melbourne accompanied by Liberal Party President, Tony Eggleton and his Foreign Affairs Minister, Andrew Peacock. According to Sales Manager Howard Gardner and Finance Director Gerry Carrington, the meeting lasted just 90 seconds.

Malcolm Fraser had been politely ushered into Casey's office. They immediately dispensed with all pleasantries and the PM began with what all described was a well-rehearsed dialogue. Fraser cut straight to the chase, outlining the morality of recognising the Soviet regime, which he said was carrying out a brutal scorched earth campaign against innocent civilians in Afghanistan. He barely took breath as he continued his support for a boycott and the need to join the other Western nations, which 'had so rightly and justly decided to boycott the Games to show support for the oppressed people of Afghanistan'. He was about to continue when Ron Casey interrupted.

'With all due respect Mr Prime Minister, may I suggest you run the country and I will run this television station.'

There was a pause. With a look of almost stunned disbelief in his eyes, Fraser then turned on his heels and stormed out with Eggleton and Peacock right behind. That night Casey, Fenton and Gardner went out to celebrate the outcome of the vote. They booked a table at Maxim's restaurant in Toorak Road, South Yarra. Around 11 p.m. after most guests had left, the door of a private room, adjoining the main dining room suddenly opened. Striding through the door was the PM and several guests. Malcolm Fraser immediately walked up to Ron Casey and placed a bottle of port on the table.

'Ron,' he said, 'I'm just dropping Tammie home. We are only just around the corner; I'll be back in five minutes.'

Keeping to his word he returned and while they spoke briefly about the day's events and the boycott vote, they drank until 3 a.m. Neither side backed down from their position, but Casey said he had a much greater appreciation for the PM than earlier in the day.

Casey left a legacy in sport and the television industry of which he was most proud. I have always believed it's not *what* you know it's *who* you know in life and I too was so proud to have been a part of his many contributions.

The last time I saw Case (as we affectionately called him) was at our luncheon together in October 1999. He died on 19 June the following year.

SIX DEGREES OF NEWS

The theory of "Six Degrees" or the "Human Webb" is that anyone on the planet can be connected to any other person through a chain of acquaintances involving no more than five intermediaries. Today, due to the technical advances in communication and travel, our friendship networks have grown larger and span greater distances than ever before. The modern world is "shrinking" as the social distance becomes smaller making the hypothesis of Six Degrees even more exciting. While a series of scientific and mathematical applications have failed to prove the theory of Six Degrees, this personal experience is difficult to ignore.

WEDNESDAY, 3 MARCH 2004

There was a quiet knock on my office door. For many of my 53 years in media I had worked against and alongside the man who had just walked into my office – cameraman Morrie Pilens.

It was a social visit by the retired Pilins and not totally unexpected as I had conveyed an open invitation to call any time he was in town. I was continually adding details to my memoirs and had requested an interview with the veteran cameraman who had contributed so much of his own life covering news. He entered with a slight limp (assisted by a walking stick) but apart from that he looked great. His blue eyes sparkled and his head literally shone reflecting a healthy tan from a recent holiday with his wife.

'Good to see you again,' he said in his familiar clipped accent as he pulled out a seat to sit on the opposite side of my desk. He had mellowed since his retirement in 1990. There was no sign of his caustic wit that we all attributed to his wartime legacy from the dark side. There was still the raised skin blemish that protruded from his head, which he wore as a sort of badge of honour having never made any effort to have it surgically removed. I grabbed a tape recorder and with his permission switched it on and left it running. Like Ron Casey and many others I had worked alongside, Pilens contributions were also part of our television history and a small part of my life.

Modrus 'Morrie' Pilens had just turned 14 when German forces invaded his homeland of Latvia driving out the Bolsheviks who had ruled in brutal fashion for over a year.

That hot summer Sunday in 1941 thousands of his countrymen stood on the streets of the capitol Riga tossing flowers as a welcome to the forces of the Third Reich. Sadly it didn't take long before they realised the victors would become as brutal as the vanquished. Within three years, one in ten Latvians would be killed while others, were conscripted into the German Army to fight the Russians. Pilens may have been too young to realise the significance of the German invasion but not young enough to avoid its consequence. He was one of those conscripted, although his weapon would become a camera rather than a gun.

Within a year of the invasion young Pilens was enlisted into the German SS and then placed under Dr Joseph Goebbels, Hitler's minister of propaganda, to be trained as a newsreel cameraman. His only credential was having worked at the office of Riga Films as an assistant.

'It was a simple case of logistics,' he said. 'We were losing so many cameramen at the fronts they needed to turn us over fast.'

After his initial intensive training course in Berlin he was attached to the 6th Latvian War Correspondent Corp where over the next four years Pilens says he saw more 'life and death' than most veteran soldiers serving a lifetime in wars. He not only survived the German invasion of his homeland but the most appalling conditions on the Polish and Russian fronts. In 1945, he was determined to survive the fall of Berlin. Defeated and in total despair Berliners were sheltering – not so much from the allied planes above – but from the sheer terror on the streets around them. In those last few days many described lying in bombed out buildings listening in fear as savage street-to-street and house-to-house fighting raged around the outskirts of the city. They described night time as the worst, with the guttural screams of looting Russians. It was a drunken violent killing spree of revenge for Stalingrad. Mornings revealed the carnage and not just from the allied bombing or advancing Russians; bodies also hung from trees and lamp posts as a warning from remnants of the notorious SS, rounding up German soldiers in hiding and executing them as traitors.

Finally, still wearing the tattered uniform of the SS, Pilens fled the besieged city escaping to a town he fondly remembers for a 'stockpiled cellar full of plundered wine', which he shared with other similar survivors. The wine, he said, became a bargaining tool for the advancing troops of the US 9th division who had surrounded the town and sent in an advance patrol to scout for any opposition. There was none – just a group of desperate souls eager to survive the war and prepared to exchange their cellar full of wine for their lives. Pilens remembers being escorted through advancing Soviet lines by those American forces but – perhaps because of that wine – he was a little vague as to how he was finally handed over to the British. The British soon determined that Pilens fell into the category of many Latvian and other Baltic prisoners who had been conscripted into the SS and as such were not party to the criminal SS, which saved him from almost certain execution.

After a brief period of internment, described as a period of "de Nazification", he was seconded to the British Control Commission Film Unit based in the historic German town of Blomberg. Occasionally, I had to interrupt Pilens as details blurred or I simply lost my way trying to keep up with his incredible tales of survival. However, something he said about Blomberg triggered a distant personal memory, but as he was on a roll I let him continue talking.

That night, after reading the news, I drove down to my mother's nursing home in the outer Melbourne suburb of Carrum Downs where she was living out her final years. My father Hugh, her lifetime soulmate, had died from cancer some 20 years earlier.

On the top shelf of a single wardrobe, too high for her to reach in her frail condition, lay a large cardboard box. Inside it contained her most treasured possessions, pictures of children, grandchildren even great-grandchildren. But in a separate package worn with age to sepia brown, along with a collection of wartime medals, were several beautiful hand-written letters.

It was not the first time I had read them, but it was the first time with the knowledge I now held. They reflected the love and loneliness of a serving soldier. I was already familiar with his post-war task of forcing shell-shocked Germans to view atrocities committed in their name through a series of films – films shot by a German cameraman who was part of their team. The letters were marked "Blomberg 1945"...

It was the early morning of 7 May 1945 when my father the British signalman intercepted a cable from Field Marshal Keitel ordering all German units of the Army, Navy, Air Force and the SS to cease-fire.

The surrender had not been unexpected but the rush of adrenalin on actually seeing it in reality had more of an effect on Hughie than he ever expected. Heart pounding with emotion he ripped the cable from the teleprinter and ran from inside the converted military van and across the car park to his commanding officer being billeted in the adjoining hotel. He thought of his wife and me his baby son and the reunion that awaited his discharge.

However, Hughie's role in post-war Germany was far from over. His background in British teleprinters set him apart from his colleagues and particularly the Americans who lacked that communication expertise which was about to become invaluable. Shattered that his discharge had been revoked, he was ordered to proceed to the British controlled sector of Berlin to help establish a communication centre in the historic German town of Blomberg.

While judicial efforts were handed over to local authorities to restore a semblance of order, the US and British military launched a program to de Nazify the entire German population through control of local media. Their aim was to prove beyond any possible doubt or challenge, that crimes against humanity had been committed and that the German people, not just the Nazis and SS, bore responsibility.

In order to implement that charter, a number of films were quickly produced with much of the material acquired from captured German newsreel cameramen now under the directions of the Allied Control Council.

Morrie Pilens was one of those cameramen who would become involved in a number of award winning 35mm documentaries such as *War in Europe, March of Time* and *Displaced Persons.*

Meanwhile, Hughie's task was not only to establish a broad based communication link with the international sectors surrounding Soviet controlled Berlin but also to organise the screenings of those films being produced at Blomberg. Neither Pilens nor Hughie would ever realise the synchronicity of their joint tasks or how they, directly and indirectly, would eventually influence television news in Australia.

Six months later Hughie received his long awaited discharged. He was demobbed and returned home to an emotional reunion with his family living in Stockport, Cheshire. In 1948 Pilens migrated to Australia. After several years of frustration, he finally picked up a camera and made a new start freelancing for Channel Seven in Melbourne, working under the station's news director, John Maher.

In 1952 our family migrated to Melbourne where coincidently Dad also picked up a camera – the revolutionary Polaroid that developed its own picture. Within eight years of arriving in Australia he became a TV household name – Roly Poly – taking happy audience snaps on Channel Seven's *Happy Show* with his Polaroid camera.

In 1964 Pilens was hired to establish a television news department for the impending launch of Melbourne's third commercial television station ATV0 (Channel Ten) where he stayed as senior news cameraman for almost 30 years.

And so it evolves that 70 years after WWII, those two adversaries, a former SS cameraman and a British signalman who both worked on the same project in the post-war German town of Blomberg, were my respected colleague and my father.

In 2013 as I stepped down from Network Ten, 89-year-old Morrie Pilens was living in retirement with his wife Ruth in one of the leafy suburbs of Melbourne. Like my father, he never hid his past nor ever had any reason to. Neither man to my knowledge was personally aware of the other – either in post-war Berlin or in Australian television. It was just another example of the many unexplained moments of serendipity that formed a familiar pattern throughout my life as a newsman.

CHAPTER 15

BLACK SATURDAY
– HISTORY REPEATS

*On 16 February 1983 around 180 bushfires swept across Victoria.
The day became infamously known as "Ash Wednesday".*

*On 7 February 2009, exactly one week short of the twenty-sixth
anniversary of Ash Wednesday, Victoria erupted again in what
history has recorded as "Black Saturday".*

Tragedy is like a black cloud that strikes indiscriminately. None of us are immune. On the same day our son James was diagnosed with life threatening cancer (lymphoma) my colleague and former GTV9 newsreader Brian Naylor lost his son Mathew in a light plane crash. Both networks moved to protect us from excessive media intrusion. Our son would survive, but tragedy, like history, has a habit of repeating and no one could have prepared us or protected us from the next black cloud.

FEBRUARY 2009

The year 2009 began under a cloud of political and economic uncertainty. World share-markets had suffered their biggest crash since the great depression. The ripple that began with property and housing caught up in the US sub-prime crisis spread like a tsunami around the world under the acronym GFC (Global Financial Crisis).

MONDAY, 26 JANUARY 2009

Melbourne endures a freak heat wave.

WEDNESDAY, 28 JANUARY

Temperature reaches 43 degrees.

THURSDAY, 29 JANUARY

Temperature peaks at 44 degrees.

FRIDAY, JANUARY 30

Temperature hits a record 45 degrees.

By the end of the week our news ratings had risen accordingly with the temperatures, garnering one of our biggest audiences of all time.

Oztam ratings showed Ten News at 5 p.m. was viewed by more than 500,000 Victorians. (a 21 per cent market share). That was one of the few things we would celebrate.

Tuesday night I removed my jacket during the evening bulletin, suggesting to the viewers that some had taken exception to being overly dressed in such conditions. No one had really complained. It was just a little theatre.

The following night I read the entire bulletin in shirtsleeves. By Friday, Channel Nine's Peter Hitchener shed his jacket too and it all became a light-hearted distraction. There would be some slight relief at the start of the following week.

MONDAY, 2 FEBRUARY 2009

The week began with Rafael Nadal celebrating his extraordinary win over Roger Federer in a five set final at the Australian Open. Our numbers fell back a little but we still recorded a healthy audience peaking at 340,000.

TUESDAY, 3 FEBRUARY 2009

PM Rudd announced a $42 billion stimulus package, which was dissected live during our one-hour bulletin and analysed by the experts.

WEDNESDAY, 4 FEBRUARY 2009

The Opposition Leader Malcolm Turnbull took a high risk gamble announcing that the Liberals would block the package in the Senate. The Senate was then put on notice for an unscheduled sitting to consider the move. They were not to know it at the time but that sitting would turn into a massive outpouring of grief and condolences.

THURSDAY, 5 FEBRUARY 2009

The family of four-year-old Darcy Freeman spoke of their shock and disbelief at reports that her father could have thrown his own daughter from the upper span of Melbourne's Westgate Bridge.

FRIDAY, 6 FEBRUARY 2009

All eyes were back on the weather. The Victorian Bureau of Meteorology had issued an ominous alert.

We are heading into the most threatening weekend in the state's history.

A short time later, the Premier John Brumby reiterated that Victoria was facing an even 'worse-case scenario than Ash Wednesday'. Comparisons to Ash Wednesday had always concerned me, like the boy who cried wolf. During our 5 p.m. news in a live cross to the CFA, I questioned this often-used analogy with the Deputy Chief Fire Officer Greg Esnouf. Esnouf dismissed this, making it abundantly clear that temperatures would be hotter, the winds would be stronger and the humidity would be even lower than on Ash Wednesday.

'Given the record temperatures Victoria has just endured,' he warned, 'the state is indeed facing its worst crisis ever.'

The warning could not have been made any clearer. A further analogy to Ash Wednesday was drawn between the freak heat wave conditions we had just endured in Melbourne and the freak dust storm, which struck one week before Ash Wednesday. So would history repeat?

After the news we all adjourned for Friday night drinks where the topic of Melbourne's weather continued. I assumed decisions had been put in place for this impending disaster but then I should have remembered the adage that "assumption is the mother of all stuff-ups".

SATURDAY, 7 FEBRUARY 2009

The day dawned with a certain dread. Temperatures quickly rose, hitting 39 degrees well before the predicted call of midday and wind gusts exceeded the predicted strength. Humidity fell well below the expected low. By mid-afternoon as we hit an all-time high of 46.3 degrees, much of Victoria was already on fire.

Early that morning, the first reporter arrived at Ten's Como News Centre in South Yarra around 7 a.m. Rikhal Eberli was one of our most junior male reporters having experienced just two years on the road. We were still operating on a Christmas holiday roster system under the directions of our head office in Sydney. Many senior staff were on a forced break. Saturday's chief of staff was one of Ten's most senior reporters but he had been assigned weekend duties on the COS desk.

Eberli and his crew were dispatched to Labertouche in

Gippsland after reports the fire in the Bunyip State Forest had broken containment lines during the night and could pose the most serious risk. They arrived round 9 a.m. and immediately began filming the water bombers attacking flames nearby.

Around 11 a.m. they returned to McGuffie farm, which was seen as a prime target for the flames and attempted to feed out their material using an FTP (file transfer system) on a laptop computer. Relying on a system that takes 45 minutes to send five minutes of footage took up valuable time. The laptop system required the vision to be condensed into a computer file before sending. Eberli then began attempting to feed out his material. Around midday the wind suddenly changed whipping up the fires and sending them out in another direction. According to Eberli, 'all hell broke loose.'

Filming the wild fire now roaring away from the farm destroying everything in its path provided new vision that was far better than the previous footage. Attempts were made to send this vision back using the same system, but by that time communications had been severed. Most of the mobile phone and radio towers had been destroyed. By the time the vision eventually found a tower sufficiently strong enough to receive a signal and send it back to Ten, it was so corrupt it was barely usable. It should have been fed up to the chopper but because of the many random breakouts the news helicopter had been diverted elsewhere for aerials.

Relying on a mobile phone card with no signal, the FTP system was totally inadequate and as Eberli later admitted, 'no one really was trained to use it properly anyway'. Back at the station, *Ten News* had only one lot of vision (which had been shot earlier that day). Listening to radio reports of fires breaking out around Melbourne, the chief of staff was becoming increasingly concerned and decided to dispatch a second reporter. She too was an inexperienced junior. Time was running out for Channel

Ten as their news was one-hour before its competitors. More importantly, weekend news was produced out of Sydney.

Across at Seven, news boss Steve Carey had his crews embedded the night before. They were in a position to capture all the breakouts as they happened. And they did. The irony was *Seven News* was now emulating the success of *Ten News* during the 1983 Ash Wednesday fires. Ash Wednesday was the turning point in Ten's struggle for news superiority. In fact, Ash Wednesday has long been attributed to Ten's winning success through the '80s.

Across at GTV9, Director of News Michael Venus had not only embedded his crews the day before but had been personally supervising events and feeding out their stories by way of Satellite News Gathering (SNG) equipment. Channel Ten Melbourne had no SNG and to require one from Sydney took at least 24 hours notice. A request had never been put in. By 5 p.m. Victoria was exploding and as our news went to air many of our viewers who had been following the crisis on radio exploded with frustration at our coverage.

> QUOTE *(Nimeton @ Feb 7 2009, 05:44 P.M.)*
> *The coverage was quite pathetic actually – for fires that are still currently burning out of control one pre-packaged, generic story and a brief phone interview, after the first ad break just doesn't cut it.*

> QUOTE *(kimberb @ Feb 7 2009, 05:58 P.M.)*
> *Disappointed Ten can't produce a local bulletin. There is so much news happening within the state of Victoria, the fires are spreading, trains, road and freeway closures, power outages and all this on the hottest day in Melbourne's history! 46.3 degrees! Instead we*

Melbourne viewers are seeing pictures of kids in Sydney sliding down water slides and eating ice creams!! Come on Ten lift your game and start delivering local editions when needed!!!!

Viewer frustration paled against mine. Sitting at home I was convinced the damage to our news brand would be irreparable. I was wrong. Late Saturday afternoon, Director of News Dermot O'Brien flew back from a holiday in Tasmania. He immediately drove directly to the station in South Yarra and took personal control. It was too late for recriminations – they would have to wait.

The lesson in catch up began with a call to the network's news boss, Jim Carol, in Sydney. Carol was already on the warpath – not because of the poor Melbourne coverage but because they had failed to carry any story of fires burning out of control in NSW. He agreed with O'Brien that weekend networking was a "dead weight around our necks" but that was a management decision out of their control. Carol conceded the coverage was disappointing but added, 'Given Victoria had hit a record heat day (which was covered briefly), NSW was battling serious fires (but had no pictures) and Queensland was facing a serious flood crisis (which featured a full coverage), all stories had some exposure but were restricted by the very nature of a network bulletin.' O'Brien then "negotiated" a Sunday morning five-minute network bulletin leading into the national golf coverage and rang me at home requesting I also host a special one-hour local news Sunday night.

Throughout Sunday morning as light rain fell across Melbourne and temperatures hovered in the low 20s we began the biggest "catch up" of our careers. Reporters began returning with their footage from the front lines including tales of harrowing survival. They also brought with them their own personal horror stories highlighting the growing impact of the tragedy. The full story was still not known. Any feeling of anger at losing Saturday's initiative quickly subsided as disbelief began sweeping through the newsroom. Throughout the day I kept updating the situation hourly as more stories emerged and the mood of the newsroom deepened further with several staff members close to tears.

After Ash Wednesday we drowned our depression at the local pub. In 2009 reporters would receive professional counselling. It was a subdued atmosphere after Sunday night's special bulletin as we gathered around to compare our efforts with Seven and Nine. Channel Seven, following its spectacular coverage on the night of the fires, appeared to have run out of steam handing the initiative to Nine who presented an outstanding coverage. However, the unimaginable and most devastating news had not yet emerged.

Shortly after 6.30 p.m. I had only just reached home when O'Brien rang. 'Brace yourself for some really bad news,' he said. 'Brian Naylor is missing at his Kinglake property.'

Naylor was a news legend in Melbourne: former news anchor at GTV9, my former colleague during our years at Seven, a competitor and a good friend. Fears were also being held for his wife Moiree, both of whom were last seen on their property at Kinglake just before the fires raced through.

I hung up, looked at Pauline and repeated my conversation with O'Brien. We were both standing in silence when Nine flashed a report: *The body of his beloved wife Moiree has just been found.*

They were still searching for Brian.

Holding back tears I immediately rang our former colleague and close friend David Johnston who had retired to live in Bendigo. The irony was the three of us were due to be playing golf this weekend but cancelled at the last moment due to the weather conditions. Johnston answered on the first ring and I assumed he had been standing near the phone waiting for the same news I had just heard. In fact, Johnston was totally unaware of the tragedy and had been trying to ring Naylor to tell him he had just become a grandfather again.

'I can't get through to Nails,' he said, 'His phone keeps ringing out!'

'You haven't heard then?' I asked.

'Heard what?'

'I'm sorry mate but there are fears that Nails may have been caught in the fires at Kinglake.' I then told him of the Channel Nine newsflash concerning Moiree.

There was silence on the other end. 'I'll call you back,' he said. He didn't.

As I hung up I was reminded again of that terrible day my son James was diagnosed with lymphoma and I thought Johnston had heard and was ringing to commiserate. But he was phoning to tell me Naylor's son Mat had just been killed in a light plane crash on his property and I wondered again at this strange symmetry we shared.

A short time later O'Brien rang back to confirm our worst fears. 'Sorry mate, Brian Naylor is dead. We have a late news service, are you able to do it?'

I said yes and hung up. I still held back the tears but wondered for how long and whether in fact I could actually read a news bulletin. The death of Naylor was not just a personal loss but as one scribe reported, it ended a very personal and professional media era.

Brian Naylor, David Johnston and Mal Walden had all made the transition from radio to television from 3DB to HSV7. All three worked together in the '70s taking Seven News to number one for more than a decade. All three former colleagues then became opponents in the bitter news-war of the '80s during which time their friendships became fractious. All three reunited and signed the truce on Naylor's retirement. In fact, all three were to play golf together on the weekend of Black Saturday.

Sunday night I struggled through the news, my voice occasionally breaking, choking back emotions and wondering how Nine's Peter Hitchener was coping as he too was a close friend and colleague of Naylor's. I went to air from the familiar surrounds of my studio, but Hitchener was presenting live from the scene of the fires just as Naylor had done during Ash Wednesday.

From that night on, the pressure mounted. The grief was relentless. Story followed story, night after night. Never had I been so proud of a news team who were constantly updating the tragedy of those devastating fires. Many were young and some were inexperienced but all showed an incredible ability and rose to an occasion few experienced journalists would ever have to face. They came from behind and caught up. The final death toll reached 173. One hundred and twenty died in a single firestorm. The fires destroyed over 2,030 houses and more than 3,500 structures. Seventy-eight townships suffered horrendously including Kinglake, Marysville, Narbethong, Strathewen and Flowerdale. Houses in the towns of Steels Creek, Humevale, Clonbinane, Wandong, St Andrews, Callignee, Taggerty and Koornalla were also destroyed or severely damaged with fatalities recorded at each location.

By the end of the week, fire victims emerged from a state of shock to one of anger often taking out their frustration on news crews. Many of the journalists themselves were shell-shocked and frustrated, resulting in several angry confrontations.

There is always a very fine line separating a need to report, a need to inform and the need to out-perform our competitors. News editors are well aware that overstepping that line and intruding on shell-shocked traumatised victims can have an enormous detrimental impact in the eyes of armchair viewers. Not since the Beaconsfield mine tragedy on Anzac Day 2006 and the subsequent rescue of miners Todd Russell and Brant Webb 14 days later had such a large gathering of media been drawn to a story of such monumental proportions as Victoria's "Black Saturday". Never had the news competition been so intense as network bosses threw all their available multimillion dollar high tech equipment and their most experienced presenters and journalists into the burnt out areas of Victoria. Aware that a Royal Commission would eventually hand down its findings into the cause and impact of the fires, Oztam ratings were providing us with a more immediate impact of how the TV coverage of the fires was being accepted.

BLACK SATURDAY, 7 FEBRUARY 2009

Ten News recorded an average of 486,000 Victorian viewers in its 5 p.m. news.

Seven at 6 p.m. – 569,000.
Nine at 6 p.m. – 509,000.

SUNDAY, 8 FEBRUARY 2009

Only 281,000 returned to watch Sunday night's news on Ten, such was the reaction to the poor Saturday coverage.

Seven at 6 p.m. – 628,000.
Nine at 6 p.m. – 825,000.

MONDAY, 9 FEBRUARY 2009

Ten News regained its lost viewers attracting 432,000.
   Seven at 6 p.m. – 417,000.
   Nine at 6 p.m. – 557,000.

By the end of that week, Ten had maintained a steady average above 300,000 viewers; Seven slipped while Nine maintained its average of 387,000 viewers, which we privately attributed to the Naylor factor. The ABC performed disappointingly, recording average viewers in the mid 200,000s.

Post-fire summaries by so-called "armchair academics" and TV critics were similar to those of Ash Wednesday. TV crews were accused of intrusion and sensationalism. There were similar claims of news crews breaching roadblocks and entering restricted areas. In both tragedies there were recriminations within our own ranks, with media organisations criticising each other for breaching codes of conduct. On Ash Wednesday 1983, Nine's Brian Naylor was accused of not having the journalistic background to report from the scene of a major news story. Naylor angrily hit back saying a good communicator had as much ability to tell a story as any journalist. In the aftermath of Black Saturday there were similar swipes at high profile presenters. There were those accused of relying too much on auto cues and studio effects to tell their stories:

> *TV stars and news presenters being followed by personal make-up artists like 'shadows in the blackened ruins with their powder puffs and mirrors'.*

Technology had certainly advanced in the 26 years but each night in the aftermath of Black Saturday the respective bulletins all managed to cover the same issues as they did in 1983. However, once the smoke had settled, it was Seven's news, which emerged clearly as Melbourne's top rating service.

Just as *Ten News* had achieved that same level of success in its coverage of Ash Wednesday, Seven emerged from Black Saturday as the most watched news service nationally but particularly in Melbourne. Seven captured the initial outbreaks, the heartbreaking losses and the raw emotion, including that of their own reporter Norm Beaman, fearing his wife Annie had been lost with their home on Mt Disappointment just north of Melbourne. I sat at home putting aside any competitive issues and watched his heart breaking live cross, sharing his frustration and fears. Beaman's live report became the personal focus of Seven's fire coverage. It was graphic, it was live and above all it was personal.

I am very much aware of the difficulty in separating personal feelings when reporting news stories – Balibo, the HSV7 chopper crash and now Black Saturday. One hundred and seventy-three people died in the fires; Brian Naylor was just one – rightly or wrongly because of his profile he became the face of Black Saturday. According to the Royal Commission finding Brian and Moiree, both 78, died while defending the property they had owned at Kinglake West for 33 years. Their home was built on a ridge with land sloping gently down before dropping into a gully. It was a solid brick home with large expanses of glass windows bordering on the Kinglake National Park and boasting spectacular views of Melbourne in the distance. They were both conscious of the need to be equipped in the event of a fire, despite very little vegetation around their home. Their confidence in facing any fire threat was backed up by their fire plan and some of the most modern fire fighting equipment available. But this was no ordinary fire. It arrived mid-afternoon. In a phone call to his daughter Brian reported the fire burning at the top of his driveway and the bottom paddock, but said it appeared to be moving away from his home. The last time his neighbour Barry Johnston saw Brian and Moiree the fire at the bottom of their gully wasn't too bad.

'It was just sort of a grass fire.' At this point Barry suddenly heard a roar from another fire coming up the nearby mountain and was forced to evacuate. He warned Naylor to leave, but as he said, 'He (Brian) could be a stubborn bugger at times.' Around 5 p.m. Moiree spoke to two family members telling her daughter-in-law they were fighting the fire 'but it would be fine'.

Brian spoke to his grandson reassuring him the fire had burnt past the house. That was the last anyone heard or saw them. It was at that moment the wind changed and so too did history.

The bodies of Brian and Moiree were discovered the following day inside the bathroom of their destroyed home. It is the opinion of forensic police that the house ignited as a result of an ember attack on the veranda, the roof or both. In a prophetic eulogy Naylor's former news editor John Sorell said he was not surprised they had died together, '…they were inseparable in life as they were when found, probably in each other's arms'.

Throughout all the personal heartbreak and frustrations of Black Saturday, the one outcome that lifted my spirits was news that Norm Beaman's wife Annie had survived unhurt. His live report subsequently earned Seven a National Press Club Quill Award for "Best News Story of the Year" and if I felt any pride or justification for that recognition it was perhaps because I was a deciding judge.

Television news is a most resilient product and with the right people and the right passion it proves catch-up by journalists can be just as rewarding as a scoop. In some cases the words of philosopher George Santayana have proved to be most prophetic:

Those who don't learn from history are doomed to repeat it.

CHAPTER 16

A YEAR OF REVOLUTION

2011

HEADLINES

Global Financial Crisis
Japanese Tsunami
Osama Bin Laden killed
Cadel Evans wins Tour de France

HITS

Raise Your Glass – Pink
We R Who We R – Ke$ha
Firework – Katy Perry

Television has always attracted high profile media tycoons, however when the largest group of billionaires in Australia gathered together to run a network, the loss they incurred and the incompetence they showed became almost incomprehensible to understand. Unless, of course, you were there!

I first became privy to our News Revolution on an afternoon in July 2010. Ten's chief operating officer and Melbourne manager Kerry Kingston rang me from his office one floor below mine with a simple invitation, 'Do you have a minute, Mal?' Just over one minute later I was in his office. He welcomed me as he scooped up a mint from a bowl on his desk and then offered me the bowl. *What was it,* I thought, *about lolly bowls on the desks of TV executives?*

Kingston sucked his mint as he stood gazing out of his floor to ceiling window overlooking the trendy Chapel Street precinct of South Yarra. He then turned and asked whether I had heard certain rumours.

'No,' I lied. I had become aware of an earlier directive that anyone found spreading rumours would be instantly dismissed regardless of who they were. One rumour had suggested Chairman Nick Falloon was secretly negotiating a management buy-back of the Ten Network. Another rumour had plans to expand the 5 p.m. one-hour news into 90 minutes. I had deliberately not sought clarification of any such speculation so as not to be accused of leaking or spreading information. Kingston accepted my reply then went on to say he needed to know my position regarding my future in television. I had reached more than 40 consecutive years reading news on Melbourne television and retirement was not out the question.

'I will be perfectly honest, I am not considering retirement at this stage.' I then reminded him it was he who had signed my contract and it was he who held the option of extending it if he wished. He quickly moved on.

'Okay then, I'll be open and honest with you. The green light has been given by the board to start up another channel and we intend giving that high definition channel to our younger viewers in the 16 to 39 demographic. This would place the Ten Network in a very strong position with its HD digital channels ahead of the imminent shutdown of the analogue system.'

I was glazing over a little because digits and demographics are not part of my charter. We all knew the network had cornered the youth market. But then, in his next breath, it all became clearer.

'Given there would now be three channels,' he continued, 'Ten (the Mother Channel), One HD (Sport) and now Eleven HD (Youth), there is a need to age Ten over the next two years until analogue is completely switched off. In ageing the "Mother Channel" it is deemed that news would be the product best suited to that particular older demographic.' Kingston then scooped out another mint and continued to explain that it had been put to the board and ticked off at a cost of $30 million. It would later be downgraded to $20 million. Details, he admitted, were sketchy but talks were continuing to hire people best suited for the role they would play.

Now he had my full attention.

'Nothing is written in stone,' he insisted. 'But the most likely format will be keeping the 5 p.m. news intact but more local. At 6 p.m. we plan to network a half-hour news program but it will not be a news service. This will be our hardest to sell as the format would be issue based with a presenter/journalist contributing as commentator.' Iconic Australian names such as Jana Wendt, Ray Martin, Jennifer Byrne and Ian Lesley were mentioned to host this 6 p.m. program. Finally, he dealt the trump card. 'At 6.30 we will introduce a half-hour major *local news* service, requiring a high profile presenter from each capital city to present their separate bulletins to take on the opposition's current affair shows.'

For some time the critics had accused *A Current Affair* and *Today Tonight* of recycling the same old stories — arthritis cures, best meat cuts, supermarket bargains etc. In fact, several weeks earlier the ABC's *Media Watch* program had reported that over a one month period *A Current Affair* and *Today Tonight* ran the same stories on the same night no less than 16 times. Every so often there had been talk of the programs being axed. Now the critics were again describing the current affair shows as looking very tired and vulnerable.

'So the timing for an intelligent alternative we feel is now. Everyone we talk to is saying the same thing and we feel the time is right to take them on. What I suppose I am trying to say is that we would like you to host our local Melbourne bulletin and wondered what your reaction is?'

I assured Kingston that I supported the network's commitment to news, particularly his new commitment to local weekend news. For more than 16 years weekend news had been networked out of Sydney, so I confirmed I was interested.

Finally, he summed up saying he would draw up a whole new contract with new conditions laid out, as he would with up to one hundred other journalists, producers and presenters in the next few weeks. Channel Ten had been first with a one-hour news format, first to bring the news at 6 p.m. and first again at 5 p.m. Now was a new challenge and based on the research Kingston had just outlined it all made pretty good sense to me, all except for one niggling doubt. It always concerned me when management interfered with news. My one doubt was based on the possibility they were expanding the news simply because they had run out of programs and the cupboard was bare. That they were expanding the news was all for the wrong reasons. It was my gut feeling, nothing more. I sat there sucking my mint and weighing up the options.

The research pointed to two million viewers arriving home every night "after 6 p.m.", having missed the news bulletins on the other channels. Yes, it would be a new challenge and even the slogan of the proposed campaign helped reinforce my decision: *6.30 p.m. news just makes sense.* I left Kingston's office buoyed and very thankful he hadn't asked me to host the national news program at 6 p.m.

And so the News Revolution began. New staff members were soon being hired, contracts were being signed, jack hammers began expanding newsrooms, the promotion started and the excitement around the network was building. Finally, former *60 Minutes* reporter and veteran newsman George Negus was announced as the host of the 6 p.m. program. Everything was all running to plan. But then, exactly 13 weeks after my meeting with Kingston, a counter-revolution was launched and no one saw it coming.

TUESDAY, 19 OCTOBER 2010 – 5 P.M.

The familiar news theme began on cue as co-presenter Helen Kapalos and I swung towards camera one to highlight the main evening stories.

> **Mal:** *Good evening, in Ten News tonight parents seek answers at an inquest into the fatal police shooting of troubled teen Tyler Cassidy.*
> **Helen:** *Security questions amid claims guards played cricket before drug kingpin Carl Williams was murdered in jail.*
> **Mal:** *And police hunt two men who tried to abduct a 17-year-old girl in Craigieburn.*

It was not a big news day but as we went to air at 5 p.m. a big story *was* breaking – a story that would impact directly on all of us at the network. There was also a certain irony the story was being broken by the online arm of *The Australian* newspaper. Given that technology was about to drive our news at Ten into new areas of expansion, it was somewhat galling that technology from the print media was scooping us.

Until then no one was remotely aware of the events unfolding. Even the communication minister Stephen Conroy was unaware that James Packer had launched a surprise takeover bid of the Ten Network. The stock market had just shut down for the day when first details emerged of Packer's $245 million raid securing 15.6 per cent of the company's shares. The news struck like a giant tsunami, whipping up waves of uncertainty through an industry of people who already walk a very thin line between ego and insecurity. By the time we had wrapped up our nightly news that insecurity was running rampant.

Totally unaware of these events, I walked into the newsroom after the bulletin. Phones were ringing, messages were being texted, calls were being made to contacts both in and outside the TV industry, but no further details were known other than "James Packer had emerged as the largest shareholder possibly with a controlling interest in the network".

Ten's CEO Grant Blackley was driving home from work in Sydney when his phone '…lit up like a Christmas tree. I got about five calls and five emails in the space of a minute,' he later recalled. 'It took us about 12 minutes, I think, to confirm that it was James Packer.'

But the big question remained – what were his intentions?

The Ten board had just announced its revolutionary $20 million plan to expand its news service and introduce a new HD Channel. Many senior executives had put their jobs on the line in backing this project while many journalists, producers and staff had already been hired. Like Blackley, the takeover announcement stunned us all.

THE CHALLENGE

The following morning media analysts and business gurus were all quoting unconfirmed Packer connections and with each story came the "same" quotes:

> *Mr Packer is concerned about Ten's cost base and management structure and multi-channel strategy, including the network's plans to expand their news service...*
>
> *Packer will press for the broadcaster to return to a low-cost strategy, focused on the 18-39 viewers demographic.*

Each story, from every news source around Australia, contained identical phrases, which raised concerns that someone was deliberately spreading this information from a prepared script. Some within Ten believed it was a conspiracy, claiming those to benefit most from this destabilising information were from the opposition – so they blamed Seven and Nine. But no one was sure. Everyone was speculating and feeding an insatiable appetite of insecurity.

> *James Packer set to wield axe... Fears for expanded news services on Ten.... Chairman Nick Falloon to be boned again by a Packer... Packer eyes digital sports channel for Sky News.*

SATURDAY, 22 OCTOBER 2010

The share raid was reported to have risen to $280 million with almost 18 per cent of shares in Packer's hands – proving you don't have to buy a network to take control – just become its largest shareholder.

How similar, I thought, was this feeling to the uncertainty surrounding Channel Ten as it emerged from receivership in 1992 when Kerry Packer was believed to have encouraged mates such as John Singleton and Robert Whyte to join the Canadian CanWest consortium. The counter revolutionaries to that plan openly questioned a conflict of interest involving Packer attempting to ensure Ten remained a low cost, weak competitor to his dominant Channel Nine. James Packer was now poised to become Ten's biggest shareholder and similar questions of conflict of interest were again being raised.

James Packer may have divested his interest in Nine but he still owned 49.67 per cent of Consolidated Media Holdings, which owned 25 per cent of Foxtel and 50 per cent of FOX Sports. Seven and Nine were both part owners of SKY News.

There was also James Packer's friendship with Nine's CEO David Gyngell. This was not my problem. My problem lay in the future of our news service, which was about to be expanded, and we were reading unsubstantiated reports that Packer would oppose it. Packer remained tight lipped on his intentions but the stories kept circulating, as did the same phrases:

Packer threatens to wield the axe … Concerned about Ten's expansion of news… Return to a low-cost strategy, focused on the 18-39 viewers demographic…

COUNTER CHALLENGE

One of the most disturbing features during those first few days was the silence from Ten.

Not one word of explanation, encouragement or reassurance was issued from management as they hunkered down to assess their own positions. Finally, at the end of the first week of uncertainty, they emerged a little shell-shocked but more confident. The confidence came as they unveiled a net profit for the 12 months to August 31 of $150 million, a reversal from a net loss of $89.4 million in the previous corresponding period.

Suddenly revenue had risen by 12 per cent while group revenue lifted by 10 per cent, suggesting that the Ten-management team was on the right track.

'So,' they argued, 'if it isn't broke, don't fiddle with it.'

They then launched a counter attack defending their plans to expand their news arguing that news was "highly efficient programming". International productions, they argued, cost Network Ten around $100,000 per hour, while local productions were quoted up to $450,000 per hour. News on the other hand, cost just $75,000 an hour.

Ten's confidence in expanding its successful news to draw an older audience also "made sense", they said, coinciding with a Nielsen survey released that same week in the US. According to the US data, the average audience of all four major US Broadcasters was now older than ever.

Next year in 2011, members of the baby boomers (that massive post-war generation born from 1946-1964) will do an amazing thing – turn 65. US networks must reconsider their targeted younger 16-39 year old demographics.
– Nielsen research

This was supported by another survey that week which confirmed: *Those baby boomers were the group with the biggest disposable incomes.* The current management was also aware of a similar shift in demographics in Australia and was using the same argument in its bid to justify expanding our news. Their argument flew in the face of James Packer's intended plans to 'return Ten to a low-cost strategy, focused on the younger viewer demographic'. Ten was also looking to convince Packer not to oppose the news expansion. However, they were not as confident with the 6 p.m. national news hosted by George Negus. Throughout the history of commercial television the skeletons of prime time network news services have never been far from the surface.

THE RISKS

In 1974 Nine's news director Gerald Stone launched the ill-fated *News Centre Nine* concept with Peter Hitchener in Melbourne and Brian Henderson in Sydney. Rivalry between the Melbourne and Sydney newsrooms along with various technical breakdowns saw it sink in the ratings, as did the ABC's *The National*, which started and suffered a similar fate ten years later.

In 1987, *Seven's News* in Melbourne dropped to a near asterisk on the perception it was networked out of Sydney after the Fairfax takeover debacle. Ten had once considered a prime time network news service but pulled out just before it was announced. Melbourne presenter David Johnston was anointed with the task of heading that bulletin out of Sydney.

In January 1990, Network Ten's CEO Gary Rice was planning to replace all local bulletins across the network with one national news program. Johnston was planning to move permanently to Sydney and was at the point of purchasing a home when he received a tip that 'something was not quite right at Ten'.

CanWest, who had taken control of the network at the time, were holding grave fears at plans to cancel local news. They felt it would reflect badly on foreign ownership, which they had overcome by a clever arrangement with local syndicates. The national bulletin never eventuated... but it had come very close. Now another attempt was being made to introduce a prime time network news show, albeit a news program rather than a news service, and veteran newsman and former *60 Minutes* reporter George Negus had signed up to host it. Negus had been building a profile on the slow burning success of *The 7pm Project*.

WEDNESDAY, 27 OCTOBER 2010

Our News Revolution took another turn when the Melbourne *Herald Sun* announced that Lachlan Murdoch was also making a move on Ten:

> *Murdoch is seeking to invest up to $155 million in the network by taking up to half of the stake Packer gained after his surprise share raid last week. Murdoch is expected to make the investment through taking a half-share in Packer's private company, Prime Capital, which bought the stake in Ten.*

This marked the second coming of the Murdoch family. In 1979 Rupert Murdoch gained a 50 per cent stake in Ansett Airlines, which saw him take control of ATV0 in Melbourne. However, that too was surrounded in controversy. The broadcasting tribunal refused Rupert's take-over of ATV0 on the grounds that it wasn't in the "public interest" to have Sydney and Melbourne channels owned by a single operator... seemingly oblivious to the fact that the Packers had owned TCN9 and GTV9 for decades. It took two years (1981) before Rupert was finally given the green light to control ATV0 and essentially control of the network.

Now, almost 20 years later, both Lachlan Murdoch and James

Packer were poised to take control of Ten. The revolution was expanding. The battle lines were drawn and first blood was about to flow.

WEDNESDAY, 3 NOVEMBER 2010

The *Australian Financial Review* reported:

> *Billionaires James Packer and Lachlan Murdoch are seeking to oust Ten Network Holdings Ltd Chairman Nick Falloon by highlighting a change in his job title, which means shareholders can no longer vote on his re-election to the board.*

A short time later Chairman Nick Falloon agreed to stand-down. Perhaps his reported pay packet of $2.8 million in the year to 31 August (not including more than $900,000 in bonuses) made his departure a little less painful. Meanwhile, as jackhammers and power drills continued to reshape expanding newsrooms around the country, the network continued its buying spree. News cars, SNG satellite newsgathering equipment, live eye news vans, camera crews, producers, journalists and presenters were all being added to our ambitious news projects.

FRIDAY, 12 NOVEMBER 2010

It was announced that Ten's CEO Grant Blackley had his contract renewed for a further two years and we all breathed a collective sigh of relief. The most significant part of that announcement was an endorsement by Lachlan Murdoch:

*This is a positive announcement for the company and will provide
continuity and stability.*

The news project appeared to be firmly back on track and more
importantly morale had been given its greatest boost yet.

MONDAY, 22 NOVEMBER 2010

Australia's richest woman, mining billionaire Gina Rinehart
suddenly swooped on the Ten Network taking 10 per cent
of shares in a move that surprised everyone including Lachlan
Murdoch. It left us all wondering, just how many billionaires
could the network handle?

Bermuda based regional TV billionaire Bruce Gordon had
recently lifted his stake to 14 per cent. Then Gina Rinehart
completed her move acquiring 10.1 per cent, a figure the financial
gurus said prevented anyone making a full takeover bid. Meanwhile,
the power drills continued vibrating through the walls of our
expanding Melbourne newsroom as the computerised pods or
seating arrangements for journalists and producers increased from
41 to 57 – including the addition of a new editing suite.

We wondered whether the Sydney boardroom would also have
to be extended to accommodate so many billionaires.

LET THE REVOLUTION BEGIN

December 2010 revolutions swept across the Middle East and
North Africa creating rebellion, repression and reform in what
became known as the "Arab Spring". Within 12 months the

uprisings brought down leaders in Tunisia, Yemen, Libya, Egypt and created civil unrest in many other neighbouring countries giving inspiration to revolutionaries around the world.

But if revolution is defined as "a movement designed to effect fundamental change or the overthrow of those who oppose that change", then those who planned the News Revolution at Network Ten in Australia failed on both counts.

In launching a News Revolution many would believe a surge of big news stories would be the desired wish of any news producer. However, it proved as disastrous for the victims as it did for our expanded services. The year began with severe flooding across Northern Queensland.

SUNDAY, 2 JANUARY 2011

The floods were described as one of "biblical proportions" the worst in Queensland's history and the rain kept coming. A week later an unexpected flash flood raced through Toowoomba's central business district before devastating communities in the Lockyer Valley.

On Tuesday, 11 January, in the early afternoon, the Brisbane River burst its banks forcing thousands of people to evacuate as water reached the Queensland capital.

FRIDAY, 14 JANUARY 2011

Thousands of Victorians were evacuated as rising floodwaters swept through towns and properties in the northwest of the state. By the end of the month Australians were counting the cost of record rainfall and a terrible toll. Up to 35 people had died as a result of flood-related incidents across the state of Queensland alone.

MONDAY, 24 JANUARY 2011

Channel Ten launched its $20 million news and current affairs revamp. It was dubbed "the biggest TV gamble of the decade". The well-established 5 p.m. bulletin became the launching pad for its new half-hour local news expansion but as the critics had already pointed out:

> *The biggest challenge lay at 6 p.m. with George Negus, a national show described by its host "as a different way of looking at what's going on in this country and the world". This will be pitted against the top rating news services on Seven and Nine presenting what management had already conceded would be a long term effort to establish. Ten is now boasting some high-profile acquisitions for 6 p.m., including award winning investigative journalist Chris Masters as a consultant and Hamish MacDonald lured home following his successful stints at Channel 4 and Al Jazeera.*
> *Six-thirty p.m. will see the introduction of state-based news bulletins with hosts including Mal Walden in Melbourne and Sandra Sully in Sydney. The block will be capped off by the '7pm Project', a more light-hearted look at current events and a slow-burn success story that was a testament to Ten's ability to take a risk and nurture a new concept.*

Our launch day began with a concerted campaign talking it up on Melbourne radio. It was akin to politicians doing the rounds after announcing an election and then battling media speculation over leadership challenges. We were still facing the spectre of a challenge from our new leadership team.

Finally at 6.30, we launched our news. It was not the best news service I had ever read. It was certainly not the best produced bulletin, and not at all helped by a live cross to a senior reporter whose stress level was obviously higher than mine.

Throughout his 40-second live cross he lost his place four times, apologising every ten seconds. Other disappointments included international stories of no relevance to Victorian viewers. One involved the death of a 114-year-old woman in Texas and another featured some graphic flooding in Germany. This was despite a month's intense promotion pointing to a "local news service" with local stories and local issues. Immediately following the news I stormed the production desk complaining bitterly.

'Even I believed it would be local news service with local issues – and I was reading the bloody thing.'

"Local", I was told, meant locally produced.

Four weeks later the strategy changed to promote a national, international *and* local news service. But by that stage the viewers had sampled the product and while some decided to stay others resorted to their years of habit and went back to the channels of their choice. The first week saw both programs draw well in excess of 400,000 national viewers. However, by the end of its second week, the figures fell and the critics were baying for blood.

MEDIA REACTION

The *Herald Sun* reported:

> *Newsy Negus is on the Nose. Channel Ten may be putting a positive spin on the woeful performance of its new current affairs baby '6pm With George Negus' – but the reality is very different.*

James Packer and Lachlan Murdoch were also reported to have told the *Daily Telegraph* they were 'concerned that the international content of the bulletin was a turn-off for viewers and an indulgence by Negus'.

Considering the national importance of the current "Arab Spring Revolution" in Egypt, which led to the toppling of President Mubarak, and Negus's personal knowledge of the Middle East, I felt the criticism totally unfounded. Ten's largest shareholder Bruce Gordon also publicly questioned the network's news strategy claim.

'I should not be overly critical ... but it has got me puzzled,' he said.

Meanwhile, I continued reading the reports with the knowledge that at least Melbourne's evening 6.30 p.m. local news was working and growing.

THURSDAY, 3 FEBRUARY 2011

Queenslanders braced for more tragedy as Cyclone Yasi struck about 1 a.m. (AEDT). It was the largest and most powerful cyclone to hit the state in living memory. With each catastrophic news event, the media threw all available resources, breaking into scheduled programs with their dramatic coverage. And just as viewers tired of the repeated vision, another even more shocking event appeared to take over.

TUESDAY, 22 FEBRUARY 2011

At least 180 people were killed when a 6.3-magnitude earthquake struck the New Zealand city of Christchurch and again media forces swung into action.

WEDNESDAY, 23 FEBRUARY 2011

At 3.15 p.m. a short time after the Australian Stock Exchange had been notified, staff at Ten received a message from Network Holdings Chairman Brian Long:

Dear all,

The Board met today and has released Grant Blackley from his contract, effective immediately. At the unanimous request of the Board, Lachlan Murdoch has agreed to act as CEO until a new CEO is appointed.

The irony of that appointment was not lost on me. Lachlan Murdoch had become acting CEO precisely 27 years to the day his father Rupert sold his interest in the Ten Network.

By now insecurity had reached new levels as talk intensified of dumping George Negus:

Alas poor George … Negus under the pump … News heads to roll. Negus and News to switch … Murdoch to put Ten's News Hour under the microscope.

No one had been expecting the next development.

WEDNESDAY, 2 MARCH 2011

The Stock Exchange suddenly announced it was halting share trading for Network Ten pending a major announcement. News boss Dermot O'Brien nervously scratched his testicles again and retreated into his office where he could be seen swivelling his chair to face the windows and reach for his phone. Within minutes the headlines flashed across our internal computer screens.

TEN APPOINTS NEW CEO

A week since ousting Grant Blackley, Ten Network has appointed a new CEO, James Warburton, who joins the broadcaster from rival Seven Media Group.

Then came another bombshell announcement.

PACKER QUITS TEN

James Packer has quit as director at Ten, heightening speculation that his partnership with Lachlan Murdoch had fallen through after Murdoch broke an agreement not to poach from Seven. The so-called agreement was between James Packer and Seven's Kerry Stokes, which it's believed, had been struck on the ski slopes of Colorado. Murdoch had breached that agreement by poaching Warburton.

On Thursday, 10 March the Seven Network announced it was taking legal action to enforce a contract it had with James Warburton. At the heart of the legal wrangle, Seven claimed Mr Warburton was unable to move to Ten as its new chief executive, until at least 14 October 2012, at the end of his contractually obliged non-compete period at Seven. It would now be left to the courts to decide.

Meanwhile, Lachlan Murdoch had approached Ten's news boss Dermot O'Brien to head up the ailing Negus Show in Sydney. During discussions between the pair it became obvious that Murdoch had some sort of passion for news but at this stage no inference could be drawn on how long his patience for that passion would last. There is nothing like a takeover in television to highlight the self-preservation mode of senior executives. Allegiances were now being abandoned, formats were being rejected and accusations were being levelled at those who supported the News Revolution. According to at least two former executives, the decision to expand Ten's news was nothing short of 'folly and futility based on naivety at best and at worst, a deliberate attempt to reject internal research that questioned the risks involved'. They claimed the risks were outlined in Brisbane 18 months before George Negus and the evening 6.30 news service were launched. Among those attending the Brisbane conference was network researcher Doug Pfeiffer, who stood before a white board to begin explaining the risks involved. The meeting was suddenly brought to a halt by a sharp rebuke from a senior executive.

'Look if you c★★ts can't do it I will simply get someone who can.'

It was followed by a moment of total silence.

Former executives have since confirmed a bullying mentality from the top. Another executive repeated the earlier claim, 'We had a gun to our heads so we had to make it work … The exercise was totally futile and to say that the risks were only minor was an example of their unbridled naivety … The decision to expand news was simply to fill the void of programming left by *The Simpson's* and *Neighbours* which would spear-head the launch of Ten's new digital HD Channel 11.'

They accused former CEO Grant Blackley of being the brainchild behind the news expansion and despite Packer's obvious opposition to the project, Blackley had persisted. At that stage only a fraction of the budget had been spent and only a dozen or so staff had been hired. However, Blackley continued spending which they claimed was mistake number one. Mistake number two for Blackley, they claimed, followed the complete failure of the Sport Channel HD1. But the nail in Blackley's coffin came when details emerged revealing how much the sales department had been under-performing. By then it was too late to halt the news project but not too late for the new board to terminate the newly re-appointed CEO. For Grant Blackley it was three strikes – out!

FRIDAY, 11 MARCH 2011

Nothing prepared us for the next major news catastrophe.

The first pictures that came through brought our newsroom to a standstill. The black tide of a giant tsunami crashed into Northern Japan from the sea following a 9-magnitude earthquake. It was by far the most graphic live vision we had witnessed since the September 11 attack in New York. Helicopter cameras captured unimaginable scenes as the giant wave swept towns and cities from the map. First the earthquake, then the tsunami and finally in a trilogy of unprecedented disasters – the terrifying threat from damaged nuclear power stations. Under normal circumstances big news stories would have been tailor made for an expansion of news. But the stories broke too soon and swept away what little support we had built as viewers returned to the news services they had built their trust on.

Then, to add to the internal crisis facing Ten, our network weekend news was suddenly shifted from 5 to 6 p.m. but someone neglected to tell the viewers. The impact was instantaneous with viewers across the country deserting to Nine who immediately slotted their national weekend bulletin at 5 p.m. and even used

Ten's established slogan *First at Five*. Ten's news strategy was in tatters and together with the weekend fiasco it appeared terminal.

THURSDAY, 17 MARCH 2011

At 7.10 p.m., ten minutes after the end of the evening news, I was called into the office of Melbourne news boss Dermot O'Brien. There was no small talk and no preamble.

'More news changes,' he said. 'Negus is being moved to 6.30.'

I expected changes but I was a little stunned to be told I was going back to 5 p.m. to head up a 90-minute bulletin with Helen Kapalos. O'Brien obviously saw my reaction and quickly outlined the sweetener.

'You will be reading four nights a week giving you long weekends. George Donikian will continue to read Friday nights and weekends.'

My immediate reaction was one of 'go to hell, pay me out,' but again, he read my mind and told me to go home and sleep on it. So much for the pledge 'we are in it for the long haul', I thought. The 6.30 news experiment may have failed to live up to expectations but it had only been given 55 days. Given that Ten's last foray into current affairs with Alan Jones in 1995 was a total disaster and dumped after just 64 days, I thought 55 days was still a little premature.

I was full of mixed emotions. I was terribly sad for former veteran Adelaide news presenter George Donikian who had waited a life time for an opportunity to read a main evening bulletin in Melbourne, but at that stage he still had Fridays and weekends. To diarise the individual changes that followed would only emphasise the folly that would continue to unfold.

Needless to say, Negus moved to 6.30 and *Ten News at 5* was extended to 90 minutes. The format of those 90 minutes also changed a number of times before it reverted back to its 60-minute duration. The weekend news also reverted back to 5 p.m. but re-established its base in Sydney. George Donikian became one of its first high profile victims and was forced to leave.

Ten Network news boss Jim Carroll had already stepped down from his role as head of news, with Lachlan Murdoch announcing Melbourne's Dermot O'Brien as his replacement. At no stage did Murdoch indicate O'Brien's appointment was only "interim". But then several months later Murdoch announced, 'Network Ten has hired TVNZ's Anthony Flannery as head of news and current affairs, replacing Dermot O'Brien.'

O'Brien arrived back in Melbourne a little shell shocked, but still loyal after Murdoch told him, 'It's not personal.' I was immediately reminded of one of those memorable quotes from Mario Puzo's *The Godfather* between Michael Corleone and Sonny, 'It's not personal, it's business.' And not unlike victims of the Godfather, staff were about to become dispensable at Ten.

It is always the silence that strikes first – the silence before the tears – and it is always associated with a crisis. Too many colleagues tragically killed, too many takeovers destined to fail.

Television newsrooms hum along on a steady sound level from banks of television monitors, scanners, ringing phones, open editing suites, newsroom banter and the occasional outbursts of frustration or humour. It all contributes to an acceptable cacophony of sound until big stories break or late stories arrive close to deadlines – then that sound level increases. But when newsrooms – which often live off other people's misfortunes – are faced with their own internal crisis the sound level drops to a self-imposed silence.

It's like a dark shroud we drape over ourselves in a bid to protect us as we cower beneath its shadow.

Up to 180 jobs around the network were targeted as a result of Lachlan Murdoch's first strategic review. It began with around 60 voluntary redundancies, including 22 editorial positions. Then the flow-on continued.

The Late News and *Sports Tonight* also became victims of cutbacks. In Sydney, Sandra Sully moved from her high profile late news desk to co-read the 5 p.m. local news with Bill Woods. Sully replaced Deb Knight who was dumped but then soon picked up by Channel Nine. One year from the day James Packer swooped on Ten, *The Project* (starting at 6.30) was re-launched with: *new name, new time, same attitude.* The second half of that announcement included:

Negus stays with Ten
George Negus will continue with the network and his rich expertise and experience will be harnessed to provide guidance across the Network on news and current affairs.

However, George Negus (despite his experience) became embroiled in a controversial comment as a guest on the morning program *The Circle*. Together with host Yumi Stynes they were accused of making disparaging remarks about Australia's most highly decorated VC winner Ben Roberts-Smith. While Stynes was described as simply being naïve, there was no such defence for Negus who was unofficially dumped from Ten's schedule. The shambles simply permeated the network and particularly our news at 5 p.m., which by the end of the year had lost almost 50,000 viewers per quarter hour. Most of the staff were pointing the finger at the top.

MONDAY, 4 JULY 2011

It had been 259 days since James Packer had launched his surprise raid on the Australian Ten Network then appointed his mate Lachlan Murdoch as acting CEO to run the place. During this period we had all been working under the constant threat of program cuts and staff retrenchments. Not for the first time had I witnessed this scenario. We had all been bracing for some bloodletting but nothing could have prepared us for the carnage to come. The first cuts were not unexpected.

First to go was Chairman Nick Falloon, then the CEO Grant Blackley. Systematically, other senior management had also been handed the poison chalice. In this case the chalice was an elaborate lolly dispenser that had sat on the desk of the CEO Grant Blackley like a mythical talisman symbolising power and leadership.

To understand this pretentious trinket of triviality you have to understand the boys' club culture that appears to embody management teams of network television. "Blackley" (Grant Blackley), "Mottie" (Program Manager David Mott), "Kingo" CEO Kerry Kingston), "Whitie" (Head of Sport David White), "Johnno", "Dicko", "Dermo".

It had already been written into media folk law that on the day CEO Grant Blackley was sacked, one of his last acts before cleaning out his office was to hand over his talisman or toy to the chief financial officer John Kelly. For one brief moment the lolly dispenser sat proudly on Kelly's desk as it had with Blackley. However, Kelly was next in line for the door and as he left his office for the last time he placed this symbol of fading influence on the desk of the national sports boss David White.

One week later White was dispensed with and with some

humour placed the machine on the desk of network news boss Jim Carroll. Carroll was next to go. No one is quite sure what became of the lolly machine because within a very short space of time there was no one left to ask.

On Monday morning as I walked into the sinister silence of our network in crisis, a voice suddenly echoed down the passage from behind the closed door of a nearby office. Shaking with emotion, one of the first victim's of Murdoch's strategic review let loose with a string of expletives and prophecies of doom that would be carried on through time.

'Tell that One.Tel wonder he will stuff up television just like he stuffed the Telco!'

The 34-year-old producer, who had been with the network for more than 12 years, was reminding anyone within earshot that James Packer and Lachlan Murdoch were still the targets of a $244 million lawsuit in the wake of the 2001 collapse of their One.Tel telecommunication giant. She then composed herself and quickly strode back to her desk. She collected her belongings and left.

Colleagues who witnessed the producer's outburst simply buried their heads behind their computers and continued to work "in silence" – in the hope they would not be next. But they were, and there would be many more to follow.

So here in Australia on 4 July 2011, as Americans prepared to celebrate their National Day of Independence, Lachlan Murdoch ended his first strategic review by giving up to 180 staff their own form of independence – albeit by redundancies or sackings.

Those first victims took some solace from the irony that Lachlan himself was then summoned to London where his father Rupert and their family empire were also strategically reviewed by a Parliamentary inquiry into the *News of the World* phone hacking scandal. But back in Australia more pain was awaiting Lachlan Murdoch and the staff at Ten.

The effects of Murdoch's first cuts impacted almost immediately on live production at Ten – particularly the news. Many of the experienced staff accepted generous redundancies and left. Trainees became trainers, juniors became seniors, subordinates became superiors and cadets became producers. Inexperience suddenly flowed through the system, creating a newsreader's worst nightmare. The stories were not being produced quickly enough and half way through one of the main evening bulletins we simply ran out of news.

As the fifteenth story of the night came to an end there was nothing left in the line-up. No hardcopy. No autocue. Just blank spaces and blank faces from the floor crew. I covered the pause best I could, but it happened again a short time later – twice in the one bulletin. At the end of the news I did what most newsreaders would probably have done – I threw up. I then complained bitterly to my colleagues. While I received more than adequate sympathy, it was made abundantly clear that everyone else was in the same boat.

News was not the only program being affected by decisions of management. Surviving staff wilted under the pressures of program failures and decisions out of their control, but no one publicly complained. They didn't need to. They left it to other media colleagues to speak out:

TEN WAYS TO KILL A NETWORK – When the corporate history is written the theatrics of the James Packer/Lachlan Murdoch led takeover will be characterised as a sad and sorry chapter.
– The Australian Financial Review

Sadly, the events that unfolded could not be confined to just one chapter. Had I not continued to write my journals during those final three years at Ten it would be difficult to believe such a litany of poor decisions and bad timing could have caused so much damage and heartache to a company whose board members included four of Australia's biggest billionaires.

SUNDAY, 1 JANUARY 2012

James Warburton was due to officially take control of the Ten Network with Lachlan Murdoch as Chairman of the Board. The previous year may have been a successful "Year of Revolution" in the Middle East but at Network Ten the revolution failed miserably. However, with a new year and the appointment of a new leader, the surviving staff prepared for a new start.

CHAPTER 17

ANCHORS AWAY!
THE PERFECT STORM

2012

HEADLINES

London hosts Olympics
Last US space shuttle flight
Barack Obama wins US Election
Australia wins UN seat

HITS

Locked out of Heaven – Bruno Mars
Diamonds – Rihanna
Die Young – Ke$ha

A former colleague once remarked that newsreaders are called "anchors" because anchors are the first objects tossed overboard in a storm.

I dismissed his cynical analogy on the basis of his state of mind at the time – his contract had been terminated. However, not even he could have imagined the toll from the wake of a "perfect storm".

In 2011, the elements had already begun to form with a gradual change in Australia's media landscape. The growth of social media and the impact of the 24-hour news cycle coincided with a dramatic downturn in the mainstream advertising market. Network Ten was already attributing some of their economic woes on decisions made by the previous management. However, new programming failures were about to become the final catalyst to send program ratings plunging to record depths, equal to the catastrophic fall of our share price. Combined, this created what could only be described as a "perfect storm".

As I have repeatedly claimed throughout my career I am never openly critical of those who run our television networks. For a start, I have never been privy to their inner decision making process believing those decisions are the results of far greater minds than mine. However, when those decisions adversely affect the day-to-day running of news then I believe no one is more qualified to be critical than me. In times of internal crisis I have always shut myself off from the dramas that flow with egos and insecurities by seeking refuge in my office.

In 2012 however, waves from this storm were forming with such intensity and such frequency I was forced to spend even more time in my private sanctuary. A two-seater couch in sickly stripes of faded maroon extended across a wall behind my door where I could stretch out unseen from the open newsroom beyond. My walls were adorned with press clippings, photos, billboards and former anchors in a display of media history that only interested people of my vintage. In my favourite frame I was waist deep in the Seymour floods of May 1974 with a microphone in one hand while pointing with the other to survivors waiting to be rescued from the roof of their isolated home in the background. It was next to a framed letter of my first appointment to radio 3YB in June 1961, offering a salary of eleven pounds a week plus overtime. It served as a reminder of humble beginnings. This was my sanctuary surrounded by my memories and of course my most cherished memories – pictures of my family.

WEDNESDAY, 25 JULY 2012 – 2.35 P.M.

My on-air partner Helen Kapalos suddenly burst into my office. She shut the door behind her, fell onto my couch and burst into tears. She had just been assessed – as all staff members are at least twice a year. This time however the assessment found her to be uncommunicative with her viewers.

'What total crap,' I responded. 'What are you talking about?'

Between sobs and nervous giggles she tried to tell me the results of the most recent research conducted by two independent focus groups to determine our so-called "Q Scores". Q Scores rank the popularity of television stars through extensive focus group research, which is often sourced by those in programming, casting or advertising. Ten had just signed an exclusive agreement with Audience Development Australia, the company behind the industry's Q Scores and its creator David Castran. Castran was described as "the best television audience researcher in Australia" and had been hired by newly appointed CEO James Warburton. Castran became the first member of Ten's new Creative Development Unit. That unit too would become another costly disaster.

Castran only lasted four months into a three-year contract before he quit under mysterious circumstances. No one wished to talk about it. However, the results of his initial research lingered a little longer than he did – long enough to cast a devastating impact on the one program around the network that was working – the news. At precisely 2.30 on the afternoon of July 25, in her feisty response to being told she was being "perceived as failing to communicate", Kapalos demanded to see the results for herself. Someone apparently complied, flipping open the page and turning it to show her. For the first time to my knowledge, a station celebrity was actually shown their Q Score. I had always been of the understanding that it was policy within all networks that Q Scores were reserved for management eyes only. I believe the results from that research by two groups of nameless faceless Victorians virtually sealed her fate.

Similar research around the network not only determined the level of perceived popularity among the dual newsreaders but also determined which one would cause the least amount of damage if a decision should ever be made for single readers on each bulletin. Their demise would not be based on age, sexuality or experience – it would be purely a business decision in the hope of cutting costs and creating the least amount of collateral damage in the process. I was reminded of my unique position as a so-called "protected species". The die was cast. The perfect storm was coming.

MONDAY, 24 AUGUST 2012

I was called into management to finalise my contract. There appeared to be an unnecessary haste for me to sign and an unprecedented agreement to all my demands. Given the terrible morale and the deteriorating situation at Ten, I decided this would become my transitional year to retirement. Management accepted my proposal to scale down to four days a week for the first six months then three days a week with a mid-year holiday regardless of the ratings. It was by far the best contract of my career. However, no one mentioned reading a one-hour bulletin solo – nor did I connect the urgency to sign quickly.

By September 2012 the state of the network was in crisis. Programs were failing, revenue was falling and the most strident critics were aiming both barrels at the Chairman of Ten's board, Lachlan Murdoch.

LACH, STOCK AND BOTH BARRELS: WHO'S KILING CHANNEL TEN

Murdoch gets points for pulling the pin on Negus, trimming costs and shifting the digital focus from sport to entertainment. But he also oversaw this year's programming strategy – including the calamitous Breakfast Show. There were high hopes for James Warburton too but all the shows he commissioned failed abysmally.

– Crikey.com

Ten had not only lost the AFL but also failed in a costly bid for the NRL. Ten then made a series of poor program decisions, such as the ill-fated and expensive breakfast show, fronted by New Zealander Paul Henry at a reported salary of $1 million (a personal choice of Lachlan's).

Meanwhile the fast-flopping *Everybody Dance Now*, hosted by Lachlan's wife Sarah, was axed after only a few episodes following a similar fate to *The Shire*, which was also a ratings disaster. In fairness to Lachlan, the AFL deal was losing Ten more than $40 million a year. Negotiating a deal with the NRL was reported to be far more lucrative. According to sources within Ten, Lachlan was confident of sealing the deal with the NRL through his close friend at News Limited, Kim Williams. As negotiations over the rights reached a head in mid-2012, only two contenders remained, Ten and Foxtel who had teamed up with Nine. Lachlan was so confident he had the deal in the bag he was left shattered to discover Kim Williams together with Nine outbid Ten at the eleventh hour.

According to the Sydney *Morning Herald*, '… being gazumped …' over the NRL was seen by Lachlan '… as a deep betrayal by his onetime friend.' However there were no excuses for Ten's other program failures. Ten needed a scapegoat and on 24 August they led him to the slaughter.

Network Ten has announced that chief programming officer David Mott has resigned after 16 years with the channel.

Mott's decision to quit followed one of the worst rating's weeks in Ten's history, regularly slipping into fourth place behind the ABC in terms of nightly audience share. Mott would recount to friends it was the greatest relief of his life. In his final weeks at Ten he began to develop a serious physical spasm in his right hand, so severe that when attending board meetings he virtually had to hold his other hand over it to prevent the shaking. Within 48 hours of his sacking the violent spasm suddenly ceased. There was no doubt he left a remarkable legacy at Ten including landmark television programs such as *Master Chef, Australian Idol, Rove Live, The Biggest Loser, Thank God You're Here, The Panel, The Project* and *Big Brother.* However the one program he couldn't claim credit for was our news. Melbourne's *News at 5 p.m.* had consistently become the most watched program on the network and it was this success that provided us with the belief that our news would be the last program management would dare touch. How wrong we were.

SATURDAY, 1 SEPTEMBER 2012

According to the Oztam Ratings system, 'Ten hit a new all-time low posting just 6.5 per cent share and only slightly higher on Sunday with 6.6 per cent.' The *Australian Financial Review* then responded with claims that, 'Ten board members are privately questioning the company's strategy.'

The pressure was now firmly on Chairman Lachlan Murdoch and CEO James Warburton.

MONDAY, 15 OCTOBER 2012

I was sitting at my office computer reworking news scripts. It was 2 p.m. and for some unknown reason I switched to the online graph at the Australian Stock Exchange. Earlier in the day a declaration was released conceding the failure of Ten to sell its $1.43 million outdoor advertising company Eye-corp. It appeared to be the final trigger to a stampede as investors simply threw their hands up and fled. I watched in morbid fascination as a thin red line plotting Ten's share price simply dropped off the page. An empty red box and an apology from the ASX suddenly replaced it: 'Unable to generate the selected chart'. The share price had plunged into unknown territory descending to the lowest point in its turbulent history.

Earlier, the Nine Network had escaped administration following long drawn out negotiations involving their $3.5 billion debt. Such were the tempestuous times in television.

We were all feeling embattled and beleaguered, almost lifeless waiting in intensive care for a life support system we knew was not available and even if it were, it would now be unaffordable.

More investors started pulling out including Ten's largest institutional shareholder Perpetual, which dumped all its remaining investment in Ten, citing concern over the company's debt or as one insider said 'concern over Ten's management team'. So much for having the nation's biggest billionaires on the board who were still holding substantial stakes but having bought in at $1.50 a share they were now valued at 27 cents (they would eventually fall to 16 cents).

One week later Ten posted a half-year loss of almost $13 million and further gloom descended amid fears of more cut backs and cost reviews. Well, we didn't have long to wait.

THURSDAY, 18 OCTOBER 2012

I arrived moments before CEO James Warburton appeared on our newsroom monitors addressing network staff from Sydney. From his opening words his message did not bode well for what was to follow. I noticed he too had developed a nervous affliction with sporadic blinking and overt neck stretching. We were all very much aware the network had just lost $12.8 million for the year ending 31 August 2012. But no one was even slightly prepared for his next words:

'As a result of a Strategic, Operating and News Review, today we are announcing proposed voluntary redundancies. As painful and unavoidable as it is, it's a fact that we need to reduce Ten's cost base. I don't like seeing job losses, but unfortunately they are necessary. It is my duty and responsibility to ensure this process happens in an orderly and respectful fashion and with dignity for the departing staff.'

Shocked and stunned we all sat in silence. Another strategic review and a second round of cutbacks; in all, 22 news staff from Melbourne, 40 from Sydney, 23 from Brisbane and untold numbers from Adelaide and Perth would be involved. A network news desk in Sydney would be established to co-ordinate all national and international stories, which I accepted as an appropriate means of reducing duplication. However, these redundancies came 12 months after an initial blood bath of 180 jobs under Murdoch's strategic review. How many reviews were necessary?

Warburton conceded the network's annual results were "disappointing" and the ratings had not been "good enough". Of course he was referring to *The Shire, Being Lara Bingle* and *Everybody Dance Now,* which had been commissioned under his watch. In fact, nearly all local productions had failed during the year – all except the news – and now we were paying the price for those program follies. That's when I whispered an expletive just loudly enough for the visiting COO Jon Marquard to hear – before I walked out. Within minutes he was in my office.

'Look, Mal. This is a difficult time for all of us.'

Tell that to the kids about to get the flick, I thought.

FRIDAY, 9 NOVEMBER 2012

The perfect storm struck one week after Hurricane Sandy swept through New York and not unlike Sandy, the warning signs had been issued but no one was prepared for the severity of its wrath.

It coincided with a personal bout of flu-like illness. I am never sick. Hypochondriacs very rarely are. But with all that had been going on around me, my immune system simply gave up and I took time off. I attempted to come back to work on the Wednesday but O'Brien simply said, 'Go home take the rest of the week off.' In hindsight, he was protecting me from a contagion that was about to affect everyone in the newsroom.

Around 6.30 p.m., shortly after Helen Kapalos had wrapped up her nightly news, I received a garbled text message from her:

Hi beautiful Mal, I won't be joining you on the needs desk again — you are a single head reader.

The pre-emptive text spelling of "needs" instead of "news" threw me initially. I immediately attempted to call her back but she wasn't answering, in fact no one answered my calls. Within a short time it was being circulated on social media that Kapalos had been sacked.

'They've sacked the wrong person,' I whispered to Pauline. 'I only have one more year to go. It doesn't make sense.'

Finally around 10 p.m., still in a state of shock, Helen called me back. She was about to fly out to New York for the start of her holidays when told her job had been made redundant. There was little consolation in that it had been a Sydney decision to shed readers around the network. Management in Melbourne faced the dilemma of telling her before she left on holidays or inform her while she was away. Had she not been told at that moment Helen would have heard through social media, which was now reporting plans for single readers around the network.

However, her sacking paled to some others. Fairfax online was first to report the sackings and began by ringing Sydney based newsreader, Bill Woods, for a comment on his dismissal. He hadn't even been told. He then rang management at Ten who denied the report.

Woods immediately tweeted his thanks to those who had offered their sympathy and support and informed them that the reports were wrong. Management even demanded Fairfax online retract the story claiming it wasn't true. Fairfax complied. On Monday when Woods arrived for work he was called into management and told, 'Sorry mate, the report was true you finish up at the end of November.'

The Brisbane newsroom was reeling from the shock of their favourite female reader Georgina Lewis having been told her services were no longer required. It had been decided the equally popular Bill McDonald would anchor their news. Georgina apparently departed almost immediately terminating her Twitter account and refusing to make any public comment. The following weekend however, Ten issued a statement to the *Brisbane Courier* announcing a reversal of its original decision. It would prove to have been a personal decision by McDonald who was caught between two job offers at the time but it highlighted a breakdown in communication, confusion and lack of leadership within the network.

However, the most insensitive act by human resources was reserved for Melbourne's head of publicity Stephanie Bansemer-Brown, who was undergoing chemotherapy at the time she received the call. After 16 years of loyal service with the company no questions were asked about her treatment for cancer.

'Just informing you,' the familiar voice said, 'your position has been made redundant.' In a final act of some redemption the voice added, 'You're better off not being here.'

The management team under Lachlan Murdoch and James Warburton was not only facing ratings and financial fiasco but now a severe moral collapse.

With the departure around the network of senior news presenters Bill Woods and Ron Wilson in Sydney, Bill McDonald's departure from Brisbane and Craig Smart in Perth, I suddenly emerged as the last remaining male newsreader on the network's main early evening news bulletins. I had become, as one scribe reported, 'the last man standing'.

Overcome by the gamut of emotions following the Friday shock dumping of Kapalos, I spent the weekend suffering a strange sense of guilt at becoming the sole survivor.

Sunday night I drove to the Ten Como Centre, took the lift to the fifth floor, passed silently through the empty newsroom and into my office. I then systematically cleaned my computer, downloading all personal material onto a USB stick. I packed up years of documents, diaries, press clippings and memories. I took three trips down to my car on the lower level at Como. On my final trip, with a single box and two large prints under my arm, the lift stopped suddenly at level 3 and two total strangers entered. I neither spoke to them nor recognised them.

The following morning at 7 a.m. the popular breakfast duo of Ross Stevenson and John Burns announced on their 3AW rumour file segment:

Rumour as fact. Veteran newsreader Mal Walden was seen last night cleaning out his office at Network Ten.

Then all hell broke loose. My mobile immediately sprang to life so I switched it off. My home phone began ringing so I unplugged it. More was to come. Around 8.30 Dermot O'Brien arrived at my home. He stood in the driveway, dark shadows beneath his eyes.

'What are you doing here?' I asked.

'I am gutted,' he replied. 'I heard the rumour file and drove into work and checked your office. Everything has been cleaned out. Why?'

'Well, where do I begin? I have lost faith in this company. I have lost total faith in this management and now sadly after more than 35 years I have lost all faith in you.'

This was the man I had taken out on his first TV news reporting assignment in the mid-70s. For 35 years we had shared weddings, christenings and untold funerals. We were both victims of the Fairfax takeover and all its brutality at Seven in the '80s. For the past 17 years we had continued our mutual friendship and stability in what we believed was the most successful newsroom in the country. Now it was as if I had king hit him. This was bringing the worst out in all of us.

Several hours later I returned to my office with a great feeling of guilt. While it may have been a cathartic experience at the time it was an impetuous act of "prima donna" frustration that caused me to clean out my office. It was a selfish act, which apparently had a very unsettling effect on young staff facing this round of redundancies and desperate for signs of stability. The following week I learnt the redundancies had been completed but no one had informed the staff.

I will never forget congratulating one young reporter for having endured what would possibly be the worst fortnight of her career. She looked up from her computer with blank red-rimmed eyes and tried to smile. Her hair had lost its gloss as she apologised for her appearance saying she hadn't slept in over a week. When I told her the forced redundancies were all over, she mouthed the words "thank you" and then burst into tears. Sydney management couldn't even tie up the loose ends properly.

MONDAY, 3 DECEMBER 2012

I walked into the newsroom and there was the silence again. This time the silence was not caused by shock or disbelief – simply the lack of people. The background hum of monitors was still there, the occasional phone rang and an editing suite echoed a repeating video cut. I could hear no voices, just a few whispers. The redundancies were complete but the newsroom, including the camera department, had now been gutted. It was not just the experience we had lost, it was the very fabric that made a cohesive environment work as well as it did – the friendships and the familiarity of people who shared a common passion in news. And I knew this feeling would be echoing around the network.

My office now echoed from having removed all my personal effects three weeks earlier. The redundancies were complete but it was becoming apparent that the cost savings were not enough.

Respected author and journalist Paul Barry wrote:

Have Lachlan Murdoch and James Packer repeated their One-Tel disaster at Ten, or is it just bad luck to have bought a free-to-air TV network at a bad time? It's looking more like a train crash.

I sat at my office desk for several hours. My door remained shut as I reflected on this "train crash" and one terrible thought kept coming to mind. The boys from Balibo were killed in 1975 and the crew from the ill-fated HSV7 chopper crash died in 1981. They all died during attempts to report news. Had they not died, would they have survived to a point in time when they too would have simply been made redundant by a network in crisis? If so, was it all really bloody worth it?

As the year 2012 drew to a close, all I could think was 'roll on 2013', it couldn't get any worse. Could it?

CHAPTER 18

GOOD MORNING, GOOD EVENING & GOOD NIGHT

2013

Caesar: Who is it in the press that calls on me?
I hear a tongue shriller than all the music.
Soothsayer: Beware the Ides of March.

Since the assassination of Caesar on the 15 March 44 BC the Ides of
March has represented a foreboding time for those in public life.

THURSDAY, 28 FEBRUARY 2013

Pope Benedict stepped down. The first time in modern history a Pope had actually resigned as leader of the Catholic Church.

WEDNESDAY, 6 MARCH 2013

Less than one week later, and on a lesser scale of historic proportions, the Liberal Premier of the State of Victoria Ted Baillieu suddenly announced he was stepping down.

THURSDAY, 21 MARCH 2013

Eleven high profile Labour party faithful fell on their swords after a failed coup to bring down Australia's PM Julia Gillard. Just three months later the PM called another leadership spill but this time she too failed to survive.

Not one of those who stepped down or fell victim to circumstance in 2013 did so without enormous pressures and influences swirling around their chosen fields.

Media was no exception.

2013 began with banners and blogs all bellowing the same headlines:

Who Killed Channel Ten?

'No one!' I wanted to scream. 'We are not dead yet. We still have a pulse.' Press reports appeared to be relentlessly revelling in the plight of the network:

War drums sounding at Ten.

And each incessant beat conveyed the same rhythmic message:

Crisis at Ten or Another head about to roll.

It was impossible to ignore the negativity that was swirling around the network as we hunkered down in our respective newsrooms and speculated on whose head would be next. The more cynical among us even ran a book. We knew the board could not be happy with the company's performance and the odds were shortening for some more bloodletting. Someone at the top had to pay the price of our boardroom folly. Come to think of it, someone had to pay the price of our boardroom.

In the course of the first painful cutbacks more than $700,000 had been spent on hi-tech renovations to the Sydney boardroom. And that was without the costly furnishings. The timing of this exorbitant spending did not go down well among the staff, particularly those who were being axed. Even Lachlan Murdoch was reported to have been "surprised and somewhat concerned at the cost", but not enough to call a halt to the renovations.

Head Office in Sydney was now leaking like a sieve and the sound of the drums continued to intensify. Then suddenly a guiding light appeared with the appointment of a new station manager for Melbourne – Russell Howcroft.

TUESDAY, 29 JANUARY 2013

The staff responded to an invitation to meet our new appointee – a man we had all come to know from his appearance on the ABC

Marketing and Advertising Show *The Gruen Transfer*. Howcroft would become the eighth General Manager in my time at Ten. As I wove my way through the crowded venue CEO James Warburton stepped forward to greet me with a firm handshake and a genuine smile. No sign of the feared reputation I had come to hear from others. However, a nervous physical twitching of his neck and rapid eye blinking had become far more prominent since we last met. I was totally unprepared for his opening words.

'I am so sorry last year was such a difficult one for you.'

I was taken aback further by his next words.

'We stuffed up. We simply moved too fast with untested programs.'

When a CEO of a major network admits he has stuffed up there is little more to say. So I just stood and listened as he attempted to talk up the network and introduce us all to Russell Howcroft. I suddenly felt that Warburton must have known his time with Ten had become untenable. It was a short introduction and by the time Howcroft responded I was left wondering how long he too would last. Enthusiasm is one thing but his television experience, which was confined to his appearance on the *Gruen Transfer,* did not inspire confidence. However, I felt if Network Ten could bottle and sell his enthusiasm they would never have to worry about revenue ever again.

Meanwhile, the war drums continued their negative stream and following a crisis boardroom meeting the following week Chairman Lachlan Murdoch issued a staff email:

The board would like to thank James Warburton for his hard work and contribution during what has been a difficult period for the company and for the broader media sector. He steps down with Ten's best wishes.

Murdoch then went on to welcome Warburton's replacement, Mr Hamish McLennan, labelling him a "world class" CEO with a "strong track record". For a number of senior executives to later claim they had been "blindsided" by Warburton's departure simply showed how out of touch with reality they all were. For God's sake, even the girls in the make-up department at Ten knew Warburton was about to be terminated.

MONDAY, 25 FEBRUARY 2013

I arrived once again to a silent newsroom as the morning producers were proudly talking of the previous night's ratings and with very good reason. Our news had not only achieved an audience peak of 235,000 but, once again, we were the most watched program on the network – the only program in the top 20.

Ten's chief of staff Mark O'Brien was doing deals with all networks for vision of stories we no longer had the staff to cover. I had already dubbed the veteran newsman "Jesus" for the miracles he was performing in allocating crews to cover the stories of the day.

However, even he admitted he couldn't "heal the sick", and with the pressure on such few staff he believed they would eventually succumb to illness. No one at Ten appeared to be mourning the loss of Warburton, however, according to social media, the wrong man had gone.

THE TEN NETWORK IN DEEP DISPAIR
When the corporate history is written the theatrics of the James Packer/Lachlan Murdoch led takeover of the past two years will be characterised as a sad and sorry chapter.
– Crickey, February 26

Sadly, the events that were unfolding could not be contained in just one chapter.

ZERO OUT OF TEN – NETWORK STILL IN STRIFE
Channel Ten will soon have its fifth CEO in two years and there is still no indication the broadcaster has a clue about how it might climb out of its governance, ratings and financial pit. The ultimate responsibility must lie with chairman Lachlan Murdoch.
– Michael Pasco, Business Day

Another revamp won't save Murdoch's Ten debacle. Hamish McLennan, the new CEO of Ten, has promised the network's third revamp in two years.
– Michael Bodey, The Australian, 5 March 2013

So we asked, who is this Hamish McLennan? According to "Mumbrella":

He's known as Hamish the Hammer and former colleagues suggest he's a "clinical henchman", but can Ten's new CEO Hamish McLennan walk the walk or is it all talk? He's a good friend of Lachlan Murdoch and has spent the past year working side by side with his dad – the media mogul Rupert – but newly appointed Network Ten CEO Hamish McLennan insists he is his own man.

Then began a series of conspiracy theories amid claims of "conflict of interest". It was almost impossible to be unaffected as we all hunkered down against this torrent of negativity. No one was expecting another blow so soon.

TUESDAY, 9 APRIL 2013

Hamish McLennan announced a $243.3 million half yearly loss, blaming program flops such as: *Being Lara Bingle* and *The Shire*. In announcing the loss he also pledged to move away from the "extreme" youth demographic, skewing its audience to target "older viewers". They were precisely the same words used by former CEO Grant Blackley and CFO Kerry Kingston when they launched the News Revolution targeting "older viewers". The only difference between the two announcements was Blackley's announcement came shortly after posting a record profit – not a record loss.

It was against this climate of uncertainty and a threat of further cuts I began to accept my transitional year to retirement.

THURSDAY, 6 JUNE 2013

I wrote out my resignation on 6 June. I chose this day specifically to coincide with my 53rd year in media. I began my career on 6 June, read my first news on Melbourne television on 6 June – so why break this synchronicity? I then put it on hold for an appropriate time, which came 20 days hence.

WEDNESDAY, 26 JUNE 2013

Our Melbourne news posted its highest ratings in three years peaking at just fewer than 300,000 viewers. There is no better time to quit than when you are on top and there was no guarantee we would ever match those figures again. I then post-dated my resignation for the following day to coincide with a planned visit by the network's news boss Anthony Flannery. I set it up in my email system to simply press "send".

THURSDAY, 27 JUNE 2013

The following afternoon I sat opposite Flannery in a coffee bar of the Como Centre in South Yarra. I leant forward and said, 'Anthony I have written out my resignation. I wish to confirm my intention to step down at the end of this year.'

There was a pause. Just a slight pause – enough to confirm my decision was right. At no stage was there any suggestion 'would I reconsider'. I was not disappointed in that. In fact I held the distinct impression this confirmation would fit well with his plans.

'Mal,' he said, 'the network will want to acknowledge your incredible career. We will want to send you off with the dignity you deserve and –'

But by then I had faded out. I have no idea what he said after that or indeed what I said in reply. I had just confirmed the end of a 53-year career and while it was all my own decision I think – in hindsight – I may have slipped into a slight state of shock.

We took the lift together to the fifth floor and while I peeled off into my office, he headed straight to the office of Dermot O'Brien. In fact, he would not even have reached that office before I had pressed the send button and my resignation became official. It was the end of a marathon balancing act in which I was once warned 'to survive in television is akin to tightrope walking. It requires a fine balancing act between ego and insecurity – one slip either way can prove fatal'. At no stage in those 53 years had insecurity been so rampant as it was now.

Having sent my resignation to all departments I sat at my desk preparing for my final six months. Suddenly, there was a shout from the newsroom. PM Julia Gillard had just called a ballot in a leadership battle against her nemesis Kevin Rudd. From that moment on nothing else mattered as we scrambled what few resources we had for a historic night's news.

By the end of the evening I was not the only one facing a new future. Australia's first woman PM had lost her job. At least I had six months to say my farewells and reflect on the lessons, the legacies and a lifetime of great memories.

WEDNESDAY, 4 DECEMBER 2013

I read my final bulletin.

Surviving colleagues and some of those who I had worked with for periods throughout my career gathered to send me off. It was a bittersweet farewell and a very high profiled retirement including a State Reception hosted by the Premier Denis Napthine at Parliament House and a lifetime achievement award from the Melbourne Press Club.

However, I was not finished at Ten. Part of the final agreement was to remain for 12 months as a mentor and news ambassador. The sad reality was in those final 12 months no one sought my advice and there was no one left to mentor. I was witness to a small-dedicated news staff simply going through the motions waiting for the next cuts. And they didn't have long to wait.

WEDNESDAY, 21 MAY 2014

Channel Ten slashed another 150 jobs, three news bulletins and another failed breakfast show *Wake Up*. Now it was left to an even smaller contingent of news staff to produce a nightly news bulletin. I couldn't contribute. The most disturbing factor was having to watch this once proud department – the flagship of the network – reduced to a reliance on Seven, Nine and the ABC to supply vision for stories they no longer had the recourses to cover. As Ten's chief of staff conceded, 'Without their help we would simply be forced to shut down.'

WEDNESDAY, 15 OCTOBER 2014

Network Ten posted another massive loss, $168 million, and it was left to others to sum up what most at Ten were in no position to say.

> *An unmitigated financial disaster – Ten bled more than $2 million a week – 40 % improvement on previous year but deeply in the red- Accumulated loss up from $701 million to $870 million – ouch! Have four billionaires ever shared such a mess?*
> – Stephen Mayne, Thursday 16 October 2014

This was precisely the same loss that forced Ten into receivership 14 years earlier. Perhaps it was only monopoly money for the four billionaire owners but this wasn't a game for the staff. The Ten news budget, which had been reduced earlier that year to roughly $40 million, had now been slashed in half. Similar pain was being felt across the entire media spectrum.

SUNDAY, 23 NOVEMBER 2014

The ABC shed 10 per cent of its work force and its news division also bore the brunt of the cutbacks. Two weeks before Christmas

2014, I deleted everything on my computer, packed up what few belongings I still possessed and quietly left the building. Before leaving I bid my final farewell to the meagre remaining staff. Four years earlier the newsroom seated 57 staff. On my final day, with two reporters out on assignment, I counted just six.

CHAPTER 19

NEWS EPILOGUE

2016

Human behavior flows from three main sources:
desire, emotion, and knowledge.
— Plato

Throughout history, mankind has always been possessed by a thirst for knowledge. We have always sought to know why things happen and then pushed the boundaries to discover what was possible thereafter. The power of knowledge has not only shaped our very existence but has given enormous prestige to the storytellers who have been charged with passing that knowledge down through the ages.

Most historians believe that storytelling has defined our humanity. Humans are the only beings who create and tell stories. Since the first cave paintings were etched more than 40,000 years ago, telling stories has been one of the most fundamental methods of recording our history. From myths to legends, fairy tales to fables, they have not only reflected the wisdom and knowledge from our past but have shaped our future.

When I first started in media back in 1961 I was convinced stories had to be complex and detailed in order to be interesting. I soon discovered simple stories were more likely to be heard – and more easily passed on. Apparently we all possess an innate human propensity to share what we know, it is part of our human psyche. How often have we all enjoyed a certain satisfaction in passing on hitherto unknown stories or information? Or being among the first to hear those stories? Like hit songs we tend to remember where we were when we first heard them.

Psychologists believe people share knowledge and information because it also allows us to each feel more involved and perhaps more important in the eyes of others.

According to Freud: *There is one longing – almost as deep, almost as imperious, as the desire for food or sleep – that is "the desire to be great." Others have called it "the desire to be important."* I believe the driving force behind becoming a TV newsreader came from an inherent desire to inform, to seek out a story and tell it. I have always considered myself a storyteller – nothing more – so I made a career out of it and like many storytellers before me I accepted any plaudits for sharing information and knowledge along the way.

Yes, it raised my profile in the eyes of a few – just as it may have done for the storytellers among original cave dwellers and just as it did among the many "bardic disciples" of the Middle Ages and beyond.

The Minstrel

The lilt of his lute broke the dawn at its stillest
Wretch'd and weary yet still eag'r to fillest
of battles and plague from a land b'rne of tears,
A king his queen their l'res and their sears
And the village stood mute in rapture 'r naught
As the minstrel f'rtold what his god had wrought

Today the lute is long gone. News was once delivered from the village square – now the global village is accessible in every home. Tales are similar: battles, wars, leaders, laws, even light-hearted trivia of modern day seers. The reporters gather the information but each night when a familiar theme rolls it's a presenter who introduces the story: presenters, anchors, newsreaders or simply "Modern Day Minstrels".

After sixty years of television the most consistently watched program on nearly all networks is still the main nightly news. In that time there has been little change to the format of our news:

from the headlines, content, sport and the weather. In fact it has all been very predictable. However, behind the headlines it was a far different story with dramatic changes continually driven by technology. I stood in awe at the introduction of satellites, welcomed the transition of black and white to color, struggled a little with film to tape then finally witnessed the birth of the digital computer age. I bore witness as millions of dollars was spent annually on production, research and promotion, then agonised with news editors and producers over ways to find that indefinable formula that would guarantee success for our bulletins.

Accepting the fact that television is all about perception, we continually tweaked our news in the hope that even a change in set design would attract more viewers. We experimented with pillars and posts, squares and circles, desks and chairs, untold "chroma key" backgrounds and multiple TV monitors. The only constant was the color blue and of course, the cost. Always rising.

As one veteran news editor lamented when his opposition boasted a million dollar set change, 'What's the point of redecorating a restaurant if the food is still crap?'

We attempted to change the "menu", providing an appetite for happy news, worthy news, tabloid news, overseas news, feature news, fanciful, factual and sensational news – anything to make a point of difference. We ended up delivering a mix of all, then sat back to watch the weekly ratings to see if the viewers approved. Not exactly rocket science but almost as costly.

And as our production costs continued to rise, alternative news sources began to increase. In the last few years TV news viewers apparently found these alternative sources and simply left us in droves. We not only lost audience numbers but somehow lost the initiative to reinvent ourselves to compete.

We were overrun by multiple digital platforms led by Facebook, Twitter and other social media outlets, and we allowed them to capture our initiative for "breaking news". Sixty years ago breaking news was the sole domain of radio. The assassination of JFK in 1963 established a formula for live breaking news on American TV, which then flowed through to Networks around the world following the introduction of satellites.

As my first TV news editor John Maher lamented in 1956 'no one complained what we did then because they knew less than we did and we knew nothing.'

Today audiences are far more discerning. They not only watched as we stumbled into this unchartered wilderness, they even led us into it.

The first group to desert us was that vital young demographic we had all so righteously boasted as our front line of defense. They left us with a diminishing group of news consumers that were all getting older. Viewers then watched as we not only lost the initiative for breaking news but attempted to make up for that loss by using reporters to fill with superfluous waffle under the pretense it was live television. We can all point the finger of blame at others but "beware who casts the first stone" as we were not blameless ourselves.

On the plus-side as we celebrate 60 years of television we can still boast an audience reach of 85 percent of Australian viewers. And as I have repeatedly said TV news is still the most consistently watched program on all networks.

I suppose in life we all hope that our contributions make some difference. I had hoped in retirement to leave the industry in better shape than when I started. Sadly I am not confident my contribution had any effect at all. The question now being posed is whether TV news can continue to survive.

I fully believe it can, but am a little unsure in what form. It's perhaps worth looking at the Ten Network for an answer. Ten recovered from receivership in the early '90s by default. They came to within 24 hours of shutting down. They emerged, admittedly with very few programs, but those few programs suddenly began attracting a young demographic. From that point on they began to program specifically to a young audience becoming the corporate success story of the '90s.

By default Ten may again have discovered a formula to survive. With the exception of exclusive stories it may become necessary for all networks to consider pooling their news recourses. Ten has set a precedent for that. Having faced "unmitigated financial disaster", Ten management all but sacrificed their news by slashing its budget and cutting its staff in order to survive. Their news only remained on air thanks to the support of all the other commercial networks including the ABC and SBS who provided them with stories they no longer had the resources to cover.

Pooling sport and politics has always been acceptable between networks but never has a network news service been dependent on pooling news stories to survive. When I recently questioned one commercial network news editor on why they were keeping Ten's news afloat his reply was, 'It's not good for the industry if one of us fails.' Taking cost cutting to further extremes may also throw into doubt the future of highly paid news presenters. Most one-hour bulletins on Seven and Nine have already been reduced to a single reader. Everything will be tossed onto the table in order for TV News to survive financial pressures brought on by the changing media landscape.

I am reminded that when television first began in 1956 there was no such workplace position as "newsreader". The job evolved, as did the industry itself, and the evolution continues. If, as the doomsayers are proclaiming, this is the "beginning of the end", having seen it all from the beginning doesn't make the end any easier. If anything, it confirms that it is the journey that matters the most.

ACKNOWLEDGEMENTS

My thanks to the many mentors and managers who saw in me something I may have failed to grasp at the time. To the hundreds of colleagues whose support I may seemingly have taken for granted – please know that each of you contributed to my life in so many various ways.

The late Eric Collins of 3YB Warrnambool may never have appreciated how he set in motion a career that would span six decades of broadcast news. The late and revered Allan McClelland of 7EX Launceston may never have known how much his creative leadership and paternal advice would impact on my life. At least Ron Casey of HSV7 was fully aware how he taught me to continually push the boundaries. But there were many others including: Keith Cairns, John Maher, Gary Fenton, Gerry Carrington, Dan Webb, David Johnston and Dermot O'Brien – not just colleagues but confidents and friends who have greatly influenced my life both personally and professionally. My indebted thanks also to good friend Gordon Bennett whose own lifetime experience began on the opening night of HSV7 November 4, 1956 and was still employed at Seven at the time of writing this in 2016.

There was equal encouragement at Network Ten – and many more managers – and not one failed to offer support when times became tough. As I have previously mentioned joining Channel Ten in 1987 was akin to being adopted by a special family. But my bittersweet memories are clouded by so many colleagues who fell victim to cost cutting and redundancies along the way – particularly those wonderful women who shared the newsdesk on a nightly basis. Like the very headlines we read – life is just not fair at times.

Gordon Grice, senior lecturer, non-fiction writing course UCLA and fellow class mates who taught me there was more to writing than my initial instructions of: 'twelve words are six words too many.'

The Herald and *Weekly Times,* Fairfax Publishing, *Melbourne Green Guide, Australian Financial Review, Business Day,* Crikey.com, Media Spy, Oztam Ratings and media lawyer Nick Pullen.

To Mark Zocchi and the team at Brolga Publishing, a small Melbourne company that took on my project after many other rejections, my sincere thanks. Encouragement for writing my memoirs can also be attributed to Nigel Dick from GTV9 whose early thesis on television provided the background to my journey. The gaps were then filled by my personal diaries and from those who spent hours recording their own experiences with me, such as cameraman Morrie Pilens, whose life was inextricably linked to a time with my greatest mentor – my father – in post-war Berlin.

It was the wish of all who contributed to my memoirs that I share their stories before we all fade to black. And to those who were there for my "final curtain call" thank you for your kind thoughts and fond farewells.

THE
NEWS MAN

MAL WALDEN

		Qty
ISBN 9781925367492		
RRP	AU$34.99	.....
Postage within Australia	AU$5.00	.....
	TOTAL★ $_____	
	★ All prices include GST	

Name:..

Address: ....

....

Phone:...

Email: ....

Payment: ❏ Money Order ❏ Cheque ❏ MasterCard ❏ Visa

Cardholder's Name:..

Credit Card Number: ....

Signature:...

Expiry Date: ....

Allow 7 days for delivery.

Payment to: Marzocco Consultancy (ABN 14 067 257 390)
PO Box 12544
A'Beckett Street, Melbourne, 8006
Victoria, Australia
admin@brolgapublishing.com.au

BE PUBLISHED

Publish through a successful publisher.
Brolga Publishing is represented through:
• **National** book trade distribution, including sales,
marketing & distribution through **Macmillan Australia.**
• **International** book trade distribution to
    • The United Kingdom
    • North America
    • Sales representation in South East Asia
• **Worldwide e-Book distribution**

For details and inquiries, contact:
Brolga Publishing Pty Ltd
PO Box 12544
A'Beckett St VIC 8006

Phone: 0414 608 494
markzocchi@brolgapublishing.com.au
ABN: 46 063 962 443
(Email for a catalogue request)